GOVERNMENTS, INDUSTRIES AND MARKETS

The New Business History Series

Series editor: Geoffrey Jones, Reader in Business History, Department of Economics, University of Reading

In recent years business history has emerged as an exciting and innovative subject. A new generation of business historians has moved away from former pre-occupations with commissioned histories of individual companies towards thematic, conceptual and comparative studies of the evolution of business. The pioneering studies of Alfred D. Chandler Jr on the rise of big business have inspired much of this work, but there is also a growing dialogue between business historians and their counterparts in business policy, management studies and industrial economics.

The *New Business History Series* is the successor to the former Gower Business History Series, which played an important role in the 1980s in encouraging thematic studies of such topics as the rise of multinationals, the evolution of marketing and the relationship between business and religion. The *New Business History Series* aims to build on and develop this innovative role by publishing high-quality studies in the 'new' business history.

G.J.

Governments, Industries and Markets

Aspects of Government-Industry Relations in the UK, Japan, West Germany and the USA since 1945

Edited by
MARTIN CHICK

Edward Elgar

Published by
Edward Elgar Publishing Limited
Gower House
Croft Road
Aldershot
Hants GU11 3HR
England

Edward Elgar Publishing Company
Old Post Road
Brookfield
Vermont 05036
USA

British Library Cataloguing in Publication Data

Governments, industries and markets: aspects of government-industry relations in Great
    Britain, Japan, West Germany and the United States of America since 1945.
    1. Industrialized countries. Industries. Relations with governments, history
    I. Chick, Martin 1958–
    338.9′009172′2

ISBN 1 85278 316 8

Typeset in Great Britain by Inhit Limited, Godalming, Surrey
and printed by Billing & Sons Ltd, Worcester

Contents

Tables and figures

Tables

Figures

Contributors

Heidrun Abromeit is Professor of Political Science, University of Duisburg.

R.A. Bryer is a Senior Lecturer at the School of Industrial and Business Studies, University of Warwick.

Forrest Capie is Professor of Economic History, City University, London.

Martin Chick is a Lecturer in the Department of Economic and Social History, University of Edinburgh.

Wyn Grant is Reader in Politics, University of Warwick.

Geoffrey Jones is Reader in Business History, University of Reading.

Michael S. Moss is the Archivist, University of Glasgow.

Richard J. Samuels is Associate Professor in the Department of Political Science, Massachusetts Institute of Technology.

Roger Sugden is a Lecturer in the Department of Economics, University of Edinburgh.

Richard H.K. Vietor is Professor at the Graduate School of Business Administration, Harvard University.

Stephen Wilks is a Senior Lecturer in the Institute of Public Administration and Management, University of Liverpool.

1 Politics, information and the defence of market power

Martin Chick

This collection of papers includes studies of government-industry relations since 1945 within certain industries (chemicals, electricity, financial services, motor vehicles, steel and whisky) and countries (Great Britain, Japan, West Germany and the United States of America). The purpose of this introduction is to identify the main factors influencing the structure and dynamics of government-industry relations as discussed in this book, and to make some speculative comments about the study of government-industry relations in general. To this end, it is helpful to explode the term 'government-industry relations'. Often, in the existing literature, the term 'government-industry relations' seems to refer primarily to the participants within the relationship. Thus, whenever government and industry meet, government-industry relations form. However, this general use of the term tends to distract attention from the often catholic range of issues involved within this general relationship. Indeed, it is my contention that if any part of the term is to predominate, then it should be 'relations' rather than 'government-industry'. Thus it is the interaction between each participant's aims across a range of issues which is of more interest than the nature of the two participants. At each point of contact between the particular set of aims of government and industry, 'government-industry relations' will form. Thus, fundamentally, government-industry relations derive from aims rather than participants. There may well be variance between each set of aims pursued by government and industry at each point of contact. It is the subsequent interaction between the sets of aims which is at the heart of government-industry relations and which is the main concern of this introductory paper.

Often, it is the government's pursuit of particular sets of aims which initiates specific government-industry relations. As is reflected in this book, the range of aims pursued at various times by government is wide. Intervention to correct 'market failure' or, as in the case of environmental protection, to compensate for 'missing markets' is frequently cited as a leading reason for government intervention (see Chick, Abromeit). However, while intervention to correct 'market failure' is theoretically concerned to improve the operation of the market, many government-industry relationships arise from the government's wish to influence the outcome of market operations. Government concern with the level of

1

unemployment (Vietor, Jones, Sugden, Wilks), the balance of payments (Wilks, Moss, Sugden, Jones), the breakdown of basic services (Vietor), financial crashes (Capie) or the distribution of wealth (Chick) have all provided grounds for the initiating by government of particular government-industry relationships. In each case, concern for the political and social response to the outcomes of particular market operations has occasioned government intervention. This is intervention to correct a more political 'market failure'; the failure of markets to produce outcomes desired by politicians.

Whatever the reasons for the initiating of particular relationships, where differences exist between the aims of government and industry, each party will seek to influence the decisions of the other. A leading factor determining the ability of one party to influence the decisions of the other is the degree of cooperation which it requires from the other. Government-industry relations are likely to be at their least complex when there is considerable accord between the two sets of aims. Sugden and Jones argue that there was frequently considerable accord between the aims of British governments and particular multinationals, and, given that there was therefore little need for incentive structures, this would go some way towards explaining the absence of monitoring arrangements noted by Sugden. However, Sugden would regard the accord between the aims of the two parties as arising not from a consensus between two balanced parties, but rather from a capitulation by the government to the wishes of the multinational. Abromeit makes a similar point in reference to relations between local government and locally-sited industry, in which such is the political concern to secure employment and income that the local government adopts a dependent position within the relationship; the willingness of local authorities to compromise in their dealings with firms being 'in direct proportion to the local importance of the firm' (Abromeit).

Government-industry relations are also likely to be at their least complex when, while there may be little accord between the aims of government and industry, one party is able to achieve its main aims without securing the cooperation of the other party. Bryer discusses how, for example, the legislative power of the Attlee Government allowed it to nationalize the steel industry in the face of opposition from the industry and despite the Labour movement's inaccurate perception of the nature of that opposition. The same government was also able to use direct controls to impose export targets on the motor vehicle and whisky industries (see Wilks and Moss). Most government-industry relations, however, are not characterized by either an accord of aims or a one-sided distribution of power. Most relationships are marked by some disparity of aims and by the need for degrees of cooperation (or coercion) between the two parties. Frequently, the subsequent interaction between the two parties will centre on the efforts of each to influence, firstly, the structure of a particular relationship and, secondly, the dynamics and workings of that relationship. In more practical terms, each party will attempt to influence both the formulation and implementation of a particular set of aims by the other party. This distinction between the formulation and implementation of aims is similar to that made by Richard Samuels between 'jurisdiction' and 'control' within particular relationships. For Samuels, jurisdiction is the territory within which authority can be exercised, while control is the exercise of that authority.

Such distinctions are useful providing the considerable interaction across the dividing line is recognized. A government's perception of what measures it is possible to implement will have a significant influence on what it attempts to achieve. A government's perception of what is possible, which in turn fundamentally influences the scope and nature of its aims, is often related to the degree of cooperation which it expects to secure from affected industries. The extent of industrial cooperation is, in turn, likely to be related to the nature of the aims that government is pursuing. In this context, there is clearly scope for implicit and explicit negotiation between parties concerning the formulation and implementation of particular sets of aims. Such trade-offs and negotiations are at the heart of the theory of 'reciprocal consent' developed by Samuels (see Samuels. Also see Abromeit and Wilks).

At this stage in the argument, it is useful to move away from considering 'government-industry relations' in general, and concentrate on analysing the interaction between government and industry on a particular issue. The issue which persistently surfaces in this collection of essays is that of government attitudes and responses towards market structure and market power. The issue has also been at the heart of much of the recent literature on privatization and regulation. Indeed, in Britain alone, the work of such economists as John Vickers, George Yarrow and John Kay on the problems of regulating monopolistic and oligopolistic industries and the associated development of principal-agent theory has done much to clarify many of the issues involved within 'government-industry relations'.[1] Used alongside the 'reciprocal consent' arguments of Richard Samuels, for example, the work of these political scientists and economists has much to offer business historians. Moreover, central to much principal-agent theory is the issue of the distribution of information, both between government and market incumbents and between the incumbents and the market. This and similar issues concerning the distribution of information underpin many of the main texts used by business historians in analysing the growth and development of companies and the increase in industrial concentration.[2] It is the concentration and internalizing of information within concentrated structures which not only characterizes the growth of the modern economy, but which also bedevils the attempts of governments and regulators to guard against the abuse of market power. The more information is internalized within a small band of market incumbents, the less information is available in the market to both consumers and regulators. Moreover, the greater the concentration of information within incumbents, the more likely it is that the regulator or government will need to work closely with the incumbent in order to gain access to the requisite information. In the following analysis of government-industry interaction on the issue of market power, not only is the importance of the asymmetrical distribution of information and technical expertise emphasized, but attention is also drawn to the political strength both within government itself and in the political economy at large which market incumbents are able to wield in defence of market power, a political strength which in turn derives from the existing market structure.

A frequent criticism made of the privatization programme in Britain is that, while the government has succeeded in transferring ownership, it has missed an important opportunity to increase significantly the level of competition within sections of leading industries.[3] In short, market incumbents have successfully defended their market power. That monopoly industries such as telecommunications and gas should have sought to defend the existing market structure is not surprising. In general, while government was concerned mainly with the issue of ownership, the industrial managers were more concerned with the issue of market structure. Managers recognized that any changes in the future structure of relevant markets were likely to have far more impact on their day-to-day operating conditions and incentives than any transfer of ownership. Thus, for years before legislation reached the statute book, such nationalized industries as telecommunications and gas devoted considerable resources to lobbying government in an attempt to influence government decision-making on future market structure in the industry's favour. The efforts would appear to have been largely successful, with the privatized British Gas and British Telecom operating in monopolistic and duopolistic markets, respectively. In part, their task was made easier by the fact that government and industry differed in the importance which each attached to the main but separate aims often associated with the privatization programme. While managers worried about future market structures, the government's main concern was with the raising of money through the sales of equity in these industries. Moroever, the concerns of the industries and of the government often coincided. The advantages to government of largely retaining the existing structures were that the sale of the industries could proceed reasonably quickly without any complicated and time-consuming attempts at restructuring industries, that the chance to buy shares in familiar monopolistic and oligopolistic basic industries might well prove attractive to investors, and that the entire process would be made easier if the cooperation of the industries concerned could be secured. Moreover, the bulk of the technical advice received by government, which came largely from the market incumbents as dominant holders of information and technical expertise, unsurprisingly emphasized the benefits of retaining existing market structures.[4] Passing such information to government was reasonably easy for market incumbents. Not only were they organizationally well suited to dealing with government, but they also possessed the resources and will needed to lobby government over a sustained period prior to legislation being passed. Thus, the market structure which had existed during nationalization largely continued into privatization. This also meant that the problem of monitoring the performance of these industries and guarding against the use of market power also continued through from nationalization into privatization. The same political, informational and technical factors which had dogged government efforts to influence the performance of the nationalized industries and which derived fundamentally from particular market structures were to continue to trouble regulators and governments in the new privatized environment.

4

The formation of regulated industries in the United States and of nationalized industries in Britain was both encouraged and sanctioned by the respective government. In both cases, regulation and nationalization were accompanied by the creation of concentrated and often closed markets. In both cases, the problems of guarding against the potential abuse of market power were underestimated. The benefits of such market structures seemed clear at the time. In the United States, regulated markets seemed to offer order in place of chaos. Similar arguments prevailed in banking in Britain. The reduction in uncertainty which underpinned this increase in 'order' in such industries was also seen by some as creating an environment in which managers, having much more control over supply side additions to capacity might make higher quality fixed capital investment decisions. In addition, there was a persistent faith in the ability of large companies to exploit available economies of scale. Such optimism was still to be found in the 1970s. The ethos of the IRC, the formation of British Leyland and of Upper Clyde Ship-builders all testified to the persistence of the view that the benefits accruing from the exploitation of available economies of scale outweighed any losses incurred through the reduction of competition. To a large extent, governments simply overestimated their ability to guard against the abuse of market power. Action was taken to check some of the clearer, more visible abuses. To prevent monopoly financial profits being earned, nationalized industries were statutorily required simply to cover costs taking one year with another. But monopoly profits and abuses extend beyond mere financial profits, from maximizing sales and volume growth irrespective of resources costs to a whole range of satisficing behaviour including the greatest of all monopoly profits, the quiet life. Such abuse was more insidious and often less visible. It was only over the longer term that its impact became apparent.

In Britain, the government hoped to check such abuse partly by appointing publicly-spirited men and women to the boards of nationalized industries. Problems arose, however, when, as in the case of the electricity industry, differences emerged as to just what constituted the 'public interest'. In an attempt to provide some internal criteria for resource allocation, attempts were made to introduce marginal cost pricing into major nationalized industries. Yet, where the introduction of such reforms clashed with the objectives of the industry, the industry was frequently able to repel their introduction. In part, political unwillingness to sanction price increases or plant closures hindered the effective introduction of such economic criteria. In part, public ownership, rather than increasing control, simply increased the likelihood that political factors would distort the behaviour and objectives of the nationalized industries. Yet, also in part, the ability of monopolies like the electricity industry to withhold information, technical expertise and cooperation from aspiring reformers severely hampered the reformers' efforts. It was the market structure which both created the problem and made its solution so difficult. Similarly, it is the persistence of such market structures which makes the regulation of many privatized industries so problematic. Much of the argument is circular. The very absence of alternative sources of information which is the foundation of market power will necessitate regulatory activity, and that regulatory process will in turn be beset by major difficulties in obtaining the information required. Regulators will seek information, not simply in order to monitor the activities and performance of the regulated, but also in order to design improved future incentive and monitor structures. Moreover, a high level of information on pricing and cost structures is required if entry deterrent measures by incumbents through cross-subsidization and price manipulation is to be prevented. The regulator is also likely to require a high level of information in order to check that the information supplied to him by the regulated industry is not being subjected to strategic manipulation by market incumbents. Both the RPI-X and the rate of return forms of regulation are subject to strategic manipulation, especially as the date of regulatory review draws near. The oft-cited Averch–Johnson effect, where firms subject to rate-of-return regulation may have an incentive to expand their capital base so as to achieve a greater absolute profit while staying within the constraint on their profit rate, is just one example of such strategic manipulation of information by incumbents, a manipulation which often has detrimental consequences for both internal and allocative efficiency.[5] As with the drug testing of athletes, one solution would be to make the timing of regulatory reviews stochastic. Devising solutions to such problems, and avoiding the associated dangers of regulatory capture, represent a continuation of the previous efforts to influence and monitor the behaviour of nationalized industries, a continuity of effort grounded in the continuity of market structure.

Market incumbents not only benefit from asymmetries in the distribution of information and expertise, but often also from considerable political lobbying power which derives from the market structure. This is not simply a matter of concentration but also of complexity. Vietor argues that one of the factors enabling the financial services industry to limit the extent of deregulation was that the industry could call upon the complex vested interests inherent within its wide-ranging, moneyed, well-organized, political interest structure. Capie too notes the sophisticated and complex political interest structure of the financial services industry in Britain, and begs the question of the extent to which such an industrial political complex will be able to influence the decisions of would-be regulators. More widely, Samuels, Vietor and Abromeit all emphasize the close relations between industrial/market structures and political interest structures. As Vietor remarks, the 'analogue to the market' is formed.

If industrial structural complexity provides powerful political support, industrial structural concentration enables that power to be deployed. It is the concentrated structure of incumbents which provides them with access to government, indeed access which is often encouraged by government. Assuming that industries are prepared to release certain information, it is easier for the government bureaucracy to communicate with and collect information from large companies within concentrated industries. In talking to ICI, the British government also talks to a major section of the chemical industry, an industry of particular importance to the government for balance of payments and defence considerations (Grant). One of the criticisms made of the relations between government and large companies like ICI is that the two organizations come to share certain common bureaucratic assumptions and perceptions (Grant). Indeed, the danger of such contacts is that of government departments being captured by large companies, especially when the leading companies from concentrated industries are the only source of valuable information which the Department can deploy in its battles with the Treasury (Grant). One of the reasons for the RPI-X form of regulation being preferred on occasions to rate-of-return regulation is that it is thought likely to reduce the chances of regulatory capture, since the regulator has only to observe that external prices are complying with the general price formula, rather than appraising and unravelling the internal cost and performance information within the industry.[6] In an effort to obtain more detailed information, the regulator draws close to the industry and becomes vulnerable to capture. In general, there is always a danger that regular and close contacts between government and large companies may lead to cosy and familiar relationships being formed. Not only is there a persistent danger of capture, but there is also concern that the views of producer groups will come to predominate within government. The net effect of such producer interest group dominance, of asymmetries of information and expertise, of the political clout of market incumbents, and of the administrative attraction of dealing with large, concentrated bureaucratic companies may well be to create an environment in which the interests of consumers in securing increased competition in product markets are quietly forgotten or played down.

It is not only large companies but also large trade unions which have bureaucratic structures which are administratively well suited to lobbying and working with government. Both groups share a common interest in persuading government to retain existing market structures. Organized labour is itself a producer interest group, seeking to take its share of monopoly profits in the form of job security, increased wages and improved working conditions. Thus, in Britain, the two main political parties were funded predominantly by producer interest groups. In this context, it is perhaps not so surprising that the British government has seemed happy to accept many of the arguments made by market incumbents against the promotion of competition within their markets. In the United States, Vietor notes how much of the initial competitive thrust of the deregulation programme was gradually toned down and neutered. Indeed, the effects might have been greater, but for the ability of some potential new entrants to file antitrust suits in the courts to prevent market incumbents engaging in entry deterrent actions. It was the FCC, for example, which, in response to an antitrust suit brought by Tom Carter, stopped AT&T's attempts to prevent its customers using Carterfone equipment, a decision which effectively destroyed AT&T's hold on interconnection and which, as Vietor notes, opened the floodgates to competitive entry by all sorts of manufacturers and distributors. Further antitrust suits against AT&T begun in 1976 and ending in 1982 further weakened AT&T's monopolistic structure, ended its deterrent cross-subsiding behaviour and lowered some of the barriers to new entry. Similar judicial pressure weakened oligopolistic/restrictive practices in other American institutions such as the New York Stock Exchange (Vietor). Perhaps significantly in Britain, there is no equivalent to American antitrust legal judgements. As in criminal law, companies in Britain are innocent until proven guilty, that is until they can be shown to have abused market power. In America, in theory at least, the possession of market power is in itself held to be undesirable. While the differences between each country's antitrust legislation are clearer in theory than in practice, the existence of antitrust legislation and judicial presence does appear to have encouraged potential new entrants and consumer groups, such as that led by Ralph Nader, to challenge market incumbents in the courts.

Providing safeguards and checks against attempts by market incumbents to deter new entrants is probably the most important and most difficult task facing regulators. This task is both so important and so difficult because the effects and costs of successful deterrent activity are, by definition, not immediately visible. Over the longer term, the accumulated effect of entry deterrence and insufficient competition does become clear. In the American air travel market, which was characterized by strong demand, the Civil Aeronautics Board allowed no new entrants to join the 16 established trunk carriers during the entire 40 years of the regulation of the air travel market in the United States. Routes continued to be allocated on a basis of rough equity between the existing couriers with a consequent freezing of industrial structure (Vietor). Similarly, in the self-regulating banking industry in Britain, it was impossible for new entrants, denied access to clearing and discounting facilities, to compete with incumbent banks (Capie). Such suppression of entry, competition and uncertainty was of course at the heart of many of the political and industrial arguments in favour of such regulatory arrangements. However, the costs of such arrangements were ultimately borne by consumers. While noting the absence of counterfactual models of unregulated equivalent industries, both Vietor and Capie argue that the costs of regulation were met by consumers, both financially in prices charged and qualitatively in terms of the service offered.

Quite apart from any benefits provided by entrants for improvements in the internal efficiency of market incumbents, new entrants can also provide an important stimulus to new and more precise thinking on where the boundaries of both markets and natural monopolies lie. Many natural monopolies are based on a given state of technological knowledge. As such, shifts in technology may challenge the bases of established 'natural monopolies', but such challenges may be suppressed by market incumbents combining to prevent new entry. Market incumbents may well wish to preserve the natural monopoly and to encourage observers to believe that far more of the industry is a 'natural monopoly' than is, in fact, the case. One such technological challenge to existing industrial and market structures arose from the development of microelectronics. The greater availability of microelectronic components reduced entry costs in many markets (equipment, for example), altered economies of scope within industries (electronic funds transfer and automated teller equipment) and redrew many existing market boundaries. This redrawing of boundaries was particularly evident in the telecommunications market, where what had once been a telephone business quickly evolved into a much larger market for information transfer and communication (Vietor). Continued technological development also reduced consumer dependence on existing networks and in conjunction with the lowering of entry costs both promoted competition and challenged many long-held assumptions on the extent and nature of natural monopolies. The extent to which the competitive potential implicit in such technological change will be allowed to come to fruition depends on how many of the factors and influences identified in this introduction work out in practice.

Many of the issues identified in this introduction are developed by the various contributors to this book. In selecting contributors, a deliberate decision was made to attract contributions from a wide and diverse range of economists, political scientists, management scientists, economic and business historians. In addition, particular importance was attached to devoting a significant proportion of the book to international analyses of the development of government-industry relations. It was recognized that the use of such international and interdisciplinary criteria in the selection of contributors was likely to result in a collection of essays of great variety in both approach and content. As editor, I have deliberately chosen not to edit the varied parts towards a more homogeneous whole. The variety, warts and all, is there for the reader to see. I think that there is much to be gained from such variety and this introduction has sought to show how some common threads might be drawn from such an international and interdisciplinary approach. Readers may or may not agree. Yet, if this book achieves nothing other than causing the reader to follow up the writings of scholars outside his or her own subject area, then this particular editor will be pleased.

Acknowledgement

I wish to thank Roger Davidson, Leslie Hannah and Roger Sugden for their comments on this paper.

Notes

1. Vickers, J. and Yarrow, G., *Privatisation: An Economic Analysis*, MIT Press, London 1988
   Kay, J., Mayer, C. and Thompson, D. (eds), *Privatisation and Regulation: the UK Experience*, Oxford 1986
2. Coase, R.H., 'The nature of the firm', Economica, 1937, 10, pp 386–405
   Williamson, O.E., *Markets and Hierarchies: Analysis and Antitrust Implications*, Free Press, New York 1975
3. Kay, J. and Thompson, D., 'Privatisation: a policy in search of a rationale', *Economic Journal*, 1986, 96, pp 18–32
4. Chick, M., 'Privatisation: the triumph of past practice over current requirements', *Business History*, 1987, 29, pp 104–116
5. Averch, H. and Johnson, L., 'Behaviour of the firm under regulatory constraint', *American Economic Review*, 1962, 52, pp 1052–1069
6. Vickers, J. and Yarrow, G., *Privatisation: An Economic Analysis*, MIT Press, London 1988, p 207

2 Regulation and competition in America, 1920s–1980s

Richard H.K. Vietor

Since the early 1970s, America's service infrastructure – transportation, energy, communications, and finance – has been thoroughly restructured. These sectors of the economy, long shaped by government regulation, have recently been opened to greater competition. Restrictions on entry have been reduced or eliminated; price controls reformed or removed; and operating standards substantially relaxed. Taken together, these developments in microeconomic policy are least as profound, and certainly more constructive, than the macroeconomic legacy of Reaganomics.

Economic regulation of privately-owned public utilities by 'independent' government agencies has been a peculiarly American institution. Only Japan, reshaped as it was by the American occupation, is at all similar. In most other industrialized countries, public utilities have been owned and operated by government, as public enterprises. Even in banking and insurance, regulation by treasury authorities was invariably more centralized than in America.

American-style regulation, an inheritance from British common law, developed in the 30 years between 1885 and 1915, as a limited response to monopoly power in industries 'vested with the public interest'. For the most part, this control of franchise, entry, and price (or rate of return) originated in state jurisdictions, since the scope of commerce was still limited. As transport and finance expanded across state boundaries, the federal government became increasingly involved. Still, with courts giving narrow interpretation to the scope of federal authority, the thrust of regulation remained minimalist – preventing abuses and overseeing sound practice.[1]

The character of regulation changed abruptly after 1932, as the American economy sunk into the Great Depression. With competition clearly not serving the public interest, President Franklin Roosevelt, with the support of Congress, moved to assert governmental control over competition. Those most affected were airlines, trucking, railroads, petroleum, natural gas, electric power, telecommunications, banking, securities, and insurance. Taken together, these sectors formed the backbone of the American economy and today account for nearly one-fifth of the Gross National Product.

Under regulation from the late 1930s through the late 1960s, these industries grew and prospered, evolving into national networks that distributed services widely and evenly. But as Figure 2.1 suggests, this regulatory regime began to experience problems late in the 1960s. Technological and economic characteristics had begun to alter market segmentation and product differentiation. In industry after industry, large customers and competitive entrants discovered incentives and technological means of bypassing regulated services priced above (marginal) cost. Entrepreneurs, in business and politics, took every opportunity to circumvent or relax regulation.

At first, regulators and their institutions seemed unable to adjust to these changes effectively, often aggravating the failures of regulation. Meanwhile, as economic growth slowed, and inflation and interest rates started to rise, government management of the economy was increasingly questioned, then attacked. Academic economists provided the evidence of regulation's inefficiencies, and by the mid-1970s, politicians began to respond.

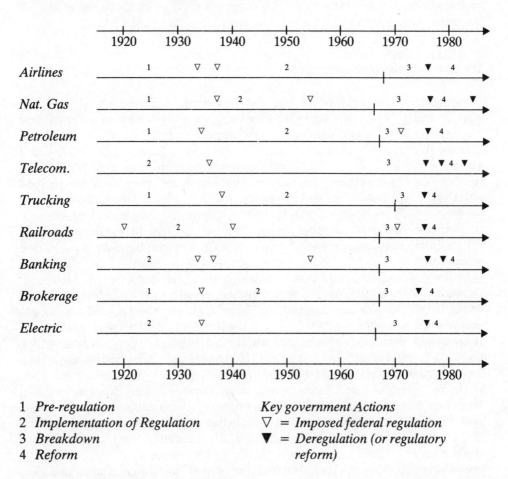

1 *Pre-regulation*
2 *Implementation of Regulation*
3 *Breakdown*
4 *Reform*

Key government Actions
▽ = *Imposed federal regulation*
▼ = *Deregulation (or regulatory reform)*

Figure 2.1   Half a century of regulation

It was actually during the Carter administration that Congress moved to rewrite the principal regulatory legislation of the New Deal. By the time Reagan took office in 1981, 'deregulation' as a political initiative had already peaked. Despite the Reagan administration's rhetoric, further administrative reforms increasingly focused on devising new types of regulation to control, rather than deregulate, increasingly competitive industries.

By the end of the eighties, the markets for infrastructural services had changed radically from the stable, non-competitive, and generally less efficient circumstances that prevailed two decades earlier. Not surprisingly, the companies in these industries had to adopt new strategies, new organizational structures, and fundamentally new, more efficient operating systems – just to survive.

The next section of this chapter will summarize very briefly the origins and impact of New Deal regulation. The third section will compare the reasons for deregulation, and the process, in airlines, natural gas, telecommunications, and banking. The fourth section will offer some generalizations about the effects of deregulation on market structure, business strategy, and public policy.

The failure of competitive markets

In the decade before the Great Depression, America's infrastructural industries were booming. World War I provided the last great growth spurt for railroads and fostered the birth of two new modes of transport – trucking and airlines. Entry barriers in these two businesses were low, and with government highway and airmail subsidies, both grew chaotically until the early thirties.[2] New technology, making possible interstate pipelines for both petroleum and natural gas, helped lower prices and foster the rapid expansion of both industries into midwestern and northeastern urban markets.[3] In telecommunications, innovations in long-distance transmission first made it possible for the Bell System to interconnect local exhanges into a national network.[4] And in financial services, the 1920s was a period of extraordinary growth, product innovation, and diversification.[5]

In the midst of this rapid system building, the American economy collapsed. Between 1929 and 1933, aggregate demand fell about 33 per cent. Nine thousand banks failed, rail tonnage dropped by 50 per cent, and the price of natural gas dropped below 4 cents per 1000 cubic feet (equivalent to 24 cents per barrel of oil). In telecommunications, residential subscribership dropped 25 per cent, and AT&T laid off 150 000 workers. In airlines, notwithstanding the mail subsidies, more than half the trunk airlines operated at a loss.[6]

The net effect of such conditions across the entire economy had a devastating impact on Americans' traditional faith in unrestricted competition. In this respect, agriculture and manufacturing fared little better. Speculation, monopoly power, and excessive competition were simultaneously blamed for the total failure of markets; as Franklin Roosevelt put it, 'because rulers of the exchange of mankind's goods have failed through their own stubborness and their own incompetence'. Yet in the face of a deep American commitment to private property, nationalization would be too extreme. In his first inaugural address, President Roosevelt asked only for 'supervision of all forms of transportation and of communications and other utilities which have a definitely public character', and especially, 'strict supervision of all banking and credits and investments'.[7] In a word – regulation.

During the next 100 days and over the next several years, Congress answered this call with legislation designed to stabilize the economy, to prevent abuses, and to insure more equitable results. Table 2.1, which lists the most important of these intitiatives, grossly understates the increase in the federal government's control over business.

In the next three decades, the regulatory institutions created during the Depression fundamentally redirected the industries involved. Market characteristics and industry structure were reshaped to comply with the social and economic objectives that Congress appeared to have chosen. Economic regulation evolved as a distinctive political process with its own adjudicatory rule-making procedures. The courts became deeply involved through their appellate responsibilities, and Congress exercised periodic oversight.[8] As time went by, all sorts of vested

Table 2.1 New deal economic regulation

Financial Services
    Banking Act of 1933 (Glass-Steagall)
    Securities Act (1933)
    Securities Exchange Act (1934)
    Banking Act of 1935
    Mahoney Act (1938)

Telecommunications
    Communications Act of 1934

Surface Transport
    Emergency Railroad Transportation Act (1934)
    Motor Carrier Act (1935)
    Transportation Act of 1940

Airlines
    Air Mail Act (1934)
    Civil Aeronautics Act of 1938

Natural Gas
    Natural Gas Act of 1938

Electric Power
    Public Utility Holding Company Act (1935)

Petroleum
    Connally Hot Oil Act (1935)

---

interests – producers, suppliers, consumers, and substitutes – organized political capabilities and institutions that formed a sort of analogue to the market.

In the airlines business, for example, World War II dramatically stimulated aviation technology and the demand for air travel. Yet despite tremendous growth, the industry structure (once reorganized in 1934 to do away with vertically integrated holding companies) scarcely changed over four decades. The Civil Aeronautics Board allowed no new entrants to join the 16 established trunk carriers. Routes authorized in the 1930s were continued, and new routes were allocated on a basis of rough equity; each carrier received its share of profitable and less profitable routes, with the smaller trunk carriers slightly favoured as an incentive to catch the 'big three' (United, American, and TWA). A similar separate structure was developed among commuter (or 'feeder') lines. Fares were set by the carriers, periodically increased by the CAB, and generally allowed to cover industry-average costs (plus a fair rate of return). Only non-price competition was allowed – meals, reservation and baggage services, frequency of departure, and aircraft modernization.[9]

This system fostered an integrated, nationwide air transport system that provided comfortable, non-stop service. But it also encouraged high costs, especially labour costs, cross-subsidies, an inefficient route structure, and excess capacity. Load factor (capacity utilization) declined from 78 per cent in 1946 to 48 per cent in 1971.[10]

In natural gas, as in airlines, a radical industry restructuring preceded the imposition of regulatory stability. The Public Utility Holding Company Act of 1935 ordered the dismantling of the huge holding-company pyramids created in the early 1930s. Interstate pipelines were separated from gas production companies and from intrastate distribution companies. In this manner, gas producers avoided federal utility regulation and the distribution sector remained primarily within state jurisdictions.[11]

In 1938, Congress authorized the Federal Power Commission to regulate interstate commerce in natural gas, on a 'just and reasonable basis.' In 1954, the Supreme Court ordered the price of natural gas production likewise regulated. Under this system, gas prices and industry structure remained virtually unchanged from the 1950s through the early 1970s. Cross subsidies abounded, with markets eventually segmented by vintage, state jurisdiction, and use. Rate cases lasted for years, with only non-price competition, in the form of elaborate contract provisions, allowed. Demand for gas naturally boomed, while exploration lagged; the inevitable result was a supply crisis of major proportions.[12]

By the time Congress created the Federal Communications Commission in 1934, the American Telephone & Telegraph Company had already achieved near-monopoly status. Western Electric, an AT&T subsidiary, manufactured most of the telephone and switching equipment used in the United States. AT&T Long Lines provided all long-distance services, and the 22 Bell operating companies provided 82 per cent of local-exchange, telephone service. In research, Bell Labs was pre-eminent.

Under federal regulation, telephone service expanded rapidly throughout

America. The high cost of local-exchange service was subsidized by long-distance toll revenues (where technological innovation was driving down costs). Statewide averaging of local rates, and nationwide averaging of long-distance rates also fostered 'universal service'. Interconnection to the Bell network by private networks or non-Bell end-user equipment was prohibited. Service was constantly improved by the introduction (and careful integration) of new technologies. Costs to subscribers were minimized by limited product choice, huge production runs, and long depreciation schedules. This was a stable, indeed marvellous, system at least through the mid-1960s.[13]

Financial Services, without the scale economies that drove AT&T's monopoly, were fragmented in thousands of small and medium-sized firms, segmented by geographic and product restrictions that were devised by multiple agencies. Figure 2.2 illustrates this complex structure of regulation-defined industry structure and service markets. By 1980, nearly 50 000 financial institutions that intermediated $3.8 trillion in assets were distinctively chartered as commercial banks (15 000), thrifts (5100), investment banks (300+), mutual funds (1000), credit unions (12 000), or insurance companies (5000+). Regulators set prices (interest rates on deposits and ceilings on loan rates), controlled product portfolios (assets) and sourcing of funds (liabilities), insured depositors, restricted entry, mergers, and acquisitions, and set accounting standards and reserve requirements. The only competition allowed was non-price competition – free gifts, free checking accounts, free parking, and as many branch offices as possible.[14]

From the perspective of the early 1970s, it appeared that government's role in the economy was expanding indefinitely – a secular evolution from unrestricted free enterprise to socialism. But this was not so.

Deregulation – the sources of change

The deregulation movement in America, ranging as it did across several industries, was obviously a complex phenomenon. As with the imposition of economic regulation during the Great Depression, multiple and overlapping forces were at play. Five of these, however, stand out as most significant in precipitating major regulatory reforms.

Change in the underlying macroeconomic and political context was fundamental to American deregulation. After two decades of vigorous, non-inflationary growth, the US economy experienced price pressures and rising interest rates towards the end of the 1960s. Deficit spending for social programmes and the war in Viet Nam appeared to be the trigger. Coupled with the collapse of fixed exchange rates and the first oil shock in the early 1970s, economic and productivity growth stagnated. Established fiscal policy (Keynesian demand management) implemented by Nixon, Ford and Carter, failed to mitigate these problems. At the micro-level, cost-based rate regulation, designed for rapid growth and declining average costs, did not respond effectively to this inversion of postwar trends in supply and demand.

These developments reverberated through the polity, shaking the ideological

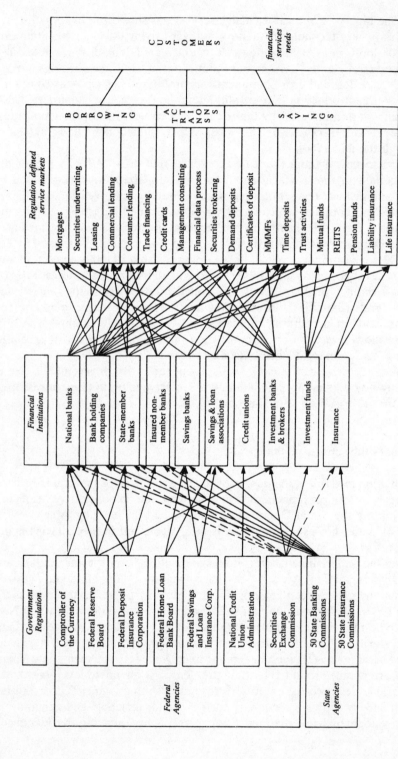

Figure 2.2   Regulation defined financial-service markets

consensus behind government interventionism. A consumer movement, inspired by Ralph Nader, attacked regulated industries and their regulators alike, across a broad front. Faith in government authority, already shaken by Viet Nam and Watergate, was challenged on all sides – by traditional liberals (such as Senator Edward Kennedy), by rural populists (Jimmy Carter), and by conservative Republicans (Ronald Reagan).

New ideas about how regulation failed (and how it might work) also contributed to the change. As early as 1962, academic economists, in empirical studies of regulation, began to document serious problems of economic inefficiency, adverse impacts on consumers, and damage to regulated businesses. Gradually at first, the political establishment – commission staffs, bureaucrats in the executive departments, and congressional staffs – began to absorb these criticisms.[15]

Technological innovation was a third force behind deregulation. Major changes in technology, commercialized some 15 to 20 years after their inception in World War II, undermined the industry economics on which regulatory policy was premised. Thus, where new technology dramatically lowered entry barriers (e.g. microwave), or increased capacity (e.g. widebodied aircraft), or changed the economies of scope (e.g. electronic funds transfer and automated teller equipment), prevailing regulatory barriers became unsustainable.

Entrepreneurship – especially in the political realm – was a fourth factor in deregulation. As technology or macroeconomic conditions changed and distorted less dynamic regulation, opportunities developed for individuals who could take advantage of the political system. In Texas, for example, Lamar Muse saw that the absence of federal regulation in the intrastate market was an opportunity to compete by offering a low-cost, no-frills airline service. Bill McGowan, chairman of MCI, used microwave technology to skim the cream from the immense cross subsidies in telecommunications; his sophisticated lobbying helped break AT&T's long-distance monopoly. Public figures, like Steven Breyer and Alfred Kahn, were similarly entrepreneurial in effecting regulatory reforms.

The fifth important factor was regulatory failure itself. When regulatory institutions, procedures, or regulators themselves could not adjust effectively to the problems of regulation, industry performance deteriorated. In fact, in some instances, the initial responses by regulators actually aggravated this tendency. The railroad bankruptcies of the late 1960s, banking disintermediation and gas shortages in the 1970s, and prudence audits of nuclear plants in the 1980s are good examples of regulatory failure.

Airlines deregulation and political entrepreneurship

Air transport was the first industry in which the New Deal regulatory legislation was rescinded, and it is the only instance to date where the regulatory agency itself was disbanded. The impact of airline deregulation was the quickest and most dramatic of any deregulating industry.

The airline industry's customary problem with excess capacity worsened abruptly

17

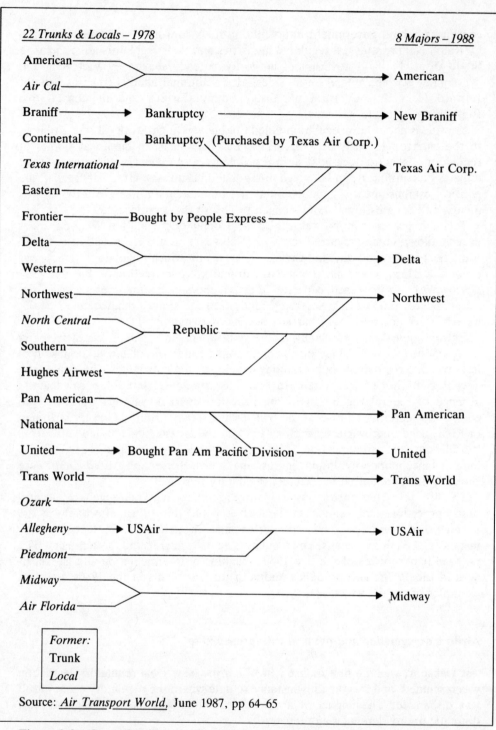

Figure 2.3 Consolidation of pre-deregulation trunk and local airlines

Table 2.2   National market shares of the largest US airlines[1]

Airline	Market Share
Texas Air	20.1
Continental[2]	10.5
Eastern	9.6
United	15.7
American	13.5
Delta[3]	11.9
Northwest[4]	9.4
TWA[5]	8.1
Pan Am	5.7
USAir	3.0

[1] Market shares are based on each carrier's per cent of revenue passenger enplanements on a national basis
[2] Includes New York Air, People Express, and part of Frontier Airlines
[3] Includes Western's market share
[4] Includes figures for Republic, which was formed by the merger of North Central and Southern
[5] Includes Ozark's market share

Source: Data derived from 'Texas Air's hard bargainer', *New York Times*, September 16, 1986

in 1969; slower economic growth, fare increases, and deliveries of widebodied aircraft all contributed. As load factor plummeted, uncontrollable labour costs, increased debt (at rising interest rates), and sharply higher fuel costs (due to the first oil shock) outran the gains in productivity that jet technology had made available.[16] Return on equity was less than half that of unregulated businesses, yet development of airline markets seemed well below potential.[17] The administration of Gerald Ford and the Civil Aeronautics Board itself recognized these problems and urged that control over entry be reduced.

The issue of regulatory reform gained real momentum in 1975. Senator Edward Kennedy, chairman of the Subcommittee on Administrative Practices, hired a law professor named Stephen Breyer to reinvigorate his subcommittee. Breyer chose airline regulation for several reasons. As a retail business with an aura of glamour, but with many problems, airline regulation could attract media and public attention. In Texas and California, there were examples of non-regulated, intra-state airlines that outperformed the regulated carriers. And above all, the airlines had a relatively simple, political interest structure – just two groups, the airlines' management and labour unions. These would oppose deregulation, but with little political clout.

Kennedy and Breyer orchestrated a highly visible series of hearings, in which airline management and regulators looked rather foolish in their defence of regulation. A carefully prepared report, with recommendations for legislative reform, got the political ball rolling.[18]

When Jimmy Carter campaigned for President in 1976, he pledged regulatory reform, among other things. After taking office, he appointed Alfred Kahn, an evangelist for marginal-cost pricing, to chair the Civil Aeronautics Board. Kahn encouraged open entry, low-cost service, and price competition in several, specific cases. The experiments, combined with his persistent and effective advocacy, encouraged Congress to pass the Airline Deregulation Act in October, 1978.[19]

Regulatory stability in airlines came unravelled almost immediately. Although Congress had intended a five-year phase out, the onslaught of competition surprised everyone – management, labour, and passengers. First entry, then price cutting, then route abandonments and restructuring by the incumbent carriers, and by mid-1980, competition was wide open, and brutal.

New airlines sprang up everywhere, with leased aircraft, non-union labour, low overheads, no-frills service, and names like Midway, New York Air, and People Express. Joined by charter companies (World and Capitol) and hitherto regional carriers (Southwest and PSA), they entered the highest density, intercity routes where prices generally exceeded costs and where the potential for traffic growth was greatest. Fares not only declined (in real terms), but declined even in markets with little or no competition. Discounting below standard fares, through marginal-cost and package pricing, was rampant. By 1987, more than 90 per cent of all coach fares were somehow discounted.[20]

Although slow to respond, the major trunk carriers eventually restructured, each with different route plans, fleet composition, marketing and service concepts, and labour relations. After 40 years of regulatory protection, their cost structures were unsustainable in the face of competition. Inefficient aircraft were sold; maintenance, operations and training facilities were centralized; headcount was reduced, wages lowered, and previously acceptable workrules eliminated.

The most startling operational change was the shift, by all major carriers, to a 'hub-and-spoke' route design. Direct flights between individual city-pairs were drastically reduced, with most flights funnelled through one or two huge centres. By concentrating operations and raising utilization rates, this concept facilitated cost reduction, creating economies of scale. And by serving more city-pair markets indirectly through a hub, with fewer aircraft, fewer crews, and higher load factors, it created new economies of scope.[21]

Taken together, the combination of more efficient routes, fleets, and labour drove cost per passenger-mile down by about 30 per cent (from 4.5 to 3.3 cents in constant dollars) between 1981 and 1987.[22] Load factor, for the major carriers has increased into the range of 60 per cent.[23]

On the revenue side, marketing, pricing, and distribution channels became critical. Computerized reservation systems, already important, became the key to winning and maintaining market share. Price-sensitive customers were offered an array of discounted seats, adjusted in real time to match demand by reservations

Table 2.3   Market shares of the largest US airlines at selected airports[1]

Airport	Airline	Enplanements	
		1978	*1985*
Chicago (O'Hare)	United	33.1	41.8
	American	18.6	30.3
Atlanta (Hartsfield)	Delta	50.1	52.3
	Eastern	38.6	41.5
Dallas – Fort Worth	Braniff	33.7	—
	American	29.8	61.1
	Delta	16.6	23.8
Los Angeles International	United	27.8	16.2
	Western[2]	16.9	14.1
	American	16.4	12.6
Denver	United	32.0	35.8
	Frontier[3]	19.9	25.4
	Continental	19.3	22.5
St Louis	TWA	39.4	57.1
	Ozark[4]	20.6	27.2
Pittsburgh	Allegheny	46.7	79.8
Minneapolis	Northwest	31.7	42.5
	North Central[5]	21.4	36.7
Houston	Continental	19.0	57.6

[1] Market shares are based on each carrier's proportion of revenue passenger enplanements at each airport
[2] Delta has since acquired Western
[3] Frontier has since sold a significant portion of its assets to United; Continental purchases the remaining assets
[4] TWA has since merged with Ozark
[5] Republic, which was formed by the combination of North Central and Southern, has since merged with Northwest

Source: Federal Aviation Administration

computers. Advanced boarding passes, comfortable lounges, free trips and service up-grades, meanwhile, maintained the loyalty of frequent business travellers.

The impact of these changes on industry performance is difficult to isolate from the effects of the second oil shock (1979–1980), the presidential firing of striking air traffic controllers (PATCO) in 1981, and the deep recession in 1982–83. Still, a few outcomes are clear. Aggregate demand for air transportation was immensely stimulated by lower prices;[24] safety appears to have been relatively unaffected;[25] but quality of service (measured by delays and complaints) did deteriorate.[26] The industry was substantially restructured (see Figure 2.3), with significantly higher concentration levels nationally, one or two firm dominance at every major hub (see Tables 2.2 and 2.3), and a dramatic mortality rate among new entrants.[27]

Finally, industry profitability all but disappeared. From 1979 to 1987, the 11 major American carriers earned $750 million, total. Their average return on equity for the period was −1.2 per cent. Clearly, the adjustment to deregulation is not yet over.

Natural gas and regulatory failure

In December 1968, the president of the American Gas Association wrote a letter to the chairman of the Federal Power Commission, warning that gas prices were too low to sustain an adequate supply. The AGA, representing gas distributors and transmission companies, had always opposed higher wellhead prices. But at last it admitted that prevailing practices of rate-base, rate-of-return regulation needed reassessment.[28]

This warning came too late. Net additions to reserves declined (for the first time since World War II), and prices in the unregulated, intrastate markets rose above regulated, interstate prices by a widening margin. Curtailments of 'interruptible' service to large users occurred in 1970, eventually to exceed 15 per cent of national demand. Domestic gas production peaked at 22.6 Tcf (trillion cubic feet) in 1973. By 1986, it had fallen to 17.4 Tcf.[29] New gas, meanwhile, was increasingly diverted into the unregulated intrastate markets, thus aggravating shortages for interstate customers.

Desperate pipeline and distributor companies launched various high-cost gas development projects, such as imported LNG, coal gasification, and an Alaskan gas pipeline. These projects, however, made sense only in a rate-base, regulated world.

Attempts by regulators to alleviate these distortions were frustrated by institutional inertia, procedural barriers, and the rhetoric of consumer advocacy. John Nassikas, appointed chairman of the FPC by President Nixon, announced his intent to raise prices. But any attempt to do so that departed from traditional 'just and reasonable' criteria ran into a barrage of opposition, and clashed with judicial precedent.[30] Finally, the Commission turned to rate setting on a nationwide basis (as opposed to specific gas fields), in which rate-base assessment and cost allocation made no sense whatsoever. This approach managed to push 'new-gas' prices closer to the thermal-equivalent price of oil, but did not significantly affect supply or demand.

Congress, meanwhile, first addressed the issue in 1971. Although it was obvious that the original Act, and the accretion of adjudicatory precedent, were preventing administrative reform, the oil shock of 1973 confused the issue. Oil and gas producers attacked wellhead price controls, while consumer activists adamantly opposed any sort of 'windfall' profits for the evil oil companies. Gas pipeline and distributor interests, although resigned to the need for higher prices, regarded legislative reform with ambivalence.

This political gridlock persisted throughout the 1970s, despite worsening shortages. In 1977, President Carter proposed a partial, phased deregulation of wellhead gas prices, as part of his National Energy Plan. After 18 more months of rancorous debate, Congress enacted the Natural Gas Policy Act (NGPA) of 1978. It was not worth the wait.

The NGPA caused at least as many problems as it solved. Political compromise had produced incredibly complex rules. To phase out control of wellhead gas prices (but not gas transport regulation) 'fairly', Congress designated nine new categories of gas, from different sources, well depths, and vintages – each with a different price schedule. 'Old' gas would remain regulated, 'new' gas would be deregulated gradually, and deep or other high-cost gas could immediately sell at a market price.[31]

Pipeline companies, desperate to replace depleted reserves, immediately bid up the price of newly discovered gas. The second oil shock, meanwhile, amplified the panic over energy supply and appeared to make fuel oil uncompetitive. Pipelines signed 'take-or-pay' contracts, agreeing to pay producers unheard-of prices, even if they could not take (and sell) the gas. There was virtually no thought of demand elasticity.

But over the next several years, increased production, conservation, and recession dampened demand. When oil prices fell after 1982, industrial users switched away from gas, leaving producers and pipeline companies with a surfeit of committed supply. By 1985, spot-market gas prices were falling sharply; pipeline companies came under intense pressure to transport 'third-party' gas, other than their own.

The energy glut, the increasingly market-driven wellhead prices, and the emergence of a nationwide pipeline network, pushed the Federal Energy Regulatory Commission (FERC, renamed from the FPC) towards further regulatory reform. First, the FERC allowed gas distributors to back out of long-term purchase contracts. It encouraged 'contract carriage', where pipelines were allowed to carry gas for distributors that purchased it directly from a producer. New rates were developed that separated the charges for the fixed and variable costs of gas transportation.

In late 1985, the FERC issued Order 436 – a landmark in natural gas regulation. Henceforth, interstate pipelines that wished to transport any third party gas would be required to do so on a non-discriminatory basis. To provide equal access to buyers and sellers, the pipeline companies would have to 'unbundle' their gas sales

Parent company	Acquired pipeline	Date
	Acquisitions by non-pipelines	
Burlington Northern	El Paso Natural Gas Co.	1982–83
Goodyear Tire & Rubber Co.	Celeron Corp. (Included Mid Louisiana Gas Co., Louisiana Intrastate Gas Corp., & Tuscaloosa Pipeline Co.)	1983
CSX Corp.	Texas Gas Transmission	1983
Williams Cos.	Northwest Energy Co.	1983
	Acquisitions by pipelines	
Northwest Energy Co.	Cities Service Gas (now Northwest Central Pipeline Corp.)	1982
MidCon Corp. (Natural Gas Pipeline)	Mississippi River Transmission Corp.	1983
Houston Natural Gas Corp.	(1) Transwestern Pipeline Co. (2) Florida Gas Transmission Co.	1984 1984
MidCon Corp.	Tatham Corp. Pipelines including Sugar Bowl Gas Corp. (renamed Acadian Gas Pipeline System), Pelican Interstate Gas Corp., Bayou Interstate Pipeline Corp.	1984
MidCon Corp.	Conversion of 457 mile crude oil pipeline (formerly Texoma Pipeline Co.) to natural gas service	1984
Coastal Corp.	American Natural Resources (ANR Pipeline Co., Great Lakes Gas Transmission Co.) (50%)	1985
InterNorth, Inc.	Houston Natural Gas Corp. (Houston Pipeline Co.)	1985
MidCon Corp.	United Gas Pipe Line Co.	1985
Tenneco Corp.	Mid-Louisiana Gas Co., Louisiana Intrastate Gas Corp., Tuscaloosa Pipeline Co. (from Goodyear Corp.)	1985
Phillips Gas Pipeline Co.	Conversion of 500 mile crude oil pipeline (formerly Seaway System) to natural gas service	1984

Figure 2.4 Mergers and acquisitions involving FERC-regulated pipelines from 1982 to present

business from their gas transport business, each with separate tariffs. Distributors could convert long-term, gas-purchase contracts to transport-only contracts. In conjunction with this, the FERC substantially deregulated most old gas.[32]

Order 436 pushed the American gas industry further into the chaos of restructuring. By 1987, the proportion of gas sold by interstate pipelines had fallen below the portion transported. As the spot market developed, brokers and independent marketers sprang up throughout the Southwest. Mergers, divestitures, and acquisitions restructured the corporate organization of the gas industry (see Figure 2.4). Interstate pipeline companies faced new competition from each other as well as from fuel oil, and were stuck with billions of dollars in take-or-pay liabilities (to producers).

Pipeline companies had to reduce costs and increase sales to compete, but they still remained regulated on a rate-base, rate-of-return basis. This, of course, was not deregulation; rather, it was a new form of asymmetrically regulated competition.

Telecommunications and technological innovation

AT&T's end-to-end monopoly in electronic voice communication came unravelled gradually, with the postwar commercialization of technological innovations. On both the supply side and demand side of the business, in both transmission and switching, new technological opportunities changed the cost characteristics of the business. It became virtually impossible for regulators to maintain the prevailing restrictions on entry, or the cross-subsidies that had facilitated universal service.

In long-distance transmission, the first break occurred in 1959, when the Federal Communications Commission allocated frequency bands above 890 megacycles to private users (such as railroads and pipeline).[33] Microwave technology, developed for radar during World War II, could carry more channels, at a lower cost, than cable. It was ideal for point-to-point, high-density service.

As AT&T had feared, entrepreneurs intent on resale, not just private use, immediately applied for licences under *Above 890*. Since regulators had allocated costs to cross-subsidize local service with long-distance revenues, AT&T's rates were well above costs. Nonetheless, in 1969, as an 'experiment with the market forces of American free private enterprise competition,' the FCC decided to issue a licence to Microwave Communications Inc. (MCI) to provide private-line service for businesses between Chicago and St Louis.[34] MCI claimed it could build the system for $564 000 (since customers would provide their own connections to MCI's terminals).

During the next several years, dozens of other applicants sought entry under AT&T's regulated pricing umbrella. MCI expanded its system into a multi-city network, and demanded interconnection with Bell System's local exchange companies (since customers, not surprisingly, were unwilling to provide their own originating and terminating connections). Eventually, MCI manipulated its tariffs to convert its private-line service into a public, switched long-distance network;

25

somehow, the FCC was caught by surprise.[35] The courts upheld MCI's initiative, and by 1978, long-distance telecommunications was fully competitive. Only then did regulators begin to address the problems posed by cross-subsidies, much less deregulation.[36]

Competitive entry into the 'customer premises equipment' segment of telecommunications developed in parallel to long-distance. Here, the invention of the transistor (1947) and the subsequent development of integrated circuits provided the key to change. As long as electromechanical technology dominated the telephone business, AT&T's subsidiary, Western Electric, had attained substantial economies of scale in the manufacture of equipment. But as microelectronic components became widely available from independent vendors in other industries (consumer electronics and data processing), entry into the equipment business became feasible, even for entrepreneurs with relatively little capital.

The most serious challenge to AT&T's tariff prohibition on interconnection (of non-AT&T equipment) came in the mid-1960s, from Carterfone. Tom Carter, a Texas businessman, made and distributed a device that connected field-mobile radios to the telephone system, by induction. Objecting to any form of interconnect, AT&T warned its customers against the use of Carterfones, under the threat of disconnection. Carter finally brought an antitrust suit. Upon demand, the FCC decided that the tariffs which prohibited interconnection were unwarranted and unlawful.[37]

This decision in 1968 opened the floodgates to competitive entry by all sorts of manufacturers and distributors. AT&T's share of the equipment market eroded rapidly, even before 1977, when the FCC removed its remaining entry restriction – a requirement for protective interfaces.[38] Three years later, in its Second Computer Inquiry, the FCC deregulated telephone equipment altogether.

In a third segment of the market – that of 'enhanced services' – the convergence of data processing and switching technologies overwhelmed the boundaries drawn by the Justice Department in its 1956 consent decree. 'It is the computer control of the telephone switching machines,' explained one engineer, 'and the telephone network capability to switch and transmit computer signals that is causing the two fields to grow together.'[39]

The FCC had begun efforts to define the separation of computing from telecommunications in 1966. In 1971, it decided not to regulate data processing (where message switching was incidental), but to regulate hybrid services in which data processing was incidental to switching.[40] By 1980, this distinction was likewise outmoded. In its Second Computer Inquiry, the FCC tried to distinguish between 'basic' and 'enhanced' services.[41] For the first time, AT&T could provide enhanced services, but only through a separate subsidiary. But just as quickly, this definition was also obscured by technological change, and the FCC had to rule anew in 1986, in a Third Computer Inquiry.[42]

Only the local-exchange segment remained fully regulated and closed to entry through the early 1980s. But in 1982, the Justice Department and AT&T announced a settlement to the antitrust suit begun eight years earlier. In that suit, the government had accused AT&T of maintaining a monopolistic structure, using its market power in the local exchange to prevent competition in long-distance and equipment. In the settlement, AT&T agreed to divest its 22 local-exchange operating companies, which were then reorganized into seven regional holding companies, each with $10 to $14 billion in assets.[43] The telephone market was divided into 161 regions (LATAs), and only the regional operating companies (and other independent telephone companies) could provide intra-LATA service. But the regional Bell operating companies could not compete in long-distance (inter-LATA) markets, nor manufacture equipment, nor provide enhanced services (other than Yellow Pages directory services).[44]

On January 1, 1984, the day AT&T's reorganization took effect, the American telecommunications was completely restructured. Almost a dozen companies competed with AT&T in the long-distance market. In terminal equipment, AT&T's market share had dropped below 30 per cent, as dozens of other manufacturers provided a range of telephone, keysets, modems, answering machines, cellular phones, and PBXs. Even in the central office equipment and switch business, several multinational firms (Northern Telecom, NEC, Siemens, Ericsson, and Alcatel) provided stiff competition for AT&T. Enhanced, information services, meanwhile, were just taking off, with packet switching, value-added networks, local-area networks, data bases, shared tenant services, and various signalling systems proliferating.[45]

Even with all this competition, telecommunications remained very much regulated. Changes in regulatory form and scope were spreading in the states, but public utility commissions still controlled key aspects of entry and exit, service, price, and rate-of-return. The federal court, supervising the consent decree in the AT&T case, controlled the activities of the Bell operating companies. And the Federal Communications Commission was more active than ever, regulating equal access (for all long-distance carriers), interstate 'access' tariffs, AT&T's prices (and rate of return), and new rules for 'open network architecture' to implement its Third Computer Inquiry.

Here too, regulated competition seemed to have displaced the drive towards deregulation.

Financial services and the new economic context

Ever since the New Deal, banking regulation had been a kind of cat-and-mouse game between regulators trying to maintain product/market restrictions, and bankers creating new financial instruments and organizational forms designed to breach them. But in 1966, government borrowing to finance the war in Viet Nam precipitated a credit crunch; short-term rates exceed long-term rates and the ceilings under Regulation Q – the Federal Reserve Bank's maximum on deposit-interest rates.[46] Disintermediation – the exchange of funds directly by lenders and borrowers – resulted.

For the thrift (savings and loan) industry in particular, this meant a decline in deposits and a squeeze on margins (as short-term costs exceeded long-term earnings). The overheated economy, meanwhile, encouraged corporate borrowing in the equity markets, where the volume of trading increased dramatically.[47]

In the 1970s, however, slower economic growth and a decline in the aggregate savings rate caused competition for market share in financial services to intensify. Floating exchange rates and petrodollar imbalances after 1973 helped internationalize American financial markets and institutions. Large government deficits and two oil shocks further contributed to inflationary pressures, forcing nominal interest rates to new heights. More serious bouts of disintermediation and inverted yields followed, in 1970, 1974, 1979, and 1981. The last of these caused the withdrawal of several hundred billion dollars from depository institutions.[48]

In this environment of heightened competition, technological developments in information processing and telecommunications offered opportunities to control costs and stimulate revenues. Applications began in back office operations, where reader/sorter document processors and mainframe computers revolutionized the computational capabilities in banking, brokerage, and insurance. Improvements in digital transmission facilitated electronic funds transfers for integrated branch-office networks, interbank transactions, and international banking. In the 1980s, this technology reached into retail markets – 'the front office' – with the development of automatic teller machines (ATMs), point-of-sale terminals, and smart cards for credit and debit transactions.[49]

By changing basic conditions of supply and demand, these new macroeconomic and technological circumstances strained the prevailing regulatory structure. Where regulations were most binding, or where loopholes were most opportune, aggressive firms devised means of breaching product and geographic constraints. Bankers at Citibank devised negotiable CDs (certificates of deposit); mutual banks in Massachusetts created the NOW Account (Negotiable Order of Withdrawal) to compete with commercial banks for checkable deposits; and Merrill Lynch developed Money Market Mutual Funds to capture savings deposits when market interest rates exceeded Regulation Q.

Bank holding companies and 'non-bank banks' (an institution that made loans or took deposits, but not both) were two of the innovative organizational forms used to circumvent the McFadden Act (restrictions on interstate branching) and the Glass–Steagall Act (separation of banking and securities). Of course, these loopholes cut both ways, allowing entry into financial services by all sorts of service and manufacturing firms. By the mid-1980s, for example, the ten largest non-financial firms earned as much from their financial-service activities as did the three largest non-bank financial institutions or the six largest banks.[50] So porous had the regulatory barriers to entry become that Citibank's chairman, Walter Wriston, complained that 'the bank of the future already exists, and it's called Merrill Lynch'.[51]

Despite these economic and entrepreneurial pressures, politicians were extremely slow to accept reform. There were several reasons for this. The American public had an abiding distrust of financial power and central banking; most Americans still associated the Great Depression with financial malfeasance. Bureaucratic competition among diverse and well-established regulatory institutions prevented unanimity on important public policy issues. And then, unlike the airline industry, the political interest structure of financial services was exceedingly complex. Financial interests representing the status quo were well organized, with deep pockets and a broad-based presence in grassroots politics.

The first significant regulatory reform occurred in 1975, when the New York Stock Exchange, under pressure from institutional investors and the Justice Department, de-controlled fees in security brokerage.[52]

Five years later, during a brutal bout of disintermediation that severely damaged the S&Ls, Congress finally enacted the Depository Institutions Deregulation and Monetary Control Act (DIDMCA) in 1980. State usury laws were preempted, S&Ls were authorized to offer interest-bearing checking accounts, and the interest ceiling on deposit accounts (Regulation Q) was phased out. At the same time, reserve requirements were standardized for the various types of banks, solidifying the Federal Reserve's monetary authority.

But DIDMCA was not enough. Record-high interest rates, inflation, and rampant disintermediation pushed the entire thrift industry into crisis. As a wave of failures gripped the industry, a panicky congress passed the Garn–St Germain Act in 1982. This emergency provision gave federal deposit insurance agencies wider latitude to orchestrate bailouts of ailing institutions and arrange interstate mergers and acquisitions. S&Ls were also authorized to broaden their product offerings (assets) and sources of funds (liabilities).[53]

In the courts and state legislatures, restrictions on branching, interstate banking, and financial-service diversification came increasingly under attack. But it was not so much free-market sympathies as the threat of insolvency that was driving policy-makers to loosen restrictions. Size, scale, scope, and diversity were increasingly seen as the best, and perhaps only, hedges against financial risk.

By 1988, interstate banking had become more the norm than the exception, with the emergence of several new regional giants. The Federal Savings and Loan Insurance Corporation was insolvent, and the Federal Deposit Insurance Corporation was wavering. Congress was deliberating over a bailout for deposit insurance, a ban on non-bank banks, and a reduction of Glass–Steagall restrictions on commercial banks.

The consequences of regulatory reform

The reduction of economic regulation in America has provided a sort of laboratory for industrial organization and political economy. Changes in market structure, political stakeholders, and business strategy have been compressed and dramatic. In fact, the market-structuring effects of deregulation have underscored the degree to which regulatory intervention originally shaped these sectors.

In all the regulated industries, entry was severely restricted. With the removal of regulatory barriers, scores of low-cost, entrepreneurial entrants flocked into the highest-volume, most over-priced markets. Entry was also accomplished by back-wards integration from users, by diversification from related business, or by restructuring incumbents. Exit too became less difficult, and as the airlines experience has shown, a major risk for entrants.

Regulatory market segmentation broke down as new segment economics undermined tariff or charter restrictions. Just as quickly, however, competing businesses developed strategies to re-segment the market, more in line with technological opportunities or customer needs.

Pricing, under regulation, was usually simple, with various services bundled together. Distribution channels were likewise underdeveloped or non-existent. With deregulation, pricing immediately became a competitive tool, far more diversified than economists had anticipated. Across all these industries, real prices generally fell and all sorts of new pricing options and packages became available: discount fares, freight contracts, variable interest rates, and off-peak telephone rates. Distribution channels became critical links to customers – the means of implementing invigorated marketing plans; computerized reservation systems in airlines, computerized dispatch in trucking, spot markets and brokers in natural gas, and automated teller machines in banking.

Cost reduction was the most painful, but central, aspect of deregulation. Reductions in headcount, wages and workrules, operations, and asset utilization affected every sector. The further deregulation progressed, the more severe the cost reduction, with airlines leading and banks lagging.

The structure of regulated industries, shaped by regulators during the Great Depression, had nothing to do with the competitive and technological characteristics of those businesses in America of the 1970s and 1980s. In airlines, railroads, and natural gas pipelines, mergers substantially concentrated market share and produced entirely new operating networks. In banking, the rationalization was well under way, and in telecommunications, the AT&T monopoly had been replaced by closely related oligopolies.

Even industry boundaries changed dramatically with deregulation. What had been a telephone business, for example, evolved into a much larger market for telecommunications and information services. Banking became but a chartered piece of the financial services sector; and trucking, railroads, barges, and shipping were merging into a global freight-transport industry.

These immense changes in market structure were accompanied by analogous changes in the political arena. Vested interests changed, political coalitions gained or lost coherence, and new pressures on the 'public interest' developed. Opposing political forces pulled and hauled at the future course of policy. On the one hand, deregulation developed a considerable momentum, driving beyond economic reason. 'Re-regulation', on the other hand, was a sort of political and bureaucratic counterforce arising from the ill-effects on special interests, from general performance problems, and from adverse structural developments.

For firms in all of these industries, strategy and organizational structure were severely tested and usually found in need of radical change. Basic corporate goals and performance objectives had to be reassessed. Operating practice, marketing, investment and finance, and personnel policies had to be re-conceived and reoriented – and above all, coordinated with political strategy.

Regulated competition – a contradictory course

Writing from the perspective of the late 1980s, it now appears as if America's fling with deregulation has either stalled, or given way to a hybrid form of public policy – 'regulated competition'. This latter prospect merits a brief discussion.

Under regulated competition, government officials attempt to manage competitive markets. This is different from the regulation of monopoly, where regulation substitutes for competition, or from deregulation, where government withdraws from the market. Although it is new to natural gas, telecommunications, and banking, it is not altogether new. From 1947 to 1978, regulated competition was attempted in airlines. It proved to be grossly inefficient, and eventually untenable.

The central problems of regulated competition are inadequate information, inadequate authority, and inadequate incentive. Setting rules for competitive markets is like determining marginal costs; Alfred Kahn compared it to finding a black cat in a black room. Even the most sophisticated regulatory methods and statistical tools are insufficiently dynamic to keep pace with the market conditions. And if they were, regulators would too often lack the necessary will or political discretion to act accordingly. And even then, the presence of regulation could not help but distort business and managerial incentives – raising or lowering risk, and restricting or underwriting profit in some manner or another.

Regulated competition poses difficult strategic problems for the firms it affects. A company faced with competition must minimize cost and pursue sales, almost by definition. Yet regulation – and especially rate-of-return regulation – tends to mute, or reverse, the incentives to do this. Regulatory restrictions invariably create loopholes, posing profit opportunities. Competition, then, creates compelling pressures to exploit them – despite their artificiality and inherent risk. Product/market innovation is distorted by regulatory barriers and discouraged by public disclosure. Risk and earnings are decoupled.

For public policy, regulated competition raises some related issues. First, and already grossly apparent in telecommunications and natural gas, is the need for more, *not less*, regulation. Competition among firms is obviously more difficult and more complicated to control than merely supervising a monopoly. Cost allocations, in any multi-product industry, become increasingly complex, as regulators must unbundle rates and dissolve cross-subsidies. Antitrust policing, to prevent cross-subsidization of competitive products, or discriminatory and predatory pricing, becomes increasingly necessary for regulators, as well as for the Justice Department. And finally, and most unavoidable, are the unanticipated, and usually undesirable, consequences of intervening in competitive markets.

Nearly 90 years ago, just as regulation was getting started, the visionary chairman of AT&T, Theodore Vail, concluded that 'effective, aggressive competition, and regulation and control are inconsistent with each other, and cannot be had at the same time'. More recently, Alfred Kahn, drawing on his experience in airline deregulation, came to much the same conclusion: 'there was no rational halfway house between thorough regulation and free competition.'

If these thoughtful observers are right, and I think they probably are, then

America's drift towards regulated competition should be carefully reconsidered, by private and public policy-makers alike.

Notes

1. For the early history of regulatory ideas and institutions, see Thomas K. McCraw, 'Regulatory Agencies', Glen Porter, ed., *Encyclopedia of American Economic History*, Charles Scribner's Sons, New York 1980, vol. II; and *Prophets of Regulation*, Harvard University Press, Cambridge 1984
2. Paul T. David, *The Economics of Air Mail Transportation*, The Brookings Institution, Washington, DC 1934; J. Howard Hamstra, 'Two decades – federal aero-regulation in perspective', *The Journal of Air Law and Commerce*, 12, 2 (April 1941), pp 108–114; and Dudley F. Pegrum, *Transportation Economics and Public Policy*, Richard Irwin, Homewood, IL 1985
3. Federal Power Commission, Docket No. G-580, *Natural Gas Investigation*, GPO, Wash., DC 1948; John Ise, *The United States Oil Industry*, Yale University Press, New Haven 1928; and Norman Nordhauser, *The Quest for Stability: Domestic Oil Regulation 1917–1935*, Garland Publishing, New York 1979
4. Gerald Brock, *The Telecommunications Industry: The Dynamics of Market Structure*, Harvard University Press, Cambridge 1981; Federal Communications Commission, *Investigation of the Telephone Industry in the United States*, in US Congress, House, *House Document No. 340* (76th Cong., 1st Sess.) 1938; and Richard H.K. Vietor, 'AT&T and the public good: regulation and competition in telecommunications, 1910–1987', Boston: HBS Working Paper 87-056, 1987
5. Thomas F. Huertas, 'The regulation of financial institutions: a historical perspective on current issues', in American Assembly, *Financial Services: The Changing Institutions and Government Policy*, Prentice-Hall, Englewood Cliffs, NJ 1983; and Nelson Peach, *The Security Affiliates of National Banks*, Baltimore 1941
6. Susan E. Kennedy, *The Banking Crisis of 1933*, University of Kentucky Press, Lexington 1933; Ari and Olive Hoogenboom, *A History of the ICC*, W.W. Norton & Co., New York 1976, pp 104–105; and N.R. Danielian, AT&T: The Story of Industry Conquest, The Vanguard Press, New York 1939, p 410
7. Franklin D. Roosevelt, Inaugural Address, March 4, 1933, in *Public Papers and Addresses of Franklin D. Roosevelt*, Random House, New York 1939, vol. I
8. For the best general studies of regulation, see Stephen Breyer, *Regulation and its Reform*, Harvard University Press, Cambridge 1982; James Q. Wilson, *The Politics of Regulation*, Basic Books, New York 1980; and Alfred Kahn, *Economics of Regulation, Principles and Institutions*, John Wiley & Sons, New York 1970
9. See Richard E. Caves, *Air Transport and its Regulators*, Harvard University

Press, Cambridge 1962, Samuel B. Richmond, *Regulation and Competition in Air Transportation*, Columbia University Press, New York 1961, and William Fruhan, *The Fight for a Competitive Advantage*, Harvard Business School, Division of Research, Boston 1972

10. Elizabeth E. Bailey, David R. Graham, and Daniel P. Kaplan, *Deregulating the Airlines*, MIT Press, Cambridge 1985, p 19; also, Richard H.K. Vietor, 'American airlines and deregulation', HBS Working Paper, Boston 1988

11. Arlon Tussing and Connie Barlow, *The Natural Gas Industry: Evolution, Structure, and Economics*, Ballinger Publishing Co., Cambridge 1984, chapter 8

12. Richard H.K. Vietor, *Energy Policy in America Since 1945*, Cambridge University Press, New York 1984, chapters 7 and 11

13. In that year, AT&T settled an antitrust suit with the Justice Department, in which AT&T was allowed to retain Western Electric and its vertically integrated structure. It agreed, however, not to enter data processing or other non-telephone markets; see Richard H.K. Vietor, 'AT&T and the public good: regulation and competition in telecommunications, 1910–1987', HBS Working Paper, Boston, MA 1987

14. Richard H.K. Vietor, 'Regulation-defined financial markets: fragmentation and integration in financial services', in Samuel L. Hayes, III, ed., *Wall Street and Regulation*, HBS Press, Boston 1987, pp 7–62

15. Martha Derthick and Paul J. Quirk, *The Politics of Deregulation*, The Brookings Institution, Wash., DC 1985

16. William E. Fruhan, Jr, *The Fight for Competitive Advantage*, Division of Research, Graduate School of Business Administration, Harvard University, Boston 1972, p 24; and Richard Vietor, 'American airlines and deregulation', pp 36–42

17. Civil Aeronautics Board, *Handbook of Airline Statistics, 1972*, Washington 1972 and Civil Aeronautics Board, *Regulatory Reform: Report of the C.A.B. Special Staff, 1975*, Washington 1975, pp 142–143

18. Stephen Breyer, *Regulation and its Reform*, pp 197–220

19. Richard H.K. Vietor, 'Chicago-Midway (A): Alfred Kahn at the CAB', HBS Case Services, No. 9-384-156, Boston 1984; and M. Derthick and P. Quirk, *The Politics of Deregulation*

20. Elizabeth Bailey et al., *Deregulating the Airlines*, pp 54–66; also, Robert Joedicke (Shearson Lehman Brothers), *Airline Analyst's Handbook*, September 12, 1988, pp 8–9

21. Richard Vietor, 'American airlines and deregulation', pp 72–75, 84–89; also, Elizabeth Bailey and Jeffrey Williams, 'Sources of economic rent in the deregulated airline industry', *Journal of Law & Economics*, vol. XXXI (April 1988), pp 173–202; also, David K. Massey, 'Hub strategies', *Airline Executive*, June 1987, pp 37–41

22. *New York Times*, March 20, 1988

23. Department of Transportation, *Air Carrier Monthly Traffic Statistics*, 1986 and 1987

24. Merill Lynch, *Airline Industry*, November 1985, and Department of Transportation, *Air Carrier Monthly Traffic Statistics*, June 1987

25. Accident rates and fatalities decreased, through continuing improvements in avionics. Only the incidence of near-collisions increased, and this seemed largely due to the sharp increase in traffic volume; Federal Trade Commission, Bureau of Economics, *The Deregulated Airline Industry: A Review of the Evidence*, January 1988, Washington, DC, pp 76–77

26. Conventional measures of service quality declined, for much the same reason. Performance by individual carriers, however, diverged dramatically, suggesting that strategic choice (or ineptitude) was also a factor; see, US Department of Transportation, *Air Travel Consumer Report*, November 1987

27. Of at least 18 new entrants in the major routes between 1979 and 1985, 15 failed or were acquired; DOT, *Air Carrier Monthly Traffic Statistics, 1986, 1987*, and *Air Transport World*, June 1987, pp 64–65. In the commuter airlines segment, 48 of the 50 largest firms have been tied to majors through joint marketing arrangements, or been acquired; Clinton V. Oster, Jr and Don H. Pickrell, 'Marketing alliances and competitive strategy in the airline industry', *Logistics and Transportation Review*, 22, 4 (1986), pp 371–387; also, 'Major U.S. airlines rapidly gain control over regional lines', *Wall Street Journal*, February 17, 1988

28. W.M. Jacobs to Lee White, December 16, 1968, reprinted in US Congress, House, Interstate Commerce Committee, Subcommittee on Communications and Power, *Natural Gas Act of 1971*, 92nd Cong., 1st Sess., September 1971, p 139

29. Richard H.K. Vietor, *Energy Policy in America*, pp 157–160, 196–198, 270; also, American Gas Association, *Gas Facts 1979*, AGA, Arlington, VA 1980, p 6

30. The Commission tried allowing pipeline companies that produced gas to charge the same rates received by independent producers; allowing pipelines to enter joint ventures; exempting smaller producers from regulation; and approving emergency sales, for a limited term, at market prices. See for example, Federal Power Commission, 'Pipeline production area rate proceeding', *Opinion No. 568*, 42 FPC 738 (1969), aff'd *City of Chicago v. FPC*, 458 F. 2d 731 (D.C. Cir. 1971); *P.S.C. of New York v. FPC*, 511 F. 2d 338 (D.C. Cir. 1975)

31. US Congress, Senate, *Conference Report No. 95-1126*, 'The Natural Gas Policy Act of 1978' (95th Cong., 2nd Sess.), August 18, 1978

32. Maryland People's Counsel v. FERC, 761 F. 2nd 280 (D.C. Cir.); FERC, *Order No. 436*, 50 *Fed. Reg.* 42, 408 (October 18, 1985); and *Order No. 451a*, June 6, 1986

33. *Above 890 Mc.*, 27 F.C.C. 359 (1959)

34. *Microwave Communications, Inc.*, 18 F.C.C. 2d, 953 (1969)

35. Steve Coll, *The Deal of the Century*, Atheneum, New York 1986, pp 51–52, 83–85; also, *United States v. AT&T*, Civil Action No. 74-1698, 'Defendants'

Third Statement of Contentions and Proof', March 10, 1980, pp 473–480, 685–688

36. *MCI Inc. v. FCC*, 580 F. 2d 590 (D.C. Cir.), cert. denied, 439 US 980 (1878)
37. *Carterfone*, 13 F.C.C. 2d 606 (1968)
38. 35 F.C.C. 2nd 539 (1972); 56 F.C.C. 2d 593 (1975)
39. *US v. AT&T*, C.A. No. 74-1698, Testimony of Ronald Ruebusch, Advanced Micro Devices (Defendant's Exhibit D-T-359), p 6
40. *Regulatory & Policy Problems Presented by the Interdependence of Computer & Communications Services & Facilities*, 28 F.C.C. 2d 267 (1971)
41. *Second Computer Inquiry*, 77 F.C.C. 2d 384 (1980)
42. FCC, Docket No. 85-229, 'Report and order', *Third Computer Inquiry*, June 16, 1986
43. Peter Temin with Louis Galambos, *The Fall of the Bell System*, Cambridge University Press, New York 1987; Richard H.K. Vietor, 'AT&T and the public good'
44. *US v AT&T*, C.A. No. 82-0192, 'Modification of final judgment', August 24, 1982; also, Gerald R. Faulhaber, *Telecommunications in Turmoil: Technology and Public Policy*, Ballinger, Cambridge 1987
45. Peter W. Huber, *The Geodesic Network*, 1987 Report on Competition in the Telephone Industry, prepared for the Department of Justice in connection with the court's decision in *US v. AT&T* 552 F. Supp . 131 (D.D.C. 1982), GPO, Wash., DC 1987
46. Albert H. Cox, Jr, *Regulation of Interest Rates on Bank Deposits*, University of Michigan, Ann Arbor 1966, p 121
47. Lewis J. Spellman, *The Depository Firm and Industry: Theory, History and Regulation*, Academic Press, New York 1983, pp 141–142; and Charles F. Haywood and Charles M. Linke, *The Regulation of Deposit Interest Rates*, Association of Reserve City Bankers, Chicago 1968, pp 38–41; also, Herbert Dougall and Jack Gaumnitz, *Capital Markets and Institutions*, Prentice Hall, Englewood Cliffs, 3rd edn, 1975, pp 169, 180
48. Thomas Cargill and Gillian Garcia, *Financial Reform in the 1980s*, Hoover Institute Press, Stanford 1985, pp 81–84
49. Office of Technology Assessment, *Effects of Information Technology on Financial Service Systems*, Washington, DC 1984
50. Harvy Rosenblum, 'Banks and nonbanks: who's in control?', *The Bankers Magazine*, September/October 1984, p 13
51. Quoted in Stephen Koepp , 'Banking takes a beating', *Time*, December 3, 1984, p 50
52. Joel Seligman, *The Transformation of Wall Street*, Houghton Mifflin, Boston 1982; also, Gregg A. Jarrell, 'Change at the exchange: the causes and effects of deregulation', XXVII, October 1984, p 277
53. Andrew S. Carron, *The Plight of the Thrift Institutions*, The Brookings Institution, Washington 1982; also, Frederick Balderston, *Thrifts in Crisis*, Ballinger Publishing Co., Cambridge 1985

3 The business of the Japanese state

*Richard J. Samuels**

The paradox

This essay starts from the curious fact that the Japanese state, reputed to be among the strongest, smartest and most centralized in the industrial world (and faced with resource constraints second to none) is nowhere a direct, commercial participant in energy markets. Despite a pervasive regulatory presence, Japan has no European-style national oil champion, no national electric utility and no state-owned coal mines.

In energy, as in other sectors, the Japanese state is a ubiquitous market player without a commercial market presence. Japan has a state-owned oil firm that does not explore, produce, transport, refine or sell oil; it has part ownership in an electric utility that is prohibited from selling power to end users; and it has not owned a coal mine in more than a century. By the mid-1980s the Japanese government had even divested holdings in the few businesses in which it had enjoyed a commercial stake: the salt and tobacco monopoly, telecommunications and national railways.

The near absence of state ownership distinguishes Japan from most of Western Europe. The Europeans build national champions with state equity, the Japanese restructure private markets. One question is why they do so. Another is whether it matters. Some would argue that it does not matter whether the Japanese state is a commercial participant in markets. Japanese state planners prefer regulation to ownership, it is often held, because regulation affords greater flexibility without compromising state authority. They prefer market-conforming policies to market-displacing policies because they believe the market is a policy instrument most efficiently controlled by indirect means.

I suggest a different explanation for the nature and extent of state intervention in the Japanese market place. In 300 years of coal and 100 years of oil and electric power development, direct state intervention has always mattered. Regulation has often been the planners' second choice in Japanese industrial policy; regulation,

* This chapter is derived from the author's longer study, *The Business of the Japanese State: Energy Markets in Comparative and Historical Perspective* published in 1987 by Cornell University Press. It is reprinted here with permission.

even when it is most extensive, has depended upon the cooperation and preferences of the private actors.

Japan is a singular case of public policy without public ownership. The Japanese state is a market-conforming player not because it is strong enough to control by other means, nor because it is smart enough to appreciate the efficiency of the market, but because in the development of Japanese commerce and industry powerful and stable private actors emerged who established enduring alliances with politicians and bureaucrats. These same actors vigilantly checked market-displacing intervention. As a result, the Japanese state, when it intervenes, usually attempts to reproduce shifting market structures and it does so by fortifying the position of existing firms.

Of course, these market-conforming actions cannot prevent significant transformations of market structure in Japan. Indeed, these shifts help explain the pervasiveness of the Japanese state in the economy; because there is no end to market instability, there is no end to efforts by the state and firms alike to order markets. As a consequence, intervention by the Japanese state is paradoxical – the Japanese state is pervasive in the economy because, as we shall see, private actors have learned how to limit and enhance state power simultaneously. They surrender jurisdiction to retain control.

The point at issue is not why the state is so pervasive in the Japanese economy but why firms find the pervasive state so congenial. The answer lies in the ways that private interests have institutionalized their access to public goods. I thus conclude that the market place and state structures are as fully the product of negotiation and opportunity in Japan as they are elsewhere. This analysis challenges assumptions of bureaucratic dominance and state-led capitalism in Japan. It suggests, rather, a comparative framework of 'reciprocal consent'. The state often helps structure market choices, but public/private negotiations invariably structure state and market choices alike. By incorporating Japan, this framework suggests the need for caution in the application of models of state-society relations which stress the autonomy and capacity of the democratic state. For the politics of reciprocal consent, negotiation and compact are the core of business-state relations.

The politics of reciprocal consent

The political interdependence of states and markets is a matter of permanent negotiation, what I call the politics of reciprocal consent. The analysis of this politics begins not with the state but with the objective of those negotiations, control of the market itself. To explore the mutual accommodation of state and market, we must first ask whose market it is. Questions about identity, autonomy, capacity and development (what is the state, whose it is, what can it do and where is it going) often obscure explanation of market outcome by paying excessive attention to public policy and state structures. Our prior question compels us first to identify structural transformations in the market, alterations in relations among producers or between producers and consumers (and/or the state) which affect the ability of any or all of these actors to pursue the market strategies of their choice. Only then do we inquire about the role of states, firms and other players, including labour. This approach assumes no barriers or permanent balances of power between state and society. Instead it uses compact and negotiation to explore how power and resources in shifting markets illuminate these other issues.

Reciprocal consent is the mutual accommodation of state and market. It is an iterative process of reassurance among market players and public officials, one that works better where the parties to these negotiations are stable and where the institutions that guarantee their compacts are enduring. This notion is consistent with Axelrod (1984), although it was developed independently.[1] I analyse these compacts with explicit regard for a subtle but critical distinction between jurisdiction and control. Jurisdiction is the territory within which authority can be exercised, and control is the exercise of that authority. By 'consent' I imply that both public and private jurisdictions in markets are negotiated and draw attention to the interdependence of public and private power. Market jurisdiction is not monopolized by states or by private firms. Likewise control, defined in terms of leadership and authority, is something better discovered than attributed. Instead of assuming the leadership and autonomy of either state or private actors, therefore, I explore their mutual accommodations within particular markets and then explain the distribution of power.

By 'reciprocity' I imply that jurisdiction can belong to private firms as well as to the state. Control is mutually constrained. In exchange for the use of public resources, private industry grants the state some jurisdiction over industrial structure in the 'national interest'. Business enjoys privilege, systematic inclusion in the policy process, access to public goods, and rights of self-regulation. It reciprocates by agreeing to state jurisdiction in the definition of market structure and by participating in the distribution of benefits.

The nature and extent of that jurisdiction is permanently being adjusted; private firms continuously seek to separate state aid from state control. Both business and government have jurisdiction; both lack exclusive control. Each, at different times, will surrender the one to retain the other. Businessmen are invited into the interior processes of government, and bureaucrats are invited into the interior processes of the market. In short, business in government is exchanged for government in business. A focus on market transformations rather than on state structures reveals how that exchange is consummated. It also reveals how each competing group defines its own vision of a national interest while trying to transfer the costs of pursuing that interest to others.[2]

The notion of reciprocal consent assumes that states, no less than markets, are a function of shifting compacts. The analysis of these compacts can accept structured relations between state and society, but it must not reify them. It must allow for state autonomy without ignoring private strategies. It assumes permanent negotiations for the distribution of public and private power without attributing a consistent monopoly of jurisdiction or control to particular groups or actors. It disaggregates states and markets to specify strategies of exchange. In sum, it recognizes there is no a priori way to sort out patron and client in most policy settings.[3] This study explores the market to reconstruct this compact and to explain how and to what extent private preferences and state preferences, when they diverge, are reconciled. It thereby provides a record of where preferences originate and how they are articulated.

Japanese energy as the critical case

Relations between state and society and between business and government, I believe, can be illuminated by a critical case study.[4] The purpose is to either support or refute propositions by applying them to the most difficult case one can find. Japanese energy policy is just such an analytically strategic case. Japan and the energy industries are each critical in different ways. Each offers a 'most-likely' scenario for state strength, state autonomy and convergence. Taken together, they represent a rare opportunity for the analysis of business-government relations in the industrial democracies.

Energy

Nowhere is there a less ambiguous test of state strength and state autonomy than in the energy sector. Energy policy, especially after 1973, should least reflect societal influences on states struggling to cope with fiscal and industrial adjustment. Strategic concerns, specifically those associated with the acquisition of stable supplies of petroleum, should a priori be less hospitable to societal demands than other sectors where society, polity and economy seem less vulnerable. Moreover, the energy sector is an obvious candidate for state intervention, if only because the state enjoys a comparative advantage over private interests in foreign policy.[5] The dependence of many industrial economies upon foreign energy supplies invites the intervention of the state.

The state should be especially strong in energy industries for another reason: energy markets are among the most standardized of markets. Because energy trade in gas, coal and oil is commodity based, policy planners need concern themselves only with production and distribution. They need not worry about market niches and product development as they might in electronics, automobiles or machine tools. As state planners and private manufacturers alike see energy industries as upstream prerequisites for industrial development, we should expect these sectors to be early targets for state intervention.

Both points are easily asserted in an era of oil crises, Middle Eastern political instability and interfuel substitution, but a similar argument holds for the interwar period and the wartime that interwar energy choices helped create. States have seldom been more assertive than they were in the 1920s, when they sought protection from foreign control through state ownership in the various energy industries, particularly oil.[6] Likewise, states seldom actively intervened when cheap oil first began to replace coal as the energy source of choice. If there is state autonomy to be discovered and state leadership to be evaluated, we are likely to find them in the energy industries.

Japan

Japan contributes even more unambiguously to a critical case for the analysis of business-state relations in the industrial democracies. Theories about state and society in Japan have long been at odds with central theoretical drifts elsewhere. In the West, liberal and Marxist approaches to state and society share the fundamental assumption that societal preferences prevail when they diverge from state preferences.[7] Japan, on the other hand, has a long tradition of explicitly including the state in the explanation of economic development. One description of Meiji Japan gives the flavour of that interpretative tradition: 'The Japanese state's awesome ability to extract unlimited compliance from its subjects and to mobilize all of the economy's resources for specific goals of the state indicates a perfect synchronization of polity, society, and economy.'[8] The analytical notion of 'bringing the state back in' is thus ipso facto curious to generations of Japan scholars who have assumed a pervasive state in the economy. Put simply, Japan is the most unambiguous case of state autonomy and strength.

Analyses of business-state relations in Japan rest on four often contradictory assumptions. In identifying the Japanese state, many analysts have posited harmony among interests in society. This study explores conflict. In assessing the relative autonomy of the Japanese state, most observers posit state independence and state control. This study separates independence from interdependence and control from jurisdiction. In evaluations of state capacity, the dominant view of Japan has been one of strength and, often, prescience. This study explores constraints and fortuity, occasionally discovering weakness. Finally, accounts of Japanese development have stressed inexorability. I examine choices and contingencies in an effort to restore bounded indeterminacy to models of the Japanese political economy. I explore each of these points briefly.

Views of a harmonious, consensual, monolithic 'Japan, Inc.' have fallen on hard times in recent years, and for good reason. A useful notion has been unfairly exaggerated.[9] It identified an interlocking directorate of competing elites from big business, the Liberal Democratic Party (LDP) and the bureaucracy who, through institutionalized and exhaustive consultation and negotiation, reached consensus. Agreements could be enforced because of the stability of the Japanese elite. State and society were difficult to untangle. In its original formulation Japan, Inc. remains a valuable description of how the system works; no more elegant formulation has yet been developed. Unfortunately, popularizers chose to ignore the competition within the ruling triangle, opting instead to explain Japanese competitiveness – and indeed the very identity of the competitor – as a monolithic, consensual, machinelike organism solely bent upon national aggrandizement.[10]

Two groups of scholars reject this simplified and teleological view of the

Japanese political economy. Liberal economists deny that markets can be so orderly or even that the state could have played so determinant a role in Japanese development.[11] Political scientists point to the political significance of groups outside the triangle, demonstrating how important decisions are made through political conflict.[12] This study builds upon these efforts looking to reconcile notions of conflict and consensus in the Japanese policy process without doing violence to the one by overstating the other. The identity of the Japanese state may, in the final evaluation, look very much like the interpenetrated, collusive Japan, Inc. of days past. But we need to identify the mechanisms of collusion and interpenetration. We also need to recognize that consensus, even where we find it, is the product of conflict rather than the alternative to it.

Questions of autonomy and development are closely connected to this point and scholars have entertained a curious ambivalence on the issue. Bernard Silberman assumes the most extreme position. He speaks of a period of bureaucratic absolutism (1868–1900), followed by a limited pluralism under which the state was *primus inter pares* with private interests (1900–1936). In his view the Japanese state ultimately emerges as the organizer of all interests during a period of state corporatism (1936–1945). He insists that 'from the very beginning of the Restoration, the state played a dominant role in the organization of interests and the determination of public policy' and that during the 1930s 'the state foreclosed on all concepts of interests'. His Japanese state is an autonomous actor driving to depoliticize interests and substitute administration for politics to solve the central problem of the era – the governability of society. T.J. Pempel and K. Tsunekawa seem to concur. They argue that Japan between 1938 and 1945 was an 'almost perfectly congruent example of state corporatism. . . . [By 1940] all autonomous interest associations were replaced by a monolithic organ of totalistic state control.'[13] In political histories, then, the Japanese state looms large.

Economic histories have always cast the state as the central actor in Japanese economic development, but they have been more careful to incorporate a role for private interests. Jerome Cohen, for example, sees early Japanese development as 'nurtured in a virtual state incubator', but he also sees how industrial interests unwilling to bow to the demands of the military and the economic bureaucracy compromised state efforts to separate management from capital.[14] Other students of the development of capitalism in Japan concur. Some Japanese scholars stress the role of political merchants (*seishō*) who learned early in the Meiji era how to use the state to protect themselves from excessive risk.[15] Others focus upon the state-sanctioned cartels and industry-specific legislation of mid-century Japan.[16] The consensus among economic historians is that, as Barrington Moore put it, 'Japanese big business successfully resisted attempts to subordinate profits to patriotism.'[17]

This point is too often overlooked because the confusion of jurisdiction with control is accompanied by a confusion of state autonomy with state capacity. The developmental state is often confused with the strong state. Chalmers Johnson suggests, for example, that most of the ideas for postwar reconstruction 'came from the bureaucracy and the business community responded with . . . "responsive

41

dependence" '.[18] Ironically, this confusion has been more pronounced than it was even during wartime mobilization. Pempel and Tsunekawa argue, for example, that MITI's power to intervene after the war 'was much more institutionalized and corporatized than anything big business had encountered during the prewar period'.[19] Analysts have groped for explanations, stressing the state's capacity to intervene in the Japanese economy at the expense of clear explanations for the ways in which markets and market players help shape that intervention. All analysts acknowledge the role of the private sector, but most stress the power of the state.

Most available descriptions of the Japanese political economy exaggerate state power at the expense of private power, as if the two were mutually exclusive; they use such terms as 'guided free enterprise', 'state-led capitalism', 'administered competition', 'quasi-capitalism' and 'bureaucratic inclusionary pluralism'.[20] In contrast, when the Japanese are asked who governs, in public opinion surveys, they uniformly ascribe far greater power to the politicians, bosses and big businessmen than to the bureaucrats.[21] But the bureaucracy gets the credit from scholars and, certainly, from elite bureaucrats themselves. Johnson's observation that 'the elite bureaucracy of Japan makes most major decisions, drafts virtually all legislation, controls the national budget, and is the source of all major policy innovations in the system' is now widely quoted, ignoring the author's own caveats and more balanced observations about pressure groups and the private sector.[22]

Because so much recent scholarship has been concerned with comparative evaluations of how and how effectively states are able to intervene in their economies, the overstatement of the importance of key actors, particularly the state, in the Japanese policy process has important implications. Few studies of Japanese economic policy by Japan specialists are overtly comparative, and many overtly comparative studies of Japan are not by specialists; perhaps as a result, most work on contemporary Japan stresses the strength of the state rather than the constraints upon it. But the developmental state need not be the archetypical strong state; the comprehensive visions and role of the Japanese state do not necessarily resemble those of France more than those of the United States.

These distinctions have a significance beyond a better understanding of business-state relations in Japan. Japan's late industrialization and economic success have reinforced the idea that there is only one economic rationality, that of a standardized efficient, and centralized productive machine. Japan has been portrayed as the very embodiment of economic modernity.[23] If this is so, it should nowhere be easier to demonstrate than when the Japanese state intervenes directly in the energy market place. Let us briefly explore the historical evidence.

Historical evidence

Coal

The lengthy debates and incomplete solutions to the multiple historic crises of Japanese coal reveal striking historical continuities. The Japanese state has been pervasive across centuries of uncertain and volatile coal markets. But it has had a commercial market presence only when domestic producers were weak and disinterested, as in the Edo and early Meiji periods; when there was a military government (and even then state participation was limited to nonproductive, 'tunnel' functions); or when a foreign occupation force advocated state control. The coal mines in Japan were never permanently nationalized, nor even effectively consolidated by the Japanese state. Prices were never set by state agencies, except when costs were subsidized and profits were guaranteed to producers. Instead, the Japanese state has served as guarantor to private firms whose own commitment to coal mining ultimately (and rationally) evaporated.

The failure to nationalize the mines in Japan is due neither to lack of effort nor to a bureaucratic commitment to free market principles and efficiency. It is directly attributable to the politics of reciprocal consent and to the several factors that have shaped these negotiations about the nature and extent of state intervention.

Consider first how market structure has constrained the state. Coal mining firms were divided in several politically relevant ways. Large mining firms were split between *zaibatsu* and local capital. These producers assembled and disassembled collusive mechanisms, only occasionally with the state's help, and their collusive history is riven with exceptions and violations. Add to this mixture the politically savvy and influential small mining firms and industrial consumers. In the absence of a well-coordinated, highly centralized, and markedly determined state, we are left with all the ingredients for an exceedingly messy policy process.

This is precisely what the policy record reveals; it is related to the way state centralization shapes the capacity of states to intervene in markets. Characterizations of 'clear state visions' in Japan and 'conflated' private interest notwithstanding,[24] the policy record shows fragmented but individually powerful private interests labouring with a divided economic bureaucracy to assure state intervention that was extensive but market-conforming. Neither business nor state was consistently unified. It was conflict among subgovernmental coalitions that set the policy agenda on coal.

Third, the breadth and stability of Japan's ruling coalition was critically important in ensuring that intervention would remain market-conforming. The impermanence of Japan's Socialist coalition in 1947 was matched by the impermanence of state control of the coal mines. Although the Katayama Cabinet made nationalization thinkable for economic bureaucrats who had long coveted such a role in the economy, the opportunity proved only fleeting. The experiment with state control was eviscerated even before its enactment and was responsible for the collapse of the only 'progressive' cabinet Japan has ever had. The bureaucracy put forward other proposals for nationalization, but as one former MITI Mining Bureau chief put it, MITI finally abandoned the idea of nationalization because 'once the LDP had consolidated its power, there was no chance such a program could seriously be considered'.[25]

Timing also mattered. It is no coincidence that the state enjoyed its most direct role in the management and ownership of Japan's coal mines when the Meiji oligarchs were starting their forced march toward industrialization. The observation conforms nicely with Alexander Gerschenkron's hypothesis about state intervention being likely where private capital is underdeveloped and where investment requirements are large and lumpy.[26] Once private capital, particularly *zaibatsu* capital, became concentrated, the state forever relinquished ownership of the mines.

The state's lingering temptation to become mineowner and manager is linked to the displacement of coal by oil as the energy of choice. Interfuel substitution, derived from import dependence, resulted in an energy revolution that overwhelmed domestic coal. As Japan's industrial economy slowly opened for foreign oil, the public treasury bore the escalating costs of the state's acting as guarantor. The political benefits of providing unlimited state subsidies to coal producers seemed always to outweigh the staggering economic costs. Johnson has noted the inefficiencies of 'the policy of extensively subsidizing the coal industry in lieu of nationalizing it'.[27] A former Coal Bureau chief, who tried and failed on at least three separate occasions to establish precisely that presence, concurs in a blunt retrospective: 'All things considered, it would have been cheaper to nationalize the mines.'[28]

In short, despite its repeated efforts to control domestic coal production, prices, and distribution, the Japanese state has participated in the market only on terms negotiated with and acceptable to other market players. Coal policy was doomed to be inconclusive because market volatility clashed with the political stability of policy choices. It seems clear that no government policy, no known technological innovation, no industry strategy could have produced a competitive Japanese coal industry in the late 20th century. Mining firms seem to have appreciated the fact sooner and more clearly than state planners did. These firms consistently shaped and used public policy to ease market transitions, and they did so in ways that frustrated the very state programs for which they had lobbied before circumstances changed.

Coal, then, is a case of negotiated jurisdiction and reciprocal consent. But coal was not exceptional. Similarly negotiated constraints on state power obtained in other energy sectors.

Electric power

In the 100-year policy record of efforts by the state, financial institutions, industrial consumers and utilities to negotiate the nature and extent of state intervention, we find that private control of Japan's electric power industry has mostly been preserved. Private utilities repeatedly blunted state efforts to displace private markets. A review of market transformations in electric power, as in the case of coal, reveals sustained efforts by producers to effect a protective collusion. It also reveals a bureaucracy eager to force the pace of consolidation under its own control. Only during the Pacific War did the Japanese state and its allies in the private sector achieve even a significant part of its vision for comprehensive transformation of the sector. This incomplete nationalization came undone quickly after the war, and though the idea resurfaces from time to time, never since has nationalization been a matter for serious debate. Instead, MITI supervises the Electric Power Development Corporation, an anaemic heir to a wartime national electric utility, Nippatsu, which is prohibited by its private shareholders from displacing any but the most peripheral markets participants. Japan has the most fully private electric power sector in the world today.

Several factors help explain this outcome; the most convincing are related to market structure. The failure to nationalize electric power in Japan reveals much about the politics of reciprocal consent where private markets are well developed. State intervention in electric power, unlike in the case of coal, began after private capitalists had already established control over the generation, transmission, and sale of electric power. Meiji-era bonds to displaced samurai may have bought the new government time to restructure the national state, but they also provided partners for such entrepreneurs as Shibusawa Eiichi and Fujioka Ichisuke. Unregulated electric businesses grew apace, immune from all state designs on private markets which private actors themselves did not help draft. Indeed, industry succour of young political parties during the Taishō parliamentary experiment helped preserve private control.

But 'private control' has not always meant 'self-control' by the utilities alone. This distinction, too, is related to the development of private capital markets in Japan. In 1932 the banks were a critical ally as the state forced a reorganization upon the industry which significantly and permanently altered the structure of competition. This bank intervention was occasioned by the 1932 currency crisis; it was related as much to the openness of the economy as to the plurality of interests operating within it.

The American Occupation of Japan provides a caricature of openness as an explanation for market restructuring. The only unalloyed state initiative ever to succeed in restructuring Japanese electric markets occurred under the extra-ordinary circumstances of foreign occupation. Only a foreign power stood between state ownership and private control. When the authorities intervened with its Potsdam Ordinance to create the private, regional utility system, the economic bureaucracy had assembled the broadest subgovernmental coalition ever to favour nationalized electric power. But once again the state was discomfited, this time by American reformers. Whether the Occupation intervened to prop up bureaucratic controls, as in coal, or to dismantle them, as in electric power, its rule was, ironically, the apex of state control in Japanese economic history.

Patterns of business-state relations emerge from the history of electric power markets in Japan to confirm those which we observed in the coal sector. It is the plurality of interests associated with the debates over state intervention which seems most important. This plurality obtained within both the state and the private sector. The Japanese state, despite widely accepted characterization of its capacity, unity and vision, was seldom well coordinated, even during wartime. Although it has a pervasive presence, it consistently exchanges jurisdiction for private control. State initiatives succeed only when bolstered by considerable private support. Electric power provides a clear illustration of the ways in which state centralization, market structure and openness combine to limit state jurisdiction in markets and to shape the politics of reciprocal consent. Like coal, however, it is not exceptional in this regard. The oil sector provides additional evidence about the negotiated limits to state intervention in private markets.

Oil

The history of structural transformation in the Japanese oil industry is a record of continuity no less striking than in the coal and electric power cases. The activist Japanese state has failed at nearly every juncture – in peace and war, as early as 1902 and as recently as 1984 – to entice the private sector to consolidate on its terms and under its control. Economic bureaucrats (and in the prewar period, military planners) repeatedly aimed for a vertically integrated, nationally unified petroleum industry. What emerged instead was horizontally fragmented and vertically truncated. Of this, Inokuchi Tōsuke has observed that state power and mobilization merely accelerated a process already under way in prewar and wartime Japan:

> The goal of consolidating the refining firms was inherent in the creation of the oil control companies, but owing to the diverse positions and interests of each of the firms, it could not be achieved. . . . The consolidation and concentration of the Japanese oil industry followed a capitalist route of development. Compared to the consolidation of the production and sales sectors, the separation of the refining sector into eight blocs was . . . not a reflection of the weakness of capital in that sector, but evidence of the ferocity with which private capital competed internally.[29]

But we need not assume inexorability to appreciate this politics of reciprocal consent. Disputes over the nature and extent of state intervention in the oil business usually ensured conformity to the market; but for the structurally diverse oil industry the question remains: to whose market did state policy conform? In the prewar period it was the market of the large oil firms, most of which grew even larger with state encouragement. Upstream, private firms welcomed state action. These entrepreneurs, growing impatient with the government's limited commitment to a national fuels policy and increased drilling subsidies, lobbied earliest and most vigorously for a public policy company. The result was a government policy not merely market-conforming and risk-reducing but market-guaranteeing and risk-eliminating. In refining, however, military planners could not make private capital accept unification of the industry. The state had to settle for much less than it sought, and ultimately it had to cope with much more than it bargained for.

But a market also belonged to rural interests, and it too had to be respected and preserved. Agricultural interests displayed considerable tenacity when their commercial rights were threatened in 1939 and again in 1954. These interests, by no means those of big capital, were nonetheless successful. Competitive fragmented markets clearly limited state intervention.

Above all else was the military market for petroleum. The relative unimportance of oil for the civilian economy distinguishes the wartime politics of oil from those of electric power and coal. The navy held three-quarters of Japan's total refined inventories when the Pacific War started, and by 1942 military refineries were producing nearly half of the nation's petroleum products. The state may have failed to centralize and consolidate Japanese oil, but its officers (military and civilian) intervened in every phase of the industry. There is little evidence of the corresponding intervention from banks, heavy industry and national commercial federations which redirected state planning in coal and electric power until after the war.

Once petroleum became important to heavy industry and financial institutions, negotiations over state intervention became more complex. Oil became only one of several key players, and infiltration of the industry by foreigners helped ensure that oil would not always be the most important. Nonetheless, consolidation would continue to elude the Japanese state. The objects of state efforts, which often involved collaboration with parts of private industry, were domestically capitalized oil firms. But for all the nationalistic posturing by MITI in the 1960s and 1970s, and despite the Petroleum Industry Law establishing MITI as a gatekeeper, the domestic firms' share of the nation's refining capacity increased by only 5 per cent between 1965 and 1982 and actually *declined* after 1975.[30] MITI ultimately learned that its postwar welcome in the market place was not much changed from its prewar welcome. Government proposals to restructure the industry were successively diluted; plans for a state-owned Japanese 'major' became in practice two separate, barely viable Japanese *minors*. Banks replace oil firms as the main obstacle to market restructuring.

In oil, as in electric power and coal, public policy was both ubiquitous and central in the transformation of the industry. As a result some have observed, in the words of Porges, that 'government intervention has been more pervasive in the oil industry than in any other'.[31] If so, then the political struggles over state intervention in the Japanese oil industry confirm the important difference between jurisdiction and control, between state support and state leadership, and between market conformity and market displacement. Although MITI's intervention in the oil market has been pervasive, it has been constrained consistently by bureaucratic politics, market fragmentation, and the vulnerabiity of the Japanese economy to external economic crises. The record of state efforts to restructure a fragmented industry, both up- and downstream, in oil as in coal and electric power, is punctuated by blunted initiatives, compromised ambitions, and outright failures that owe as much to conflict within the state itself as to conflict between business and state.

Alternative energy

Competition among business and state actors has decided control of investment in alternative energy in Japan. Confrontations and coalitions have shifted with perceptions of market opportunities. As a result, close business-government collaboration has been bought at a high price – both for the public purse and for the egos of MITI bureaucrats. In synfuels and in nuclear power, state intervention has been stimulated by the vulnerability of the Japanese economy and limited by an oligopolistic configuration of political resources. Both cases illuminate the relationship between openness and market concentration, as well as the frustration of apparent imperatives of openness by bureaucratic politics. In short, these cases suggest the political relevance of state and market structures. Let us explore each of these in turn.

Business offered no competition to state initiatives in synfuels until it became clear that alternatives to petroleum could provide attractive markets in their own right. State designs on private markets were moderated soon after the second oil crisis had made alternatives for competitiveness seem profitable. The market role of MITI's proposed Alternative Energy Public Corporation was transformed from producer to banker; the corporation's board of directors was immediately colonized by private-sector leaders. The same private elites that championed nuclear power assumed control of synfuels development. The same Japanese heavy industrial firms and private utilities that design and build nuclear reactors (with considerable state funding) help direct the public-funded development of alternative energy technologies.

These changes were facilitated by the oligopolistic politics of heavy industry. The capacity of utilities and power plant vendors consistently to pressure the state contrast markedly with what obtained in petroleum. This coordination seems to be related to lucrative and common markets and undoubtedly has contributed to the success of private industry in setting the pace, shape and direction for Japan's alternative energies. Where commercial applications have been low in risk and immediately apparent, for example, as in light water reactors, development has involved the initiative of private industry coordinated with the (often grudging) support of the state. Where risks have been high and applications distant, as in advanced thermal reactors, fast breeders and synfuels, the state has been enticed into accepting the bulk of financial responsibility without a commensurate degree of policy control. Roger Gale's observation about nuclear power applies to the synfuels program as well: 'The private companies, while philosophically supportive of an ambitious nuclear power program, are reluctant either to finance the development of new technologies or to see them owned and managed by the government.'[32]

State structure is relevant to the explanation of state intervention in alternative energy markets. Here private oligopoly is matched by divisions within the state, divisions that often have slowed the expansion of the state's role in these markets. Bureaucratic struggles, especially between the STA and MITI, have been as important as public-private disputes in determining the nature and extent of state intervention. The Science and Technology Agency, it should be recalled, originated in private and LDP moves in the 1950s to limit MITI jurisdiction in nuclear power. Industry and its associates in the conservative ruling party created in the STA their most important ally for blocking MITI's ambitions in both nuclear power and synthetic fuels.

Compared to many national experiences with synfuels and nuclear power, the Japanese story is one of success. In the United States the prices softened in the mid-1980s. Yet although decreasing revenues from imported petroleum reduced its budgets, Japan's New Energy Development Organization continues to fund private firms. On the nuclear side, Japanese reactors are among the world's most efficient.[33] They are also among the least expensive to construct and operate. The first half of the 1980s saw not a single new plant order in the United States; meanwhile Japan's nuclear power programme moved steadily forward. Relatively minor accidents in 1982 and 1986 failed to slow its momentum.

One obvious lesson from these battles to control markets is that market success is not determined by prescient planners. It does not emerge organizationally from centralized, strong states or from pure market competition. Market and state are both products of the negotiated politics of reciprocal consent. State structures can be created by private preferences, just as private markets can be distorted by state intervention. There is ample evidence that the reverse proposition is also true: state structures can shape private preferences, and private markets can distort themselves. Japanese successes in alternative energy are no more derived from the collaborative instincts of state planners than they are from the conciliatory politics of private interests. We do better to attribute those successes to the way state structures evolve to conform to and guarantee private markets that are, ironically, distorted by oligopolistic collaboration among private interests.

Conclusion: the Japanese state as guarantor

Chalmers Johnson has correctly observed that 'Japan offers a panoply of market-conforming methods of state intervention, including the creation of government financial institutions . . . [and] an extensive reliance on public corporations . . . to implement policy in high-risk or otherwise refractory areas.'[34] This configuration, unique among the industrial democracies, deserves explanation.

Why is the commercial role of the Japanese state so limited? Why *does* Japan, often paired with France as exemplar of the strong, centralized, planned, neo-mercantilist economy, depend so heavily upon market-conforming financial mechanisms of public intervention? What *do* the limitations upon commercial activities by the Japanese state reveal about relations between the private sector and what is reputed to be the most dominant central bureaucracy in all the industrial democracies?

The most popular answers posit bureaucratic dominance and state leadership. They acknowledge the role of the private sector but stress the power of the state. It is often an article of faith that Japanese economic bureaucrats are *primus inter pares*, directors of the Japanese economy. To one version the fact that Japanese public corporations are seldom market players matters very little; these firms are seen nonetheless as instruments of the state, populated by seconded bureaucrats who answer to their home ministries as they enforce state priorities over private ones.[35] The most extreme statement of this view is historical. Bernard Silberman, for example, concludes that the prewar Japanese state was able to 'foreclose the whole notion of interests . . . [and] to incorporate those private interests into a public one dominated by the state bureaucracies'.[36] A more moderate version portrays the Japanese state-as-guarantor emerging from the uniquely Japanese confluence of bureaucratic legitimacy, administrative centralization, information exchange, market reliance, and state capacity.[37]

Common to most assessments are MITI-men and other bureaucrats with a great and prescient faith in the market place. More important still, these bureaucrats are said to have exceptionally broad power to intervene, to use market forces as instruments of public policy.[38] It is often argued that economic bureaucrats wisely choose to intervene in moderation because of their awareness of the potential costs of market distortion. The state has no separate commercial presence because it does not need one: the state can control without owning, and if it wants to, it can achieve ownership with little effort. Raymond Vernon, for example, suggests that 'when a special entrepreneurial push from the government has semed useful, MITI has had no great difficulty in securing the needed authority to create a publicly controlled enterprise'.[39] Johnson likens Japanese economic bureaucrats to their distant Venetian cousins. 'The genius of modern Japan, much like that of medieval Venice, has been the ability to fuse in an ad hoc manner the effectiveness of the absolutist state with the efficiency of the bourgeois market.'[40] Daniel Okimoto observes the Japanese state's lack of 'institutionalizcd involvement in the market-place' and argues that a 'diversity of access points permits the Japanese government to stand back and watch the market function while retaining the flexibility to intervene at any time'.[41]

In short, it is widely held that the Japanese state is not in business because the bureaucracy can regulate the market more efficiently than participate in it. Market conformity is widely understood as the industrial policy instrument of choice. It provides evidence of state capacity. Thus it is by virtue of bureaucratic choice and bureaucratic power that the Japanese state is less a market player than European states. Although the emphases on policy networks and public bureaucracies vary, analyses of Japanese economic and industrial policy are dominated by statist assumptions about bureaucratic power.

This view, in turn, has been widely accepted in the comparative literature on states and markets. Japan is the archetypical statist regime, virtually always paired with France.[42] And there is indeed much that is similar about French and Japanese patterns of economic policy making. Both countries have developed sector-specific planning mechanisms that systematically include big business and state bureaucrats and that seem to exclude labour and small business. Both rely upon an elite career bureaucracy that consistently favours scale and consolidation.[43] John Zysman speaks of the French and Japanese economies as 'both tied to state-led growth', a model he characterizes as one in which 'the government bureaucracy attempts to orient the adjustment of the economy by explicitly influencing the position of particular sectors, even of individual companies, and by imposing the solutions on the weakest groups in the polity'.[44] He suggests that both are distinguished by the way in which 'prices in crucial markets are determined by government'. Peter

Katzenstein rejects the 'Japan as *smart* state' hypothesis but celebrates the French and Japanese state structures and institutions that 'preempt the costs' of economic adjustment.[45]

If one accepts these comparisons and the analyses of Japan specialists upon which they are based, one must conclude that institutional differences between the French state-as-rival and the Japanese state-as-guarantor are trivial. My evidence, however, suggests otherwise. The origins of the state-as-guarantor reveal political dynamics of policy making in Japan which suggest a reinterpretation of why Japanese economic policy is market-conforming. Although the Japanese state pervades the market, it does not lead, guide, or supervise private interests. There is little evidence that state actors have ever been able to resist political pressures in the absence of alliances with parts of the private sector. In 300 years of coal markets and a century of oil and electric power, where have state actors systematically denied access to particular groups in the policy process? Where have they ignored the demands of labour or small business with impunity? Where have state initiatives been adopted without evisceration and without guarantees? Transformations of energy markets have always preceded state intervention and state intervention has always conformed to and reconfirmed evolving energy markets. Again we ask, not why the Japanese state is so pervasive in the economy but why the pervasive state is so congenial to private firms. We return to the paradox that frames our answer. The Japanese state acts as guarantor because its power in the market place is enhanced and circumscribed simultaneously by the routines of mutual accommodation we refer to as reciprocal consent. It achieves jurisdiction and is denied control in an iterative process with private interests within an environment of unusually stable elites and extraordinarily durable institutions. The Japanese bureaucracy does not dominate, it negotiates.

So do bureaucracies elsewhere, of course. Reciprocal consent is not uniquely Japanese. In Western Europe similar negotiations over the nature and extent of state intervention have resulted in a market presence for the state – often with considerable support from industry and labour. In Japan the state has been diverted away from market competition entirely. What makes Japan different is the routinization of economic policy which the durability of elites and their constituencies makes possible. Japan is not merely a vat of competing interests; neither is Japan a European government in an American business environment. Rather, the institutionalized routine of negotiation, reciprocal consent, is the tie that binds. It deserves closer scrutiny.

The politics of reciprocal consent has been central to the development of Japanese capitalism. Earlier in this century politics centred upon the Japanese state's failed effort to separate management from capital. More recent negotiations have centred upon the state's effort to augment private ownership with state control. Historically it has been a consistent dynamic: Japanese capital has struggled quite successfully, across wars and depressions, to separate state aid from state control. Reciprocal consent, therefore, is quite different from 'consensus', that model of Japanese politics which stresses harmony and cultural adhesives instead of conflict and structural stability.

Conflict and stability have produced an undeniably pervasive, developmental state.[46] But the evidence from the energy industries makes any inference of state leadership problematic. Market objectives are more commonly achieved through the state than state objectives are achieved through the market. The pervasive Japanese state has nearly always been congenial to private interests, in large measure because private firms have learned how to surrender jurisdiction while retaining control of markets. By privately ordering markets to conform to a perpetually negotiated, state-sanctioned economic order, private investors have found one solution – some would say the optimal solution – to the vagaries of capitalist development.[47] Risk is frequently socialized, costs often transferred. This solution entails the intimate involvement of state agencies, of course, and as a result the politics of reciprocal consent is often confused with state leadership, mutual trust with the mutual sanction from which it is derived. Regulation and jurisdiction, in sum, are often confused with control. But the energy industries provide no evidence that the Japanese state was ever able to force the pace of market transformation or to shape markets in its own image.

On the contrary, in achieving jurisdiction without control the Japanese state merely enshrined bargaining and negotiation in the definition of and access to markets. Conflict over the mechanisms for this 'private ordering' was public and consequential. Private firms have always encouraged the sort of state intervention that would permit them to limit production legally, to allocate markets, to control prices, and to collude in sales. Battles over state control (*kokka tōsei*) and self-control (*jishu tōsei*) before the end of the war were resolved by state-sanctioned cartels that guaranteed private ownership and private management. This solution profoundly affected the major institutions of the Japanese economy, and especially the limits on the state as market player, by defining the Japanese notion of what the capitalist state is and ought to be.

It is and ought to be pervasive. It does and ought to enjoy extensive jurisdiction in the economy. It can and must provide for the common defence through collective management of market diseconomies – especially excessive competition. Neither economic bureaucrats nor business leaders ever developed a deep faith in the salutary effects of the free market. The Japanese economic elite, as Okimoto aptly puts it, has long felt that the market was far from sacrosanct, that 'capitalism needs the visible hand of the state'.[48] In 1930 economic bureaucrats were suggesting that 'in order to obtain the largest possible return from the capital investment, it is necessary, besides amalgamating enterprises in the various industries, to encourage the adoption of business agreements among the enterprises . . . concerning the amount of production, division of markets, sales process, and other measures for the prevention of unnecessary competition'.[49]

Arguably matters are not much different today. The 1980s have witnessed as much concern among Japanese businessmen and bureaucrats about excessive competition as the 1930s did. Because of the stable and largely oligopolistic politics of reciprocal consent, Japan never developed the hostility to private monopoly that dominated policy debates in the United States. While the American state was invested with powers to regulate the trusts, the Japanese state was invested (often by the Japanese trusts themselves) with jurisdiction to assist in their healthy development. Even today concern about the evils of excessive competition dominates discussions of economic policy. Fratricidal hypercompetition is to Japanese economic planners every bit the *bête noir* that excessive concentration is to American antitrust officials. Clearly, as this study has shown, neither the Japanese government nor Japanese capital trusts the market. As in France, state bureaucrats or private firms have never held *a priori* that markets will adjust in the best interests of capital or citizens. This, then, has been a story of cartels, trusts, control, and other non-Smithian initiatives taken both by the state and by private actors. Yet markets and even oligopolies often prove impossibly undisciplined; whether the problem is producers, consumers, or the state, the Japanese have evolved a sophisticated system of negotiation whose results have been consistently market-conforming. Conflict does not get subsumed by consensus, it gets enshrined by reciprocal consent.

Thus emerges a Japanese guarantor-state, not from its own inherent capacity but from the complexity and stability of its interactions with market players. Comparisons to European strong states may misrepresent the fundamentally *conservative* character of the Japanese state. Indeed, comparisons to the United States may be more revealing about the origins of state intervention in the economy. Japan offers remarkable parallels to what Theodore Lowi has called 'the state of permanent receivership'. Lowi argues that the federal government of the United States increasingly and inexorably underwrites risk for established and well-organized interests: 'Any institution large enough to be a significant factor in the community may have its stability underwritten. . . . Above all (the state of permanent receivership) respects the established jurisdictions of government agencies and the established territories of private corporations and groups.'[50] In Japan, however, there is less pretence about respecting the sanctity of the free market. Ironically, a state that does not trust the market supervises interventions that consistently reproduce shifting market structures, while firms that insist on their autonomy in the market place welcome and help shape state jurisdiction.

Notes

1. Robert Axelrod, *The Evolution of Cooperation*, Basic Books, New York 1984
2. Feigenbaum 1985:25 captures this point nicely
3. Heclo 1978 speaks of issue networks in this context. Gourevitch (1978:907) puts the question succinctly: where business and the state work closely together, 'Who has coopted whom?' The literature on subgovernments is instructive. On the American case see J.L. Freeman 1965; Heclo 1978; Milward and Wamsley 1979. On the Japanese case see Campbell 1984
4. See Eckstein 1975:116
5. This is closely tied to Krasner's 1978 argument about geopolitics and foreign economic policy as relatively 'insulated parts of the state's domain'. As

Sampson 1975:73 puts it in the case of petroleum: 'Oil was too important to be left to the oil companies' (quoted in Feigenbaum 1982:1110)

6. The criticality of energy as a test of state strength and state autonomy can be overstated. Indeed, American political historians familiar with the operation of the Texas Railroad Commission (see Nordhauser 1979 and Lovejoy and Homan 1967) and the frequent collusion among private multinationals and the State Department (Adelman 1972; Vernon 1983; Anderson 1981) might not recognize energy as a sector where autonomous state power necessarily prevails over private interests. Nonetheless, in few sectors of the American economy is state regulation more intrusive. Recent analysts of American energy policy have emphasized the state's regulatory capacity and the indirect but significant instruments of state leadership in setting energy policy goals (Neff et al. 1983; Ikenberry 1986). Moreover, the United States is in many ways the extreme case. Virtually every other industrial state, both self-sufficient in energy and not, intervene more directly and (sometimes) more profitably in their oil, coal and electric power industries than in any other

7. Cf. Nordlinger 1981:147

8. Sumiya and Taira 1979:189

9. James Abegglen was the first to use the term

10. See Kaplan 1972 for the most important popularization of Japan, Inc.

11. See, for example, Patrick 1986; Trezise 1982; Saxonhouse 1986; and Pepper et al. 1985

12. Krauss et al. 1984; Horne 1985; Steiner et al. 1980; Fukui 1970; Okimoto forthcoming

13. Silberman 1982:229; Pempel and Tsunekawa 1979:244. See also Hadley 1970 for an account that stresses state leadership

14. Cohen 1949:3, 31. Smith 1965 and Marshall 1967 are excellent and balanced accounts of this period

15. Hoshino 1956; Tōhata 1960

16. The seminal works are Lockwood 1955; Allen 1946; Bisson 1945; Cohen 1949 and Nakamura 1961. Also see Duus 1984 and Tiedemann 1971

17. Moore 1966:301. See also the Japanese *Kōza-ha* tradition of Marxist economics, as well as Yanaga 1968. Few who have looked carefully at the implementation of industrial control legislation, beginning in 1931 with the Important Industries Control Law, fail to acknowledge that large capital retained significant control of the hundreds of state-licensed cartels. The number of cartels expanded from under 100 in 1930 to over 625 in 1935 (see Fujita 1935:67); the Mitsubishi Economic Research Bureau 1936 provides a comprehensive list. It notes that: 'control through these cartels rested merely on mutual consent, and there were frequent cases of violation of agreements, particularly by outsiders. On the other hand, there still were many large-scale industries in which no cartel had been formed owing to the conflicting interests of the manufacturers concerned.' Lockwood 1955:568 notes that invariably the president of each control association was the chief executive of

the largest firm in that sector, 'and as a result, the control associations were utterly dominated by the *zaibatsu*'

18. Johnson 1982:24
19. Pempel and Tsunekawa 1979:258. For accounts of the wartime economy that stress the independence of private enterprise despite controls common to all the belligerent economies, see Cohen 1949 and Samuels 1987
20. Respectively, Vogel 1978; Pempel 1982; Tsurumi 1978; Young 1984 and Inoguchi 1983
21. See, for example, the *Asahi Shimbun* survey of 12 September 1983, in which only 10 per cent of those surveyed felt that the bureaucracy held power, whereas the LDP and big business together accounted for 53 per cent. 'Bosses' (*kuromaku*) got 12 per cent. For more on the role of bosses (*kuromaku*) in Japanese politics, see Samuels 1983
22. Johnson 1982:20 and 1986:564
23. See Dore 1973 for the most sophisticated statement of this proposition. See Vogel 1979, Ouchi 1981 and Athos and Pascale 1981 for more popular accounts. Friedman 1986 vigorously rebuts the proposition with historical evidence from the machine tool industry
24. Recall Silberman's (1982:247, 229) characterization of interest groups in the 1930s as having been 'foreclosed' by the state and of small business interests in particular as 'conflated into the structure of large-scale economic organizations'. Vogel (1985:chap. 4) presents a more seamless web of creative state policies and 'clear vision' that transformed Japan's largest coal mining district. He is impressed with 'how quickly state leaders achieved policy changes in response to changing world conditions'
25. Interview, 27 January 1984
26. Gerschenkron 1962
27. Johnson 1978:130
28. Interview, 8 March 1984
29. Inokuchi 1963:310, 311–12
30. From 49.6 per cent in 1975 to 47.9 per cent in 1982. See Sekiyu Renmei 1983
31. Porges 1979:19
32. Gale 1981:90
33. The unit capacity factor of Japan nuclear reactors, 76 per cent in 1985, was behind only those of West Germany and Sweden (*Japan Petroleum and Energy Weekly*, 7 April 1986)
34. Johnson 1982:318. See Johnson 1978 for a short review of the varieties of public companies. Here I do not differentiate among the Japanese euphemisms for 'nationalization', 'state-owned corporation' or 'public policy company'. (Consider the following list: *kokuyūka, kōyūka, shakaika, minshuka, kokkakanri, tokushi hōjin, kokusaku gaisha, kōsha, jigyōdan, eidan* and *kōdan*.) Lockwood (1965:493) labels the Japanese proclivity to finance but not to own commercial enterprise 'sponsored capitalism'
35. The most exhaustively researched and best-argued representation of this view

is Johnson 1982. See also Johnson 1978:11. Additional evidence to support this 'bureaucratic dominance' thesis is in Pempel 1982

36. Silberman 1982:230–31
37. Okimoto forthcoming is a comprehensive and sophisticated political economy of Japan, focusing most closely upon telecommunications and electronics. Okimoto is less willing than others to look exclusively at the economic bureaucracy. His analysis incorporates private interests and explores their formal links to one another and the state. See also Okimoto 1984:78–133 and Inoguchi 1983. Most 'pluralist' accounts of Japanese politics, however, are not comparative, nor do they examine economic policy making. See, for example, the essays in Krauss 1985 and Krauss and Muramatsu forthcoming
38. See Katzenstein 1980
39. Vernon 1983:88
40. Johnson 1984:64
41. Okimoto forthcoming:chap. 3
42. The most prominent among these are Krasner 1978; Zysman 1983 and Katzenstein 1985b
43. See Cohen 1977:chaps. 1–5
44. Zysman 1983:91
45. Katzenstein 1985b:21–23. Elsewhere (1980:37) he distinguishes between 'Hegelian' French statism, which emphasizes political leadership and bureaucratic initiative, and 'Weberian' Japanese statism, which is derived from closer business-government ties and mitigates the need for forceful political leadership
46. Johnson 1982 speaks of this developmental role for state bureaucrats who, through their market jurisdiction, contribute to economic growth and to the competitiveness of particular sectors of the economy. Some challenge this view on the grounds that the developmental state has been anything but effective. See Patrick 1986, Pepper et al. 1985, Saxonhouse 1986, Trezise 1982 and Friedman 1986
47. On private ordering see Young 1984
48. Okimoto forthcoming:chap. 1. Note that the 1884 *Kōgyō Iken* has a nearly identical statement
49. Fujita 1935:72
50. Lowi 1979:280

References

Adelman, M.A. *The World Petroleum Market*, Johns Hopkins University Press, Baltimore 1972

Allen, G.C. *A Short Economic History of Modern Japan, 1867–1937*, Allen & Unwin, London 1946

Anderson, Irvine H., Jr. *Aramco, the United States and Saudi Arabia: A Study of the Dynamics of Foreign Oil Policy, 1933–1950*, Princeton University Press, Princeton 1981

Athos, A.G., Pascale, R.T. *The Art of Japanese Management*, Simon & Schuster, New York 1981

Axelrod, R. *The Evolution of Cooperation*, Basic Books, New York 1984

Bisson, T.A. *America's Far Eastern Policy*, Macmillan, New York 1945

Campbell, J.C. 'Policy conflict and its resolution within the governmental system.' In E. Krauss et al., eds, *Conflict in Japan*, University of Hawaii Press, Honolulu 1984

Cohen, J.B. *Japan's Economy in War and Reconstruction*, University of Minnesota Press, Minneapolis 1949

Cohen, S. *Modern Capitalist Planning: The French Model*, updated ed., University of California Press, Berkeley 1977

Dore, R. *British Factory, Japanese Factory: The Origins of National Diversity in Industrial Relations*, University of California Press, Berkeley 1973

Duus, P. 'The reaction of Japanese big business to a state-controlled economy in the 1930s', *International Review of Economics and Business*, 1984, vol. 31, no. 9, pp 819–32

Eckstein, H. 'Case study and theory in macropolitics.' In F. Greenstein, N. Polsby, eds, *Handbook of Political Science*, Addison-Wesley, Menlo Park 1975

Feigenbaum, H.B. 'Public enterprise in comparative perspective', *Comparative Politics*, 1982, vol. 15, no. 1, pp 101–22

Feigenbaum, H.B. *Politics of Public Enterprise: Oil and the French State*, Princeton University Press, Princeton 1986

Freeman, J.L. *The Policy Process: Executive Bureau-Legislative Committee Relations*, rev. ed., Random House, New York 1965

Friedman, D. *The Misunderstood Miracle*, Cornell University Press, Ithaca 1988

Fujita, K. 'Cartels and their conflicts in Japan', *Journal of the Osaka University of Commerce*, 1935, vol. 3

Fukui, H. *Party in Power: The Japanese Liberal Democrats and Policy Making*, University of California Press, Berkeley 1970

Gale, R.W. 'Tokyo Electric Power Company: its role in shaping Japan's coal and LNG policy.' In R. Morse, ed., *The Politics of Japan's Energy Strategy*, University of California Institute of East Asian Studies, Berkeley 1981

Gerschenkron, A. *Economic Backwardness in Historical Perspective*, Harvard University Press, Cambridge 1981

Gourevitch, P. 'The second image reversed: the international sources of domestic politics', *International Organization*, 1978, vol. 32, no. 4, pp 881–912

Hadley, E.M. *Antitrust in Japan*, Princeton University Press, Princeton 1970

Heclo, H. 'Issue networks and the executive establishment.' In A. King, ed., *The New American Political System*, American Enterprise Institute, Washington, DC 1978

Horne, J. *Japan's Financial Markets: Conflict and Consensus in Policymaking*, Allen & Unwin, Sydney 1985

Hoshino, Y. *Gendai Nihon Gijutsushi Gaisetsu* (An outline of the history of modern Japanese technology), Dainippon Tosho, Tokyo 1956

Ikenberry, G.J. 'The irony of state strength: comparative responses to the oil shocks in the 1970s', *International Organization*, 1986, vol. 40, no. 1, pp 105–38

Inoguchi, T. *Gendai Nihon Seiji Keizai no Kōzu* (The composition of the political economy of contemporary Japan), Tōyō Keizai, Tokyo 1983

Inokuchi, T. *Gendai Nihon Sangyō hattatsushi, II: Sekiyu* (The history of modern Japanese industrial development, vol. 2: Oil), Gendai Nihon Sangyō Hattatsushi Kenkyūkai, Tokyo 1963

Johnson, C. *Japan's Public Policy Companies*, American Enterprise Institute, Washington, DC 1978

Johnson, C. *MITI and the Japanese Miracle: The Growth of Industrial Policy, 1925–1975*, Stanford University Press, Stanford 1982

Johnson, C. 'La Serenissima of the East', *Journal of the Israel Oriental Society*, 1984, vol. 18, no. 1, pp 57–73

Johnson, C. 'The nonsocialist NICS: East Asia', *International Organization*, 1986, vol. 40, no. 2, pp 557–65

Kaplan, E. *Japan: The Government-Business Relationship*, US Department of Commerce, Washington, DC 1972

Katzenstein, P.J. 'State strength through market competition: Japan's industrial strategy', manuscript, Ithaca, NY 1980

Katzenstein, P.J. *Small States in World Markets: Industrial Policy in Europe*, Cornell University Press, Ithaca 1985

Krasner, S.D. *Defending the National Interest: Raw Materials Investments and U.S. Foreign Policy*, Princeton University Press, Princeton 1978

Krauss, E.S., Muramatsu, M. 'The conservative policy line and the development of patterned pluralism', vol. I of Japan Political Research Committee Publications, Stanford University Press, Stanford 1989 (in press)

Krauss, E.S., Rohlen, T.P., Steinhoff, P.G., eds. *Conflict in Japan*, University of Hawaii Press, Honolulu 1984

Lockwood, W. *The Economic Development of Japan: Growth and Structural Change, 1868–1938*, Oxford University Press, London 1955

Lockwood, W. 'Japan's "New Capitalism".' In W.W. Lockwood, ed., *The State and Economic Enterprise in Japan*, Princeton University Press, Princeton 1965

Lovejoy, W.F., Homan, P.T. *Economic Aspects of Oil Conservation Regulation*, Johns Hopkins University Press, Baltimore 1967

Lowi, T.J. *The End of Liberalism: The Second Republic of the United States*, 2nd ed., Norton, New York 1979

Marshall, B.K. *Capitalism and Nationalism in Prewar Japan: The Ideology of the Business Elite, 1868–1941*, Stanford University Press, Stanford 1967

Milward, H.B., Wamsley, G.T. 'Policy networks: key concept at a critical juncture', paper delivered to the Annual Meeting of the Midwest Political Science Association, Chicago, April 19–21, 1979

Moore, B., Jr. *Social Origins of Dictatorship and Democracy: Lord and Peasant in the Making of the Modern World*, Beacon, Boston 1966

Nakamura, T. *Senzen no Nihon Keizai Seichō no Bunseki* (An analysis of prewar Japanese economic growth), Iwanami Shoten, Tokyo 1961

Neff, T. et al. 'Energy and security: an analysis for the State of California', MIT Energy Laboratory, Center for Energy Policy Research Working Paper, Cambridge, July, 1983

Nordhauser, N.E. *The Quest for Stability: Domestic Oil Regulation, 1917–1935*, Garland, New York 1979

Nordlinger, E.A. *On the Autonomy of the Democratic State*, Harvard University Press, Cambridge 1981

Okimoto, D.I. 'Political context', in Okimoto et al., eds, *The Comparative Edge: The Semiconductor Industry in the U.S. and Japan*, Stanford University Press, Stanford 1984

Okimoto, D.I. *Between MITI and the Market: Japanese Industrial Policy for High Technology*, Stanford University Press, Stanford 1989 (in press)

Ouchi, W. *Theory Z: How American Businessmen Can Meet the Japanese Challenge*, Addison-Wesley, Reading, Mass. 1981

Patrick, H. 'Japanese high technology industrial policy in comparative perspective.' In H. Patrick, ed., *Japanese High Technology Industries: Lessons and Limitations of Industrial Policy*, University of Washington Press, Seattle 1986

Pempel, T.J. *Policy and Politics in Japan: Creative Conservatism*, Temple University Press, Philadelphia 1982

Pempel, T.J., Tsunekawa, K. 'Corporatism without labor? The Japanese anomaly.' In P.C. Schmitter, G. Lembruch, eds, *Trends toward Corporatist Intermediation*, Sage, Beverly Hills 1979

Pepper, T. et al. *The Competition: Dealing with Japan*, Praeger, New York 1985

Porges, A. 'On import cartels and industrial organization in Japan', memorandum prepared for the Office of the Special Representative for Trade Negotiations, Washington, DC August, 1979

Sampson, A. *The Seven Sisters*, Coronet, London 1975

Samuels, R.J. *The Politics of Regional Policy in Japan – Localities, Incorporated?*, Princeton University Press, Princeton 1983

Samuels, R.J. *The Business of the Japanese State: Energy Markets in Comparative and Historical Perspective*, Cornell University Press, Ithaca 1987

Saxonhouse, G. 'Why Japan is winning', *Issues in Science and Technology*, Spring, 1987

Sekiyu Renmei, ed. *Sekiyu Kankei Kiso Shiryō* (Basic petroleum-related data), Tokyo 1983

Silberman, B. 'The bureaucratic state in Japan: the problem of authority and legitimacy.' In T. Najita, J.V. Koschman, eds, *Conflict in Modern Japanese History: The Neglected Tradition*, Princeton University Press, Princeton 1982

Smith, T.C. *Political Change and Industrial Development in Japan: Government Enterprise, 1868–1880*, Stanford University Press, Stanford 1965

Steiner, K., Flanagan, S., Krauss, E., eds *Local Opposition in Japan: Progressive Local Governments, Citizens' Movements, and National Politics*, Princeton University Press, Princeton 1980

Sumiya, M., Taira, K., eds. *An Outline of Japanese Economic History, 1603–1940: Major Works and Research Findings*, University of Tokyo Press, Tokyo 1979

59

Tiedemann, A.E. 'Big business and politics in prewar Japan.' In J.W. Morley, ed., *Dilemmas of Growth in Prewar Japan*, Princeton University Press, Princeton 1971

Tōhata, S. 'Keizai Shutai no Keiseishi' (A typological history of economic actors), *Keizai Shutaisei Kōza* (Readings on economic policy, vol. 3), Chūō Kōronsha, Tokyo 1960

Trezise, P. 'Industrial policy in Japan.' In M.E. Dewar, ed., *Industry Vitalization: Toward a National Industrial Policy*, Pergamon, Elmsford, NY 1982

Tsurumi, Y. 'The case of Japan: price bargaining and controls on oil products', *Journal of Comparative Economics*, 1978, vol. 2, pp 126–43

Vernon, R. *Two Hungry Giants: The United States and Japan in the Quest for Oil and Ores*, Harvard University Press, Cambridge 1983

Vogel, E. 'Guided free enterprise in Japan', *Harvard Business Review*, 1978, May–June, pp 161–70

Vogel, E. *Japan as Number One*, Harvard University Press, Cambridge 1979

Vogel, E. *Comeback*, Simon & Schuster, New York 1985

Yanaga, C. *Big Business in Japanese Politics*, Yale University Press, New Haven 1968

Young, M. 'Judicial review of administrative guidance: governmentally encouraged consensual dispute resolution in Japan', *Columbia Law Review*, 1984, vol. 84, no. 4, pp 923–83

Zysman, J. *Governments, Markets and Growth: Financial Systems and the Politics of Industrial Change*, Cornell University Press, Ithaca 1983

4 Government-industry relations in West Germany

Heidrun Abromeit

West Germany: a case of 'industrial non-policy'

The central difficulty in studying government-industry relations is that, for the most part, they are not conducted in public; 'intimacy' is the basis of their success. There is only one field where close government-industry contacts are deemed entirely legitimate and hence in most countries assume a more public character: that of industrial policy. Unfortunately, if 'industrial policy' is taken to mean a government's actively shaping the industrial structure of a country and attempting to direct its permanent modernization, then such a policy could not be said to exist in West Germany. Indeed, officially, West Germany denies that it has any industrial policy.

It could be argued, of course, 'that all governments have an industrial policy even if it is by default when they do not realise the implications of their actions' (Wilson 1985:37). On the other hand, one might be led into some dire logical problems when concluding that a decided non-policy is a policy after all just because 'something happens'. And West Germany very definitely decided not to pursue any industrial policy but rather to adopt a course of non-intervention in the structural development of industry.[1] In line with these principles no 'department of industry' has ever been established, while on the subject of the proper task of an economics minister it has always been upheld that he 'does his work well only if he does nothing at all. Ludwig Erhard's economic miracle was just based on the fact that he had done nothing' (VEBA chairman Rudolf von Bennigsen-Foerder, in May 1988). The German report to the OECD, about the aims and instruments of its industrial policy, therefore states quite truthfully 'that the concept of an "independent industrial policy" does not exist in that country' (OECD 1975:10).

The policies of the Federal Ministry of Economics (BMWi) have always been based – openly and publicly – on the doctrine of 'Soziale Marktwirtschaft', that is, on the belief that industrial modernization and structural change should best be left to the market. For, it is argued, government agencies would never be put in possession of enough (as well as the right kind of) information to be able to 'pick winners', while to 'protect losers' would be a sin against the free market economy. It was not only in the fifties, the period of the 'German economic miracle', that

61

ministers clung to this belief. The BMWi continued to be the 'institutional stronghold of free market philosophy' (Kreile 1978:199) in the period of deepening structural crises since the seventies, sticking to its public rejection of direct intervention.[2]

This does not mean, however, that successive West German governments have remained passive throughout and have done nothing at all to support industry or to influence industrial modernization. Publicly-held non-interventionist doctrine and actual practice have by no means always been in accord. Firstly, the BMWi was not the only (state) actor in this field; secondly, the BMWi itself, even in the heyday of 'Soziale Marktwirtschaft' in the fifties, could not refrain from allocating money, directly or indirectly (i.e. via tax relief or investment subsidies), to specific 'bottleneck' or 'key' industries and from providing special incentives for investment in 'future' industries. However, such interventions have never been integrated into an explicit, cohesive industrial or structural policy. Mainly they have been ad hoc reactions to industrial developments in and around Germany, making for an 'unintentional' (Vogel 1987:92) or 'implicit' industrial policy (Neumann and Uterwedde 1986:25) at best. To the political scientist, an 'implicit' policy is one for which nobody has ever accepted public responsibility, one that has never been controlled in the normal democratic fashion. Thus government-industry relations have never been a matter of public attention and public control.

The ineffectiveness of regulatory policies

Competition policy

Instead of selective intervention, the emphasis of West German policies towards industry lay on general support as well as on general regulation. Since the passing of the 'Leitsätzegesetz' in 1948 their key element (and thus the key element of German 'implicit industrial policy') has been antitrust policy. This was in keeping with the belief that once a good 'investment climate' was established and competition sufficiently fostered, the effective operation of the market would preclude the need for intervention. It is debatable, however, whether or not these policies have 'encouraged competition to a degree that is unique in Western Europe' (Curzon Price 1981:55). Industry itself was by no means as convinced of the benefits of competition as was the economics minister Ludwig Erhard. Private industry, spearheaded by West German industry's peak association, the BDI (Bundesverband der Deutschen Industrie), fought Erhard's bill 'against Restraints of Competition' (GWB) in a fierce seven years' battle ('die siebenjährige Kartellschlacht'), attempting in the process to exploit the BDI president's (Fritz Berg) close contacts with the chancellor Konrad Adenauer. Hence the Act that was finally passed in 1957 was a compromise pacifying the BMWi's doctrinaires – in stating a general prohibition of cartels – as well as industry's 'practitioners', in granting them a sufficient number of exceptions from the general rule and assuring them that any cartel could be permitted 'on prevailing grounds of the public good'.

Industry's interests also exercised a major influence in the implementation of the Act. This was made easier by the fact that the Act itself opened up quite a number of channels for influence, in prescribing a successive appeal structure; namely: Federal Cartel Authority, Supreme Court Berlin (Kammergericht), Federal Supreme Court (Bundesgerichtshof), and BMWi. As a result, during its first ten years the Federal Cartel Authority opened proceedings against violators of the GWB in 4546 cases and passed verdicts in 704, but imposed fines in only seven; in a mere five cases was the fine actually paid.[3]

In practice, however, formal cartelization has proved to be no longer the most serious threat to workable competition. The real dangers arise from firstly the 'cooperative' behaviour typical of oligopolies and secondly concentration of ownership. The first is particularly well developed in Germany where even in the early industrialization period of the 'rugged entrepreneur', cooperation was considered much healthier than 'ruinous' competition. Over the decades, the traditionally deep-rooted habit of cooperation was facilitated by the coordinating services provided by sectoral business associations; enforced by the banks sitting on the supervisory boards of competing firms (and having considerable stakes in them which they were loath to lose) and thus being in a position to coordinate their investment projects, encourage product specialization etc.; and finally perfected by manifold interlocking directorships. Such old habits do not change quickly (particularly not when the major institutions favourable to them stay on), and contrary to Ludwig Erhard's beliefs, leading industrialists still tend to think it rather 'uneconomical . . . if several firms compete with the same product . . .' (Bayer chairman Kurt Hansen, in April 1965). Against their habit of 'concerted behaviour' ('abgestimmtes Verhalten') the GWB provided no sanctions. In fact, in the 'Teerfarbenfall' of the early seventies, the Federal Supreme Court explicitly denied the Federal Cartel Authority the right to sanction 'abgestimmtes Verhalten' in any way.

Nor did the GWB provide sanctions against the second threat, that of concentration which was actually encouraged by the federal government, both by its tax policy as well as by the soothing noises typically made by BMWi officials whenever a big merger was imminent. Nevertheless, in the mid-sixties the conviction grew that legislation ought to be passed to halt the ever quickening pace of concentration. All the signs indicated a new fierce battle between government and industry on the issue, in fact a renewed 'Kartellschlacht'. However, the social-liberal government which eventually passed the Merger Control Amendment ('Fusionsnovelle') in 1973 was very careful not to alienate industry (see Grottian 1974). From the start it sought informal agreements with the various parts of the 'business community' (for instance in the 'Industriekränzchen' where industry representatives met with the BMWi's competition division every six to eight weeks) and took great care not to put in clauses meeting with opposition from *all* of them. Instead it tried to realize as much as possible of the give-and-take policy variety (merger control versus facilitation of cooperation, for instance). Furthermore, it did not listen at all to what other interest groups – unions or consumer organizations – had to say; the information-gathering process was decidedly lop-sided.

As a result there is now a nominal ex ante control of mergers. The Federal Cartel Authority can inhibit a merger (of a certain size) if it can prove that it will 'seriously restrict competition'. The problem is how to prove this, the more so since neither Act nor Amendment define the 'essential competition' ('wesentlicher Wettbewerb') which is to be upheld, or specify the circumstances under which competition is deemed to be 'seriously restricted'. Small wonder, then, that little has changed in practice. The number of mergers has risen steadily: from 242 in 1973 to 887 in 1987 (of which number the Federal Cartel Authority tried to veto only three!). Of about 1670 attempted mergers in the years 1985 and 1986 the Authority prohibited 9, managed to dissuade the prospective partners in about another 150 cases and gave permission coupled with a few injunctions in a further 5.

The weapons of the Federal Cartel Authority still prove to be blunt. In particular, it is still doomed to inactivity in the face of 'concerted behaviour' (as is practised, most conspicuously, by the oil multinationals and by the banks). Since 1979 there have been renewed talks about amending the GWB, though these have so far proved futile. Anyway, the new conservative-liberal government wants to see such improvements limited to the retail sector. Meanwhile, the government continues to encourage mergers, especially those of the very large ('Elefantenhochzeiten') – for instance, the subsequent buy-ups, on the part of Daimler-Benz, of MTU, AEG, Dornier and (now under discussion) MBB, which will make Daimler-Benz Europe's largest armaments producer and the giant in West Germany's economy.

Environmental policy

The strategy of general regulation has not proved particularly successful in the field of competition policy. It has met with even less success in environment protection. Interestingly enough, in the first period of environmental conservation (1949–1969),[4] the BDI seems to have been one of the main driving forces; as a user, industry was itself interested in water regulation. While there was little conflict over the issue in this period of 'primacy of economic interests', things began to change when the social-liberal government included environment protection – under the heading 'higher quality of life' – in its comprehensive programme of reform in the early seventies. Still there was but little opposition from industry as long as the costs implied in the forthcoming measures remained unknown and the BDI assumed that no specific regulations and standards would be devised without the BDI's cooperation. However, in the mid-seventies the issue became politicized and interests became polarized, while, with the outbreak of the oil crisis and the subsequent recession, the government shifted its attention and priorities from reform policy to crisis management. As a result, environmental policy in this period (1974–1982) oscillated between a 'primacy of economic necessities' and a 'primacy of societal needs', varying with the severity of the unemployment threat, on the one hand, and the pressure from the growing green-ecological movement (presenting a growing electoral threat to social democrats), on the other. Accordingly government-industry relations on this subject oscillated between cooperation and conflict.[5]

Conflict came to an abrupt end in 1982 with the incoming conservative-liberal government, which immediately embarked on a course of environmental policy 'conformable to the market', laying stress on incentives instead of coercible standards (as exemplified in the treatment of leadfree petrol and catalysator cars) and allowing wide margins for industry. In short, this last period of environmental policies has again been one of 'cooperative policy'.

However small the achievements, reached with or without cooperation from industry, the picture is further marred by what has been termed the 'implementation deficit' of German environmental policies (Mayntz 1980; Ullmann 1982; Peacock et al. 1984: 116 ff.). In principle, environment protection in Germany is a 'classic' case of regulatory policies. Legislation is passed fixing standards and defining threshold values for various kinds of pollution and thus regulating, in a general way, the behaviour of numerous addressees. State authorities then supervise compliance with these standards and impose sanctions if they are not obeyed. The first weakness in this system is that standards can hardly be enforced if they are 'unrealistic'. In order to achieve compliance, norms and standards have to be devised with an expert knowledge which – as it seems – nobody but the addressees themselves can provide. Hence the need to ensure the cooperation of industry, and the great stress placed on minimizing conflict in this field.

The second weakness stems from the fact that, since the Acts passed were intended to be 'general' and long-term, legislators included quite a number of undefined norms ('unbestimmte Rechtsbegriffe'), such as 'best available technology', 'recognized rules of technology', 'economically feasible' and the like. Norms defined in this way are as imprecise as can be and allow wide room for bargaining, because authorities are generally not in a position (not being equipped with research facilities etc.) to determine the best available technology or the technical and/or economic feasibility themselves. The Bundesimmissionsschutzgesetz probably goes furthest in this direction, in explicitly authorizing the federal government to fix pollution standards (the so-called 'technical instructions for air' [TA Luft]) 'after duly hearing the industries concerned'. The conclusion to be drawn is that hitherto legislation to protect the environment does little more than allot bargaining positions which safeguard industry's influence and ensure that no material norms are fixed without due recourse to industrial expertise (see Maus 1987: 138). The 'capture theory' of regulation is thus proved right once again: the 'regulation game' (Peacock et al. 1984) leads to bargaining processes empowering the regulated with the 'power of definition' and with dominant influence on the stringency of measures; they attain a position enabling them to determine for themselves the regulation that will affect them.

Their bargaining power will, of course, vary. Firms will have an additional advantage if the matter at hand is one of 'corrective action' (Peacock et al. 1984: 119), i.e. when the bargaining is about already existing plants. Their position is further strengthened during a recession. Indeed a third weakness of the regulatory system is that in order to save (or create) jobs the federal government as well as Land governments are prepared to forego the enforcement of legal standards or even their right to pass respective decrees. Instead they try to reach 'gentlemen's agreements' which fall considerably below the levels prescribed by legislation (see Gessner and Winter 1986: 266 ff.). The temptation to do so is the more pronounced since the responsibility for implementation rests with Land governments and actual implementation is local government's task. Naturally, the relationship between firms and authorities is the closer the more local the level, and the latters' readiness to compromise is in direct proportion to the local importance of the firm.

'Implicit industrial policy': between conservation and innovation

Sectoral and regional policy

In supporting industry West German governments did not really restrict their policies to general measures such as tax relief and the 'creation of favourable circumstances'. Even Ludwig Erhard, otherwise a doctrinaire, made concessions when the situation seemed to demand them. In the early fifties he intervened quite actively to secure the reconstruction and modernization of the coal and steel industries. These industries received not only special depreciation allowances; on the basis of the Investment Assistance Act of 1952[6] about DM 1 billion were shifted, by way of a compulsory bond, from consumer goods industries to the coal mining and iron and steel industries as well as to the energy and water industries and the railways. Though it was clearly the federal government which selected the companies benefiting from the raised capital, Erhard insisted on camouflaging the operation as a 'normal' capital market proceeding, i.e. as if the bonds had been issued by the benefiting firms. Another means of directing investment used by the BMWi in those early years was the – highly selective – distribution of Marshall Plan aid, which generally favoured the same sectors. But again some pretence of a 'free market economy' was maintained, with the distribution being placed officially in the hands of the Reconstruction Loan Corporation (Kreditanstalt für Wiederaufbau). This corporation was organized on the same lines as a commercial bank (and at the time headed by the private banker Hermann Abs) and was expected to act like a bankers' bank. The Reconstruction Loan Corporation, incidentally, still exists, its main task now being to direct financial assistance – about DM 3–4.5 billion a year, provided by the federal government through the ERP programme – to small and medium-sized firms.

Allegedly, state subsidies to industry are comparatively low in West Germany. Nevertheless, subsidies granted by the federal as well as the Land governments amounted to about DM 80 billion annually in the early eighties.[7] The percentage received by manufacturing industries has indeed been continually low, with the exceptions of the shipbuilding and aircraft industries (for figures see Neumann and Uterwedde 1986: 147, 150 f.); more than 75 per cent of the subsidies are directed into agriculture, housing, transport and coal mining. On the Land level especially the majority of subsidies are spent on declining industries.

In order to alleviate the Lands' burden, to allow for a more even distribution of wealth among the regions, and to tidy up the jungle of subsidies, the second half of the sixties saw several attempts at bringing about a systematic structural policy. Such efforts include the passing of the 'Principles of Sectoral Policy' in 1966 and the Federal Act of Regional Planning (Bundesraumordnungsgesetz) in 1965 as well as the creation of a 'Joint Task for the Improvement of the Regional Economic Structure' in 1969. All three initiatives were aimed at securing an improved coordination of federal and Land policies, but they cannot be adjudged as outstanding successes. The 'Principles' failed to provide a stringent concept from which sectoral priorities could have bcen deduced; in the good old tradition of 'Soziale Marktwirtschaft' they merely stated (restrictive) criteria, derived from the free market philosophy, for state intervention. Accordingly, subsidies ought to have been reduced drastically in the following years, yet exactly the reverse happened.[8] The main effect of the 1966 'Principles' – still the official line of BMWi – was purely ideological, in that they re-stated the BMWi's favourite dogma and put any structural/sectoral/industrial policy firmly in second place.

Of course, there was the social-liberal interlude of the seventies, when structural policy or 'active industrial policy' was much talked about. However, this did not amount to much, in practice; in fact to little more than a regular 'Structural Report' provided by the five big economic research institutes, which was intended to furnish firms with the proper informational basis for their investment decisions. Any attempt to go beyond that was immediately condemned in public as being the first step towards investment control. Hence this interlude – sometimes dubbed the period of development of a 'Modell Deutschland' – was, in this and other respects, a period less of achievements than one of proposals.

The Bundesraumordnungsgesetz hardly achieved any more. While allotting the respective planning responsibilities to the federal government, it omitted to provide the necessary instruments. The 'Joint Task', on the other hand, did provide some of those and prescribed certain procedures as well as preconditions for how and when grants were to be given for investment in certain regions. It omitted, however, to lay down the concept needed for the coordination of the various (Land) regional development policies. The results of this medley of patched-up politics have only rarely been economically sensible.

If a region has (after a fairly complicated decision-making procedure in a Joint Planning Commission) been declared an 'assisted region', firms are granted a 15–25 per cent subsidy on investment there (50 per cent of which grants are paid by the federal government) – with nobody asking whether or not they belong to a sector specifically worthy of support or whether they would not have made that investment anyway. Meanwhile the one (and only) stipulation that has been added is that investment should *not* be in one of the rapidly declining industries such as shipbuilding or steel. So far, the effect of this costly measure (amounting to DM 1.4 billion per annum in the early eighties; see Gemper 1985: 50) has been that the vast majority of subsidies (two-thirds at least) are paid for replacement investment or extension projects of firms already existing in the respective regions, usually creating few if any new jobs (see Neumann and Uterwedde 1986: 230). This trend is explained (again) by the usually first-rate relations of those firms' managers with local and Land authorities. Small wonder, then, that regional policy so far has not lessened the existing income disparities and great differences in employment between Lands/regions.

Research and technology policy

The obvious shortcomings of sectoral and regional policy in West Germany can partly be explained by the fact that federal authorities as well as other important industrial actors did not relish those policies anyway. Of the BMWi at least it may fairly be assumed that they did not really like anything in the nature of an active structural policy which so patently clashed with their free market philosophy. Their attempt at Keynesian 'global steering' since 1967 had been 'radical' enough already and, apparently, had absorbed all their respective energies. However, the BMWi was not the only (state) actor in this field. Over the years, the Federal Ministry of Research and Technology (BMFT) has taken a rather different stance.

It took the federal government some time to decide that state authorities should support industrial research and technology. At first, the belief prevailed – in accordance with the non-interventionist dogma – that innovations and the preceding research and development were wholly industry's own business with which governments were not to meddle. It was not until the mid-fifties that some sort of technological backwardness – especially in comparison with the United States – made itself felt and that the conviction grew that government ought to do something about it.

When the federal government began to encourage industrial research and development, it did so primarily from military considerations. This imparted a certain lopsidedness to the ensuing research and technology policy. The first supportive agency, and the actual predecessor of the BMFT of today, was the Federal Atom Ministry (BMAt) founded in 1955. From the start it was complemented by the German Atom Commission, an advisory body consisting entirely of representatives of the fast evolving atomic lobby (see below). In 1962/63 the BMAt was abolished and a new Ministry for Scientific Research established – obviously a reaction to the dawning recognition that it was not only in the nuclear sector where West Germany needed to close the comparative 'technological gap'. Financial assistance for R&D was therefore extended from the original (principally military-defined) areas of nuclear power, aviation and aerospace and other military research to those of the so-called 'new technologies', data processing, oceanography and environment protection. The federal government's expenditure on R&D rose accordingly from DM 0.8 billion in 1953 to DM 17.8 billion in 1981.[9]

During the seventies the social-liberal government tried to fit these expenditures into a more general 'strategy of active structural change', with the aim of thoroughly modernizing the German economy and adapting it to world market developments (see Hauff and Scharpf 1975). However, as was the case with a number of other reform projects, the postulated 'anticipatory policy', steering structural change on the basis of highly selective state aid, never reached the stage of actual implementation. Moreover, the part the state was to play in the presumed steering process would have been a rather ambiguous if not limited one. The targets of modernization to be 'anticipated', for instance, were not to be societal, but in a strict and narrow sense commercial ones (mainly the competitiveness of German industries in the world markets). There has been much criticism of the 'anticipatory structural policy' leading to a 'self-instrumentalisation of state for . . . single firms' purposes' (Fach and Simonis 1987: 71). Even so, this 'strategy' was opposed by private industry which at the time saw the ghost of investment control lurking everywhere. The new government installed in 1982 was able to allay those fears and made it immediately clear that it would never revert to any other than the old free market economy approach to R&D.

This is not the place to describe in detail how the project-oriented research and technology assistance (still the bulk of federal R&D expenses) of the BMFT is administered (see Bruder 1986). Suffice to say, there is some doubt about its effectiveness, the main criticism being that, instead of inducing new research, it merely shifts R&D expenses from the private to the public sector ('Mitnahme-effekt'). However, indirect assistance is even more ineffective, coupling the 'take-up-effect' with a sprinkler effect.

In the absence of sprinkler effects, an unmistakable bias towards large-scale firms prevails. The 'distinct preference for a few large companies' (Donges 1980: 196) has been a pervasive trait of West German R&D policies.[10] During the seventies the ten biggest industrial clients received fairly steadily more than 50 per cent of total BMFT funding (and in 1973 even 68.9 per cent; see Bruder and Ende 1980: 17). Interestingly enough it was the new conservative-liberal government which appeared to be well on the way to changing this trend, by declaring that they would shift the stress from direct to indirect state aid and actually changing the ratio between both from 4.3:1 (1981) to 2.8:1 (1983; see Bruder 1986: 63). As a result the percentage of funds going to the ten biggest recipients fell, for the first time in more than a decade, to below 50 per cent. Meanwhile, however, research and technology minister Dr Riesenhuber has decided to turn the wheel back, explicitly on the grounds of the inefficiency of the sprinkler method of indirect assistance. BDI and the VDMA, the engineering industry's association, while complaining bitterly as well as in vain, now reckon the ratio between direct and indirect assistance to be one of about 10:1, with the electronics multi Siemens getting the lion's share (see Frankfurter Rundschau, 2 April 1988).

In addition, with respect to these big firms the BMFT appears to be restricted to an entirely reactive role. From the start, the BMFT as well as its predecessors had been content to adapt to ideas and objectives coming from industry, instead of developing concepts of their own. The demand to close the 'technological gap', for instance, originated in the BDI which, in its 1966 memorandum, insisted that the state had a definite share of the responsibility for maintaining competitive standards of industrial performance (see Bruder and Hofelich 1982: 23). In the years that followed, the BDI was obviously satisfied with the way in which the federal government lived up to industry's expectations, as was shown in the statement, in its 1968/69 annual report, that wherever the BMFT had created new 'areas of support', it had taken care to establish as a first step a harmonious and fertile cooperation with industry (BDI 1969: 160). In fact, a former high-ranking civil servant of the BMFT disclosed that the contents of research programmes as well as the conditions to be met by firms being funded, were actually, and in the last resort, decided within the BDI's president's committee (Berger 1978: 171).

The social-liberal government made some futile attempts to alter the dominance of industry by reforming the system of advisory bodies to the BMFT. These 'Fachausschüsse', advisory committees, and experts' circles play a decisive part in shaping the ministry's policies after industry's wishes, by providing the information that leads to the perception and selection of the 'right' kind of problems (subjects for research) and the 'right' kind of problem solutions (direction of research). No administration is more dependent on outside experts for detailed information than an R&D department. It lacks almost necessarily the specialized scientific skills needed for the appraisal of the various aspects of projected innovations. Hence in this specific policy arena a particularly high degree of dependence of administrators on their clientele is only to be expected. There remains the question of which parts of this clientele to turn to for advice chiefly: it is here that some scope exists for reducing administrative dependence on informed vested interests. However, less and less use is made thereof. In the last decades the presence of academics from universities on the BMFT-'Fachausschüsse' has decreased steadily, their place being taken by scientists from the large research institutions (Max-Planck-Gesellschaft, Fraunhofer-Gesellschaft) and by experts drawn from the industries concerned (whose representatives have for some time now amounted to more than 50 per cent of all BMFT committee members). These two groups practise a harmonious division of labour, the first being responsible for elementary research and the latter for industrial research; both interlock well in the joint research ('Verbundforschung') much encouraged by government. But the committees dealing with industrial research are not just 'dominated by industry'. They are dominated, quite specifically, by the large companies Siemens (heading the others by far), BBC, MBB, AEG, BASF and some (few) others (for the above see Berger 1978: 177 ff.).

Accordingly, it is not surprising that the lion's share of BMFT funds goes to those (three) sectors and those (ten to twelve) firms which are most strongly represented in the committees (see Neumann and Uterwedde 1986: 179 f.). There is an obvious identity of interest between those who provide information, those who 'advise' and those who benefit from the resulting policies. In other words, German research and technology policy involves little more than reacting to and implementing the policies of large-scale industry. Small wonder, then, that concepts such as technological assessment and 'social desirability of technologies' ('Sozialverträglichkeit') or projects like alternative energies or 'humanization of work', though from time to time much discussed in public, have but little chance within this closely-knit network of industry and administrators. Other groups in society which might bring forward such projects – or, in fact, any alternative options – are not represented in the advisory system.

Energy policy

While most of the research and technology policy hardly awakens any public interest, the commitment of successive governments to the development of nuclear energy has attracted growing public attention. Yet, the nuclear energy programme has always been something of an exception to various major rules of West German politics: that of non-intervention in market processes, that of the proper 'subsidiary' role of the state ('Subsidiaritätsprinzip'), and that of the federal government's preference for reacting instead of initiating.

One crucial factor is that no market in nuclear energy had ever existed; it was the government which created one. It has been argued that this was done against the interests of and in the teeth of opposition from industry. However, the situation was more complex than this characterization might suggest (see Kitschelt 1980: 46 ff.; Keck 1984:52 ff.). Rather it was a case of the electricity generating industry being rather sceptical about rushing into a premature instalment of nuclear power plants, while the big companies of the electrical engineering industry (Siemens, BBC, AEG and others) were strongly in favour of the federal government's initiative in 1955. Both groups were adequately represented in the German Atom Commission, the advisory body of the BMAt, which in the years to come shaped German nuclear energy policy. In passing, it should be noted that this Commission, while exerting the decisive influence, was never in any way under parliamentary control or legitimized in democratic fashion. Its members (about 25 in number, although more than 200 if one adds the Commission's five special committees and various working groups) were coopted as 'private persons' by way of informal networks and a sort of sinecure system. Furthermore, its proceedings were confidential. It is obvious that great care had been taken to keep the nuclear issue as depoliticized as possible. The Atom Commission was dissolved in 1971, to be succeeded by the BMFT advisory committee 'Nuclear Research and Nuclear Technology', 8 of whose 15 members come from the industries represented in the old Commission, while four are drawn from the great research institutions (particularly the Nuclear Research Centre Karlsruhe), two from universities, and one member represents the state (see Kitschelt 1980: 219 ff.). Neither the old nor the new advisory body has ever counted among its members a representative drawn from the strong ranks of the opponents of nuclear energy.

Industry's interests may have been split on the issue at first, as is illustrated by the fate of the 'Eltville Programme' of 1957. This was the first of the Commission's programmes (the subsequent ones were usually presented, without any alterations, as 'the Federal Government's Atom Programme'), which foundered on the opposition of the risk-averse electricity generating industry. Yet by the early sixties the industries concerned had united into one homogeneous 'atomic lobby'. Since there were no clashes of interest with government either – the BMAt, to be precise, for other government departments did not interfere anyway – the nuclear energy issue, during the first 15 years at least, was dealt with in an entirely harmonious 'closed policy arena' (Kitschelt 1980: 125), with the resulting deficiencies of perception, concerning future energy demand, alternative options of energy policy, risks and unsolved problems (about what to do with nuclear waste, chiefly). It took the fierce opposition of the anti-nuclear movement growing during the seventies to bring not only these questions, but in fact the whole nuclear issue to the fore of public attention.

Up to now, however, this citizens' movement has been fighting lost battles. In the first place, the 'oil shock' of 1973, while persuading the federal government to deal with the energy issue comprehensively for the first time, led to a renewal and enforcement of its preference for nuclear energy. Secondly, progress had been made too far, and irreversibly so, in that direction. The first two nuclear programmes may not have been too successful;[11] but by around 1967 nuclear energy in West Germany matured into its 'commercial stage'. Electricity generating companies ordered nuclear plants in increasing numbers. Neither they nor the reactor industry were any longer in need of direct state subsidies, i.e. the federal government lost most of its ability to influence the course of events. Finally, the reactor industry has in the meantime become concentrated into a monopoly which no government can force to 'listen to reason'. Of the original five groups sharing the business (German Babcock & Wilcox, Siemens, BBC/Krupp, AEG, Interatom) since 1982 only one survives, the KWU (Kraftwerksunion), which in its turn since 1976 is wholly owned by Siemens.

In recent years there has been just one instance of the federal government trying to regain the 'law of action': its decision to develop a fast breeder reactor (a project which now has got stuck in Kalkar). This decision, however, apart from resulting in obvious failure, was not really one of the government's own, but originated in the Nuclear Research Centre Karlsruhe (see Keck 1984). It might be viewed as the futile attempt of a kind of 'technostructure' to recover lost ground against industry's 'commercial' nuclear energy policy.

Nuclear energy policy appears to be one of the very few examples, if not the only one, of the federal government's having a concept of its own about sectoral policy, and trying to initiate and shape future development. Unfortunately its concept was miles apart from societal needs and even from commercial interests. Hence, while its policy may be said to have been successful in giving birth fairly quickly to a German nuclear energy sector, by granting the firms concerned large amounts of public money, its real economic success, i.e. selecting those types of reactors which allowed for the commercial running of the business, has been achieved more or less in spite of its programmes. Success was not least due to the fact that the decentralized structure of the West German electricity generating industry drastically limited the federal government's influence. Meanwhile, the state's capacity to exert any influence on a sector whose operations constitute a gigantic risk to society as a whole has proved to be limited even more drastically by the tight monopoly into which the reactor industry has developed and by the way in which it has become firmly interlocked with the big electricity companies.

It now influences and even 'buys' those authorities which are meant to license and supervise its risky business, as the latest scandal about NUKEM and its subsidiary Transnuklear (shuffling nuclear waste all around Western Europe) and the farces about 'licenses for partial constructions' ('Teilerrichtungsgenehmigungen') of highly disputed new power plants illustrate.

Crisis management

One may fairly conclude from the above, that on the whole the federal government does comparatively little to 'pick winners'. Does it, then, busy itself more with 'protecting losers'? Again, compared with other nations, the West German state tends to keep a rather low profile (though some Land governments have, every now and then, tried to assume a more active role). It does not take recourse to protectionism, even if it is sometimes accused, by other governments, of 'indirect protectionism' via rigid technical norms and standards. Neither does it undertake 'rescue nationalizations', nor is it very generous with subsidies to declining industries, excepting agriculture. In fact, what is typical of West German dealings on such matters is a type of arrangement that has been termed the 'informal crisis cartel' (Esser and Fach 1983: 112 ff.) which allows the state to stay in the background and to avoid direct and open involvement.

One of the examples of this sort of crisis regulation is the coal mining industry in the Ruhr region which has been in ever-deepening crisis since 1958 (see, for the following, Bahl 1977; Jákli 1980). A first attempt to deal with the problem by means of self-organization was the establishment, without any state help, of a coal-oil cartel. It was doomed to failure because it lacked both sanctions and compulsory membership. A second attempt, this time in the shape of a coal sales cartel, was proscribed by the High Authority of the European Coal and Steel Community. Subsequent steps eventually resulted in the establishment of the Ruhrkohle AG in 1968, which rounded off former agreements to coordinate pit closures by means of a reshaping of ownership and company structure. Throughout this process the federal and the Northrhine-Westfalian governments more or less stood by, merely lending indirect assistance and restricting support for the ailing industry to the subsidization of the use of coal by the electricity generating industry.[12]

Such indirect assistance proved insufficient. In 1971 only public money prevented the Ruhrkohle AG's bankruptcy. Since they did not mean direct subsidization to continue, the two governments now put some pressure on the electricity generating industry (and especially on their association VDEW), coupled with threats of 'dirigiste' measures such as compulsory allocation of coal to single power plants, to force it into an understanding with the coal mining association, embodying a guarantee to take on certain fixed quantities of German coal. After prolonged negotiations such an agreement – called the 'Century's Treaty' – was reached in 1977; it was renewed in 1980 and is intended to last until 1995 (although it was challenged by the French government and the EDF in 1988). The additional costs arising for the electricity generators from the use of home coal are to be met by a compensation fund fed by the 'coal penny'. On the basis of this agreement the single companies are meant to – and have done so till now – fix single contracts concerning the amounts of coal taken. Thus, the arrangement is a decidedly individualistic one, allowing for a high degree of flexibility, as well as one of 'private politics'. Over the decades, the state's role has been restricted to that of midwifery, to the organization of the financing of additional costs, and to otherwise providing some financial assistance at the margins.

Crisis regulation in the iron and steel industry has followed similar lines of 'private politics' (see Esser, Fach and Väth 1983), starting, in its first stage in the mid-sixties, with industrial self-organization in the shape of the four rolled steel sales cartels of 1966 ('Walzstahlkontore'), rearranged into four rationalization groups coordinating investment and production. These arrangements were encouraged not by the state but by the banks, for not even when the steel crisis deepened in the mid-seventies did the federal government possess anything in the nature of an explicit 'steel policy': 'The relationship between state and steel is . . . embedded in general economic policy. Like all other industries the steel industry acts on its own responsibility . . .' (Ollig 1980: 427). In upholding such principles West German steel (non-)policy contrasted sharply with that of other European nations. Consequently, the federal government did not particularly favour the Davignon Plan and was directly opposed to the European policy of allowing state subsidies for the ailing steel companies. It finally decided on a steel programme in 1981 (in order not to let the home steel industry run into serious competitive disadvantages) but still 'continued to cling to the view that adaptation of the steel industry was primarily a matter for the social partners and for the bank-industry nexus' (Esser and Fach 1983: 112).

This position became difficult to uphold when the steel industry of the Saar region was threatened with bankruptcy in 1978. In order to leave the principle of non-intervention at least nominally untarnished, the federal and the Saar Land governments negotiated in privacy with the metal workers' union IG Metall and with the ARBED, a Luxemburg company which had signalled its readiness to take over the Saar iron and steel works under certain conditions. The federal government, in its turn, was ready to grant some money on the condition that ARBED submitted a restructuring programme for the Saar plants which was judged to be adequate by the government's experts. The programme brought forward by ARBED embraced concentration of ownership (ARBED Saarstahl as the only remaining company), and integration of crude steel and rolled-steel production as well as other rationalization measures, including a reduction of workforce by 8,800.[13] The government duly judged the programme 'commercially reasonable' (Esser, Fach and Väth 1983: 86) and agreed to support it by financial aid of more than DM 1 billion (adding direct subsidies and loan guarantees). The IG Metall, seeing no alternative, undertook to keep the workforce quiet, and so this 'informal crisis cartel' was established. Unfortunately ARBED Saarstahl ran into trouble again in 1982. By then, the 'crisis cartel' had broken up, inducing the now SPD-led Land government to become more closely involved.

Although the federal government had tried to keep a nominally low profile throughout the Saar steel crisis, its financial involvement was still held by some to flout the principles of Soziale Marktwirtschaft. Therefore, when the Ruhr steel industry also ran into crisis in 1980, the federal government tried to keep its public profile even below that threshold. In principle, dealings followed the same lines. When Hoesch and Krupp asked for state subsidies, the government urged a comprehensive restructuring, concentration and centralization of the industry into a single 'Ruhrstahl AG'. The details of how this was to be done were left to the existing companies and IG Metall to arrange. The Ruhrstahl plan (strongly supported by the Deutsche Bank) was well under way when Krupp, discovering that it could do better for itself by merging its high-grade steel production with that of Thyssen, left the 'crisis cartel'. This, of course, rendered the state actors' position a trifle difficult. The federal government had tied the promise to grant financial assistance to the proposed restructuring. It proved in fact as good as its word. It remained passive and apparently even lost all interest, while the Northrhine-Westfalian government continued to cling to the Ruhrstahl concept, but without possessing the sanctions with which to force it on the reluctant companies.

During the winter of 1982/83 the federal government launched a rather lukewarm new initiative, in association with the steel companies, by commissioning three 'steel moderators' (distinguished by their connections to the steel as well as to the banking sectors, and this time without any union participation) to propose a solution to the Ruhr steel problem. Their restructuring programme envisaged two steel groups: the Rhine group (Thyssen and Krupp) and the Ruhr group (Hoesch, Klöckner and all the remaining German steel producers). This wholly unbalanced scheme met with opposition from the Land government and the IG Metall and, like the Ruhrstahl plan, landed in the filing cabinet. The problem therefore remains as unsolved as does the state remain inactive.

The federal government remained inactive in other cases where single large firms were concerned, illustrative cases being the VW crisis in 1974 or that of AEG 1975–79 which shall not be detailed here. Suffice to note – as outside observers sometimes wonderingly do – 'that firms in difficulty in Germany are allowed to collapse' (Curzon Price 1981: 53). This, however, has probably less to do with an 'exceptional self-restraint on the part of the Federal Government' (ibid.) than with the prevalence of bank-led rescues. The big banks have developed a habit of stepping into the breach, enforcing restructurings, bringing in new chairmen of their own choice, and closely monitoring their performance, frequently before the governments even take notice.

Actors and re-actors

Government as fire brigade or innovator? A summary

In summary: West German governments have often appeared to be somewhat stand-offish in their relations with industry. In particular, they have abstained from developing a coherent industrial policy, mainly on the ideological grounds of its clashes with the predominant doctrine of 'Soziale Marktwirtschaft', but also because in an economy that had been prospering over decades a specific industrial policy for a long time seemed to be superfluous. Every now and then there have been demands, from leading social democrats, unionists, and sometimes even from businessmen (as for instance AEG chairman Heinz Dürr, in June 1988) to proceed to a 'new' or 'creative' industrial policy, including 'industrial targeting' and active state shaping of the future structure of the economy. However, such an 'anticipatory sectoral policy' aimed at the thorough 'modernization of the economy' (Hauff and Scharpf 1975) has never got beyond the rhetorical stage, during either 'social-liberal' or 'conservative' administrations.

This is not to say that the West German state has not supported industry; in fact it has done so rather massively. There are its general endeavours to create a 'climate' favourable to industrial investment (preferably by way of tax relief in various forms); there have been attempts at regional policy; there is special state assistance concerning R&D; and there is some (preferably indirect) help for declining industries. The point is that these measures have usually evolved ad hoc and never been coordinated (nor have, for that matter, the various actors in the highly fragmented structure called the West German 'state') and integrated into any semblance of a well-considered programme-oriented policy.

Therefore the role that West German governments have adopted towards industry and industrial development cannot be said to have been that of an innovator, particularly if one considers that innovation deliberately initiated by the state would have to be based on targets and concepts. Not even in the field of research and technology policy had the West German state bothered about such targets and concepts. Instead, it strictly limited its own role to that of reacting, providing financial assistance to a handful of giant corporations to pursue concepts of their own (which, as likely as not, they would have pursued in any case, with or without state aid). In only one instance does the federal government seem to have stepped out of that narrow role and played the innovator, that occasion being its efforts to stimulate the emergence of a nuclear energy sector. Even here, though, the 'law of action' soon passed to some of these industry giants, and in the one case where the government tried to cling to its right to exert the decisive influence on the development and construction of the fast breeder reactor, it ran into failure.

Being committed, in practically all other instances, to a reactive role, government's attitude towards industry might have been expected to resemble that of the 'fire brigade'. But not even this can be said to be a proper description of the West German state's role, for acting as a fire brigade would, very definitely, prescribe intervention as soon as any sector (or single firm) were in need of it. As was seen in the few examples of German 'crisis management', the federal government, true to its free market ideology, rather determinedly tried to avoid just such involvement, however much the urgent desire to stay in the background may have led to mere camouflage in the end.

While being generally disinclined, in most areas of industrial policy, to act in their own right, West German governments have always stressed the need for cooperating with industry and for achieving a broad consensus about any policy measures affecting industry. In all their dealings with top industrialists (and even more so with top bankers) successive governments, including the social-liberal one, have always sought 'to minimize conflict'.

Most contemporary advocates of 'real' industrial policy, whether economists, businessmen or politicians, consider cooperation with industry to be one of its major prerequisites. 'The success of industrial policy depends, perhaps above all, on the existence of adequate contacts between government and industry' as well as on 'mutual understanding' (OECD 1975: 19). Hence 'The primary responsibility for the development and implementation of a workable concept of an industrial policy . . . ought to rest with industry itself (primacy of industry)', and governments should just 'promote' the latter's concepts (Gemper 1985: 17). This is less cynical than it sounds. Firstly, even for the mere shaping of an industrial policy governments need information which only industry can provide (about future market developments, investment projects and the like); secondly, for the achievement of industrial policy goals governments need industry's compliance which in private capitalist economies can only be obtained by building on industry's own preferences.

In its regulatory policies, where the federal government did in fact have some objectives of its own (competition, environment protection), the latter proved to be a particularly complex matter. To gain compliance, any bills had to have been 'agreed' with industry's representatives before they reached the parliamentary legislative stage. In fact, *all* bills which affect the interests of any of the important organized groups of West German society have to try to secure prior agreement of the organizations concerned. All the 'main groups' are entitled to be consulted during the drafting stage of legislation. Of course, the respective departments could consult more than one group, on any particular matter; but as an overwhelming number of examples might illustrate – ranging from anti-cartel law over anti-pollution Acts, programmes and standards decided upon in the BMFT, matters of energy policy, to the even more obvious case of agricultural policy – they do not normally do so. In practice, they listen to nobody but their clientele and do not make use of the expert advice any 'countervailing power' could give, thus dramatically narrowing down their own autonomy.

The 'regulation game', however, implies more than the regulated being well able to shape the regulation norms. In the process of the latter's application the emphasis is, once again, on 'cooperation and consensus'. Legal power is not just obeyed; to gain compliance and minimize conflict with industry West German administrators at all levels renounce their right to enforce compliance and acquiesce with results somewhat below legal standards. Since one of the chief characteristics of the pre-legislatory consulting process is that such standards will not just be toned down, but normally be fixed in a way vague enough to allow the firms' experts to decide themselves on their 'technological feasibility' and economic advisability, it is fairly obvious that 'cooperation and consensus' rob government's regulatory efforts of all their regulating powers, that is, of all effectiveness.

As for the rest of the scattered remains of West German industrial policy, this tendency of the state to relinquish voluntarily its own steering powers is even more pronounced. The whole system of advisory bodies in the areas of research and technology or nuclear energy, centres incestuously around the handful of large companies which seem to have monopolized all possible expertise. Thus BMFT administrators never get a fair chance to do some independent thinking of their own: they don't get any unbiased information anyway. Consequently, in all matters concerning the 'modernization of the economy', the West German state tends to adopt the role of some sort of 'public utility' for industrial giants such as Daimler-Benz, Siemens and a few others. Some authors have been worried recently about the growing danger of a 'politicization of business' (van Schendelen and Jackson 1987). There seems to be little doubt that the West German case illustrates the reverse: the 'commercialisation of politics' (ibid. 153).

Who acts?

Although this process appears to leave large-scale industrial firms in the role of chief 'economic actors' in West Germany, they are by no means on their own; particularly when 'crises' arise. Sectoral business associations have been known to attempt some sort of coordination of investment or 'concerted' capacity reductions in declining industries, although these have not, as a rule, been wholly successful. The power and importance of West German business associations, including their peak organization BDI, tend anyway to be over-rated (see Abromeit 1983). They lack the sanctions to enforce 'concerted behaviour' if members are unwilling, which frequently if not typically will be the case in fragmented sectors. Members will more easily 'see reason' in concentrated, oligopolistic sectors; evading any 'prisoners dilemmas' they will, in fact, tend to self-organization even without the help of any particular organization, reducing their sectoral trade association to the status of a mere public relations agency. In other words, these associations also lack the power of sanction; it is just that occasions to notice this weakness are rare.[14]

As for the BDI, its role has never been that of a promoter of industrial self-organization. It deals chiefly with the government. Since the part it plays in politics – as befits the interest organization of capital in a private capitalist economy – is essentially negative, its task consisting mainly in warding off state intervention, reforms and the like, it appears to be more powerful and 'more important when a government is in power with which industry . . . have some general disagreement' (Grant et al. 1987: 44). Yet this is a superficial view. What in fact happens is that in such situations the 'political role' of a trade association[15] comes more openly to the fore. Its power to exert pressure on an unwilling government is neither greater nor more real than in any other situation, because it rests entirely on the determination of its member firms – especially the large ones – to react by, for instance, withholding investment in a 'climate unfriendly for business'.[16] Without such determination the association's threats would be empty; hence what looks like the BDI's power is nothing but a manifestation of that of its more powerful members.

While one might be tempted to over-rate the German trade associations' power as 'actors', it is indeed difficult to over-rate that of the German banks.[17] Their influence dates back to the Bismarck Reich and has so frequently been described (from Shonfield 1965 to Zysman 1983 or Cox 1986) that a short summary will suffice here. The banks' specific power rests on a combination of roles. They are not only 'Hausbank' and source of credit for their clients, but usually also own a considerable share of the latters' equity, the impact of which can easily be increased by the German system of proxy voting (in shareholders' meetings). Finally, the banks are represented on their clients' supervisory boards. This puts them in a position to influence their clients' policies as well as to control the latter's performance. Since the big banks especially have respective dealings with most major companies, they have received privileged information on a range of industries, which allows the banks to do what the West German state never would or could do, namely to influence the direction of industry's development; in other words to embark on schemes of 'active industrial policy'.

Being rather risk-averse, they appear to have taken some care not to meddle too much in the development of new technologies. On the other hand, they traditionally play a 'promoting' role, in so far as they make it possible for companies to invest on the basis of long-term considerations (a tradition the federal government tried to exploit in the early fifties, when it placed responsibility for the reconstruction of the West German economy in the hands of the Reconstruction Loan Corporation and, therewith, the banking sector). The most conspicuous use of their privileged position, however, shows in the banks' efforts to rescue and restructure big firms that have run into trouble (one of the best-known if slightly ambivalent examples being that of the AEG), to reshape and restructure whole industries in crisis (they took on the leading role, for instance, in bringing about the 'Walzstahl-kontore' of the mid-sixties) and to lead declining industries into orderly retreat. In fact, one might say that while in other countries it is the state which steps into the breach in any kind of crisis, in Germany it is the banks which act as the fire brigade.

In this way the actors in the German banking sector quite deliberately take care that no need arises for the development of an 'economic actor state'. 'The intimate capitalist self-organization that (is) characteristic of Germany' (Dyson 1983: 44 f.) keeps the state away from the inner circles (to say nothing of the 'commanding heights') of the German economy. 'Active industrial policy', 'modernization of the economy' and other similar programmes do exist in West Germany, but are performed by actors other than the state; in fact, 'am Staat vorbei' (Ronge 1980). Small wonder, then, that German government-industry relations tend, on the whole, to be rather harmonious; there is but little cause for conflict between a passive state and a self-organized 'business community'.

Industry's perception of government-industry relations

The relationship between government and industry in West Germany has been highly asymmetrical, allowing little elbow-room for the state, reducing governments to agents for implementing industry's policies, or even leaving them out of things altogether. On the whole, this is exactly how top industrialists and business associations' managers themselves would describe the relationship (see, for empirical evidence, Abromeit 1981 a and b). They definitely see themselves in the leading role, putting governments firmly in their place, and viewing state administrations generally in the role of service agencies. Wherever regulation or any kind of intervention seems to be unavoidable, the stress is on the 'continuous dialogue', on 'cooperation and consensus', to bind government policies as closely as possible to industry's interests. Government, it is felt, would at any rate be helpless and completely at a loss, and in grave danger of getting things entirely wrong, without the information and expertise which only industry can provide, while, at the same time, the public-mindedness of big corporations is the best safeguard of public interests against the short-sightedness of election-minded politicians. Interestingly enough, some outside observers have fallen into this PR-trap and argued that government intervention was hardly necessary in Germany because industry acted in the public interest on their own accord (see, for instance, Grant et al. 1987: 37 f., 41).

However, government behaves as if industry indeed acted in such a public-minded way. Remaining inactive, it does its best to prove industry's PR right. West German government behaviour also proves right industry's view of its own rightfully taking on the lead, in all matters of industrial policy. Being as asymmetrical as they are, government-industry relations in West Germany are thus, acccording to this view (barring the odd petty friction), basically in an ideal state.

Notes

1. It did so, paradoxically, even before it was born: with the currency reform and the 'Act of Principles' (Leitsätzegesetz) of 1948
2. In this course it is still supported by the majority of 'informed' public opinion as reveals the ongoing public debate about whether or not West Germany needed an industrial policy (i.e. whether it was to follow the French or Japanese examples), and whether this could be reconciled with the doctrine of 'Soziale Marktwirtschaft'
3. Moreover, these fines were treated as being tax deductible, and quite legally so, according to a Federal Finance Court ruling in 1984; a slip which was legislatively corrected in the following year
4. For the periodization as well as for the BDI attitude see Weßels 1968
5. On the whole, however, relations after 1969 were pretty poor, industry launching, for example, a campaign to overthrow the social-liberal government in 1971/72

6. The Act was challenged by industry as not being in line with the Constitution and led to the much-quoted 'Investitionshilfe-Urteil' of the Federal Constitution Court in 1954
7. The figures, provided by the Hamburger Weltwirtschaftliches Archiv (HWWA) in 1983, include tax concessions, grants, interest-subsidized loans and EEC payments; see Gemper 1985: 48
8. Still, the rate at least of federal subsidies declined steadily during the seventies: from 2.2 per cent of GNP in 1970 to 1.7 per cent in 1982; see Neumann and Uterwedde 1986: 83
9. Of this latter sum only DM 2.3 billion went into the military sector and spaceflight; see Keck 1984: 25 f.
10. This preference is not confined to federal R&D policies, as the examples of Baden-Württemberg and Bavaria – with their loving care for Daimler-Benz and MBB, respectively – illustrate
11. Interestingly enough, the first successful projects had not originated from the programmes at all, but had been reactor types developed independently – by Siemens – or imported from overseas
12. This is based on the 'Acts on Conversion into Electricity' (Verstromungsgesetze) of 1965, 1966, 1974 and 1976, the 1974 Act introducing the famous 'coal penny' which has recently been challenged by the South German electricity generators
13. Until 1983; 1976 the workforce had been about 36 500
14. It could be noted, however, when the Wirtschaftsvereinigung Eisen und Stahl, the iron and steel industry's association always deemed to be one of the most powerful of its kind, found itself unable, several years ago, to force Klöckner to keep to its production quotas
15. As contrasted to its 'economic role'; for this distinction see Abromeit 1981a, 38 ff.
16. This is what they did, in the mid-seventies, to force the social-liberal government to withdraw several reform bills; see Abromeit 1977
17. This has recently been disputed, however, by Grant et al., on the grounds that some companies are too 'liquid' to allow for any bank influence; 1987: 51 ff.

References

Abromeit, H. 'Interessendurchsetzung in der Krise' in *Aus Politik und Zeitgeschichte B* 1977, vol. 11/77, pp 15–37

Abromeit, H. *Staat und Wirtschaft*, Campus, Frankfurt a. M./New York 1981a

Abromeit, H. 'Der Führungsanspruch der Wirtschaft gegenüber der Politik' in *Aus Politick und Zeitgeschichte B* 1981b, vol. 11/81, pp 19–39

Abromeit, H. 'Unternehmerverbände', in *Pipers Wörterbüchur zur Politik, Vol. 2: Westliche Industriegesellschaften* (ed. Manfred Schmidt), Piper, München/ Zürich 1983, pp 454–61

Bahl, V. *Staatliche Politik am Beispiel der Kohle*, Campus, Frankfurt/New York 1977

BDI. Jahresbericht 1968/69, Köln 1969

Berger, R. 'Zum Verhältnis von Aufgabe, Struktur und Interessen in der Forschungspolitik' in *Politische Vierteljahresschrift, Sonderheft 9/1978: Politische Wissenschaft und Politische Praxis* 1978, pp 169–91

Bruder, W., ed. *Forschungs-und Technologiepolitik in der Bundesrepublik Deutschland*, Westdeutscher Verlag, Opladen 1986

Bruder, W., Ende, W. 'Forschungs-und Technologiepolitik in der Bundesrepublik Deutschland' in *Aus Politik und Zeitgeschichte B* 1980, vol. 28/80, pp 3–21

Bruder, W., Hofelich, P. 'Interessengruppen und staatliche Forschungspolitik' in *Aus Politik und Zeitgeschichte B* 1982, vol. 35/82, pp 19–33

Cox, A., ed. *State, Finance and Industry*, Wheatsheaf, Brighton 1986

Curzon Price, V. *Industrial Policy in the European Community*, Trade Policy Research Centre, London 1981

Donges, J.B. 'Industrial policies in West Germany's not so market-oriented economy' in *The World Economy 1980/2* 1980, pp 185–204

Dyson, K. 'The cultural, ideological and structural context' in K. Dyson, S. Wilks, eds, *Industrial Crisis*, Martin Robertson, Oxford 1983, pp 26–66

Dyson, K., Wilks, S., eds. *Industrial Crisis*, Martin Robertson, Oxford 1983

Esser, J., Fach, W., Väth, W. *Krisenregulierung*, Suhrkamp, Frankfurt a. M. 1983

Esser, J., Fach, W. ' "Social market" and modernization policy: West Germany' in K. Dyson, S. Wilks, eds, *Industrial Crisis*, Martin Robertson, Oxford 1983, pp 102–27

Fach, W., Simonis, G. *Die Stärke des Staates im Atomkonflikt, Frankreich und die Bundesrepublik im Vergleich*, Campus, Frankfurt a. M./New York 1987

Gemper, B.B., ed. *Industrial Policy – Structural Dynamics*, HWWA, Hamburg 1985

Gessner, V., Winter, G., eds. *Rechtsformen der Verflechtung von Staat und Wirtschaft, Jahrbuch für Rechtssoziologie und Rechtstheorie*, vol. VIII, Westdeutscher Verlag, Opladen 1982

Grant, W., Paterson, W., Whitston, C. 'Government-industry relations in the chemical industry: An Anglo-German comparison' in S. Wilks, M. Wright, eds, *Comparative Government-Industry relations*, Clarendon Press, Oxford 1987, pp 35–60

Grottian, P. 'Problemlösungsstrategien der Staatsadministration anhand der Konzenstrations-und Wettbewerbspolitik' in P. Grottian, A. Murswieck, eds, *Handlungsspielräume der Staatsadministration*, Hoffmann und Campe, Hamburg 1974, pp 236–61

Hauff, V., Scharpf, F.W. *Modernisierung der Volkswirtschaft*, Europäische Verlagsanstalt, Köln 1975

Jákli, Z. 'Staatliche Intervention und private Politik im Energiesektor' in V. Ronge, ed., *Am Staat vorbei*, Campus, Frankfurt a. M./New York 1980, pp 30–82

Keck, O. *Der Schnelle Brüter*, Campus, Frankfurt a. M./New York 1984

Kitschelt, H. *Kernenergiepolitik. Arena eines gesellschaftspolitischen Konflikts*, Campus, Frankfurt a. M./New York 1980

Kreile, M. 'West Germany: The dynamics of expansion' in P.J. Katzenstein, ed., *Between Power and Plenty*, The University of Wisconsin Press, 1978, pp 191–224

Maus, I. 'Verrechtlichung, Entrechtlichung und Funktionswandel von Institutionen' in G. Göhler, ed., *Grundfragen der Theorie politischer Institutionen*, Westdeutscher Verlag, Opladen 1987, pp 132–72

Mayntz, R., ed. *Implementation politischer Programme*, Athenäum, Königstein/Ts 1980

Neumann, W., Uterwedde, H. *Industriepolitik: Ein deutsch-französischer Vergleich*, Leske + Budrich, Opladen 1986

OECD. *The Aims and Instruments of Industrial Policy. A Comparative Study*, Paris 1975

Ollig, G. 'Staat und Stahl in Deutschland' in *Annalen der Gemeinwirtschaft 4/1980*, pp 423–37

Peacock, A. et al. *The Regulation Game*, Oxford 1984

Ronge, V., ed. *Am Staat vorbei*, Campus, Frankfurt a. M./New York 1980

Shonfield, A. ed. *Modern Capitalism*, OUP, Oxford 1965

Ullmann, A.A. *Industrie und Umweltschutz*, Campus, Frankfurt a. M./New York 1982

van Schendelen, M.P.C.M., Jackson, R.J., eds. *The Politicisation of Business in Western Europe*, Beckenham 1987

Vogel, D. 'Government-industry relations in the United States: an overview' in S. Wilks, M. Wright, eds, *Comparative Government-industry Relations*, Clarendon Press, Oxford 1987, pp 91–116

Weßels, B. 'Politik, Industrie und Umweltschutz in der Bundesrepublik' in D. Herzog, B. Weßels, eds, *Konfliktpotentiale und Konsenssstrategien*, Westdeutscher Verlag, Opladen (forthcoming)

Wilks, S., Wright, M., eds. *Comparative Government-industry Relations*, Clarendon Press, Oxford 1987

Wilson, G.K. *Business and Politics. A Comparative Introduction*, Macmillan, Basingstoke/London 1985

Zysman, J. *Governments, Markets, and Growth: Financial Systems and the Politics of Industrial Change*, Martin Robertson, Oxford 1983

5 The first nationalization of the UK iron and steel industry: a test of socialist principles

R.A. Bryer

Introduction

In July 1945 the first ever majority Labour Government swept to power with an extensive programme of nationalization. However, its commitment to 'Socialist Principles' was not seriously tested until it turned to the nationalization of the iron and steel industry.[1] Here, for the first time, it encountered determined resistance from the Opposition and the industry. As *The New Statesman and Nation* observed,

> During the Government's first year of office, the enemy . . . appeared to be on the run; the opposition, not merely to large measures of social reform, but even to the nationalisation of the Bank of England and the coal mines, was perfunctory. . . . [But] . . . [w]hen it came to steel . . . the enemy's tactics were quite different. . . . [It] . . . refused point blank to co-operate.[2]

Although when faced with resistance important elements of the Government were reluctant to nationalize steel, the Left of the Labour Party eventually forced it through as an explicit test of the Government's commitment to 'Socialist Principles'. Their objective was to extend public economic planning to a 'strategic' industry that manifestly needed radical restructuring into large, integrated works so as to make it technically efficient by international standards.[3] Set against this objective nationalization was a failure. One month after the return of a Conservative Government in 1951 the industry was effectively denationalized and, although steel was under public supervision throughout Labour's six years in office,[4] no attempt was made to encourage or force the industry to radically restructure itself.

A plausible explanation is Miliband's well-known view that 'Of all the Labour Government's nationalization measures, the nationalization of iron and steel was the only one which entailed a serious threat to the "private sector" '.[5] Certainly, private sector interests would explain the hostility of the Opposition and the industry, and is consistent with the reluctance of the more conservative elements within the Labour Party, '. . . whose enthusiasm for a head-on clash . . . [with the private sector] . . . was lukewarm'.[6] However, it does not explain why, although the Labour Left had sufficient political power to eventually force the Government to take steel into public ownership, it allowed nationalization to be persistently delayed, and did nothing to force the Government to impose restructuring upon the industry.

The fact that nationalization occurred at all is evidence that the Labour Left were not averse to challenging 'private sector' interests. Yet their challenge was ineffective. Although lack of leadership and incompetence are possible explanations,[7] there seem to be no reasons why these factors should have afflicted the Labour Left only over steel. Ruling out lack of political power, willingness to challenge 'private sector' interests, leadership, and competence as adequate explanations for the failure of steel nationalization, we appear to be left with the possibility that it was caused by the 'hard' nationalizers' 'Socialist Principles' themselves. To explore this possibility is the purpose of this chapter. To do so we must investigate both the threat posed to 'private sector' interests by the nationalization of steel, and the adequacy of the Labour Left's Socialist Principles as a representation (or model) of that threat and, hence, the scale of opposition which they should have expected and been prepared for.

Quantifying and analysing 'private sector' financial interests are the central concerns of accounting and finance. Underlying its concepts and techniques is a well-defined and tested model of capitalism. Thus, our first task must be to outline the Accounting and Finance model of capitalism and contrast it with that entertained by the Socialists. We shall then use it to identify and analyse the financial interests at stake in steel nationalization. We will then be able to appreciate, firstly, the significance of the industry's development plans, the fierce opposition to nationalization, and the Government's reactions to both and, secondly, the realism of the Left's understanding of the challenge to the 'private sector' posed by the nationalization of steel, and the role which their Socialist Principles played in its ultimate failure. We shall conclude that although the evidence suggests that one cause was the reluctance of important elements of the Government to challenge 'private sector' interests, another was the Left's vast underestimate of the challenge nationalization posed, and therefore the extent of the preparations thought necessary to make it successful. For this misperception the Labour Left had nothing but their Socialist Principles to blame.

The Socialist and the Accounting and Finance models of capitalism

As an exemplar of the Socialist model of capitalism I shall use Miliband's analysis in *The State in Capitalist Society*.[8] As we shall see later, his model was shared by the 'hard' nationalizers of steel. Miliband is well aware of the importance of the very unequal distribution of the ownership of company shares for the very unequal distribution of wealth, and accepts that managers and shareholders share a 'basic community of interests'.[9] The modern manager must submit to the 'imperative demands' of the system, the most important of which is to make the 'highest possible' profits.[10] However, he also believes that with the separation of ownership from managerial control '. . . the managerial element is largely immune from the control and even from the effective pressure of individual shareholders; and the bigger the enterprise, the more dispersed its ownership, the more complete is that immunity likely to be'.[11] Thus, he concludes, '. . . it may readily be granted that there does exist a *plurality of economic elites* in advanced captitalist societies; and that *despite* the integrating tendencies of advanced capitalism, these elites constitute distinct groupings and interests, whose competition greatly affects the political process'.[12]

In the world view of Accounting and Finance, we have here an image of the organization of 'advanced' capitalism not markedly different from 'early' capitalism's fragmentation into owner-managed firms. In Miliband's model the increasing scale of economic enterprise has simply meant individual owner-managers replacing individual owners (shareholders) dependent upon the management of individual companies. The economic elite remains a loose coalition of individual shareholder and management interests. While all elements whole-heartedly endorse the defence of the capitalist social order and the purpose of economic existence, they agree about precious little else. This conception may explain why Miliband has provided no evidence in support of this thesis that the first nationalization of steel represented a challenge to the 'private sector' as, within his framework, there is no necessarily coherent interest at stake.

In contrast, from the viewpoint of Accounting and Finance, the identification and analysis of the 'private sector' interests at stake in the nationalization of steel follows naturally from its structure of ownership and control. In this model it is presumed that, as the major steel companies involved were quoted on the London Stock Exchange, and were owned (either directly, or indirectly via financial institutions) by 'investors', they were run in their financial interests. Dominant amongst investors are the wealthiest 5 per cent of the population who own some 80 per cent of all quoted shares held by individuals.

It is significant that in his enumeration of the 'integrating tendencies' of advanced capitalism, Miliband does not mention the huge growth of both financial reporting and capital markets from before the turn of the century, whose organization and avowed purpose was, and still is, precisely to transcend the divorce of ownership and control. As the Select Committee on Joint Stock Companies concluded in 1844, 'Periodical accounts, if honestly made, and fairly audited, cannot fail to excite attention to the real state of a concern; and by means of improved remedies, parties to mismanagement may be made more amenable for acts of fraud and illegality'.[13]

In both the UK and USA the development of capital markets from the 1880s became a necessary extension of the joint-stock company as the scale and complexity of business enterprise increased, and the pace of economic change accelerated. It was no coincidence that at that point 'scientific investment' was discovered or, as we would say today, the benefits of holding a 'well-diversified portfolio' became a part of the folklore of the owners of capital.[14] As Modern Portfolio Theory has rigorously demonstrated,[15] all serious investors should hold well-diversified portfolios of shares (and the evidence is that they do), because the total risk to which their wealth is exposed is reduced whilst their expected returns remain the same. The ultimately diversified portfolio would consist of all assets, each held in proportion to their market value. This is the 'market portfolio' which *dominates* all other portfolios.[16]

However, holding diversified portfolios exacerbates the divorce of ownership and control. Thus, it was also necessary to develop and elaborate a system of financial reporting to the capital markets, both to ensure the fidelity of management reporting (by the use of professional auditors and the prescription of required disclosures), and to subject management to the *collective* scrutiny of investors and their agents in the capital market. Thus, successive Companies Acts have imposed more onerous duties and financial reporting requirements on directors and auditors; Stock Exchange requirements and professional accounting and auditing standards have proliferated, and the body of accountants, financial analysts and portfolio managers has grown to a previously unimagined size.

The result, confirmed in extensive research, is a capital market in which shares are 'efficiently' priced by impounding all publicly-available information on the expected risks and returns from holding them.[17] The fundamental characteristic of an efficient capital market is that, in the long run, no-one can earn 'abnormal returns' – that is, returns not justified by the level of risk incurred. As one investor's abnormal return is another's abnormal loss, if the capital markets were 'inefficient' we would expect significant wealth transfers between investors, loud complaints from the losers, and a general loss of confidence by investors in the fairness of the capital markets. Typically we do not. Vociferous complaints about insider dealing are the exceptions which prove the rule.

In short, in the world view of Accounting and Finance share prices reflect the *collective* wisdom of investors and their agents about expected risk and return. Thus, in contrast to Miliband's model which stresses the importance of the *conflicts* between elements of the economic elite, the Accounting and Finance model stresses the importance of their *agreement*, particularly as this is reflected in capital market prices.

Within Miliband's 'elite pluralism' share prices have no significance for management decisions as '. . . there is . . . precious little that shareholders can normally do to make effective what discontent they may feel, save of course to get rid of their shares'.[18] However, in the world view of Accounting and Finance, capital market prices exert a powerful influence over managerial decisions. As a modern classic text on finance puts it, because of the existence of 'extensive and well-functioning capital markets', although 'Separation of ownership and management is a practical necessity for large organizations. . . . The remarkable thing is that managers of firms can all be given one simple instruction: Maximize net present value.'[19] Share prices are unbiased estimates of the present value of expected future dividends, and the most important single source of information which investors use for these estimates is the accounting reports which management is obliged to make publicly available.[20] Thus, the existence of efficient capital markets and financial reporting enables investors to observe whether managers are making decisions in their best financial interests.

It is important to note that the maximization of net present value is not at all the same as Miliband's 'maximization of profits' which makes no reference to the amount of capital employed, the time-scale involved, or whether 'maximum' profits are acceptable to investors. By contrast, implicit in the concept of net present value is the notion of a 'required return' on capital invested. As investors hold well-diversified portfolios the return they require on the capital invested in a particular firm must be determined in the context of the returns available on the portfolio as a whole, the 'market portfolio'. Thus, the required return on an investment is determined by the return available on the market portfolio in excess of the return available for riskless investment (in, say, government securities), adjusted for its relative riskiness.[21]

Thus, to conclude, whereas within Miliband's world view of capitalism it is impossible to speak of 'the' interest of capital, within the world view of Accounting and Finance the collective interest of investors is represented by the return they require on their capital invested, and the likelihood of it being earned. Thus, to understand how the collective interest of investors was affected by the first nationalization of the steel industry, we must understand what type of investment prospect it represented for them, and what this implied, both about the desirability of retaining it in their hands, and for the investment strategy they wished managers to follow.

The steel industry as a postwar investment prospect

Investors demand a higher rate of return for bearing a higher level of risk. A key measure of financial performance for investors is return on capital investment. The steel industry's returns on capital and those of manufacturing industry as a whole from 1920 to 1962 are shown in Figure 5.1 in the Appendix at page 101.[22] As the steel industry is notoriously riskier than most other manufacturing industries, investors will have demanded a higher return from steel than for manufacturing industry as a whole.[23] Thus, if the steel industry were earning the return required by investors on its capital employed we would expect its rate of return to be *greater* than the rate of return on capital in the manufacturing sector as a whole. However, we can see from Figure 5.1 that over this period the steel industry only earned higher returns on capital in 1920–21. Thus, it can be concluded that from the early 1920s the returns on the current cost of capital invested in steel were not satisfactory to investors.[24]

Why, then, did steel's managers not simply close the older, inefficient plants and replace them with new ones to try and improve profitability, particularly as the long-standing consensus was that the industry required extensive reorganization and re-equipment to make it internationally competitive?[25] The answer, from investors' point of view, is straightforward. Broadly, for decision-making, investments should be valued on three alternative bases – their present value (PV), replacement cost (RC) and resale value (RV). Depending on the relationship between these values investors will want different investment/divestment strategies to be followed. If an investment's PV > RC investors will want it to be replaced, when necessary, or duplicated. If, on the other hand, an investment's RC > PV investors will not want it to be replaced or duplicated, but they will not want it to be sold until RV > PV. Thus, the three strategies are to either *replace* (or duplicate) investments, to *hold* investments, or to *divest*. Which strategy for the steel industry best describes investors' interests over this period?

As the steel industry earned less than the required return on the current cost of its capital we can infer that the ratio of its present value to its replacement cost was less than 1.[26] It follows, therefore, that investors' interests were best served by not replacing the investments that had been made, but by holding them to the point where their resale value was greater than or equal to their present value.[27]

We shall see below that there is plentiful evidence consistent with the suggestion that from 1945 both the industry and elements of the Government were pursuing a 'holding' strategy on behalf of investors – that is, the maintenance of the industry with its existing technology, scale and location. However, clear direct evidence emerged in the debates on the terms of compensation for nationalization that the industry's replacement cost was at that time considerably greater than its present value.

The 1945 Labour Government decided, in keeping with its long-standing policy, to base compensation for the compulsory acquisition of steel shares at their average stock market price during specified months from 1945 to October 1948.[28] Investors could choose the highest price and, as prices had risen to a high point in October 1948, this fixed the terms of compensation. The Conservative Opposition and other supporters of investors argued that a more appropriate basis for compensation would be the 'value' of the net assets to be acquired. Naturally, these 'values' were considerably greater than the aggregate share valuation. Thus, Sir John Anderson, who led for the Opposition on this issue, produced a summary prepared by the Iron and Steel Federation of asset values for 18 major firms scheduled for acquisition. As he pointed out, 'The value of the assets of these firms . . . as compared with the £172 million of compensation is £238 million'.[29] It is not clear from his speech whether the assets were valued at current or historical costs, but for our purposes this is immaterial. On either basis the valuation ratio of these firms was clearly less than one.[30]

A more precise estimate was provided by *The Economist*, in whose view

> Half an hour with a handful of consolidated balance sheets shows that the Corporation will be picking up undertakings that are so well endowed with current assets that the value to be imputed to their fixed assets – given the limitation of compensation to Stock Exchange values – will be a small fraction of their true value, reckoned either by earning power or replacement costs.[31]

In a later note it gave details of a broker's estimates of the current replacement costs and stock market valuations of the four major steel companies summarized in Table 5.1.[32] On the basis of this evidence the steel industry clearly had a valuation ratio significantly less than one.

However, the Opposition argued that the share prices of steel companies were artificially deflated, both by the threat of nationalization and by voluntary dividend

Table 5.1 Estimates of steel companies' replacement costs and stock market valuations

	United Steel	Dorman Long	Stewarts & Lloyds	Lancashire Steel
Current replacement cost of net assets (excluding goodwill)	£37.8m	£26.3m	£47.4m	£12.7m
Stock market valuation	£15.5m	£7.2m	£25.2m	£6.1m

restraint, and also because the owners of steel shares were not willing sellers. As *The Economist* put it, the essence of the argument was that '. . . the basis of Stock Exchange values is indefensible in principle and grossly inequitable in practice'.[33] In modern terminology, the Opposition and their supporters were, in effect, claiming that the Stock Exchange was 'inefficient' – that share prices did not fully and unbiasedly reflect all relevant publicly-available information about expected risks and returns. The Government were easily able to demonstrate the flimsiness of the Opposition's case even though they did not have the benefit of the voluminous evidence and theoretical understanding of capital markets accumulated since the 1960s, which overwhelmingly supports the view that the UK and US Stock Markets are highly efficient,[34] and were almost certainly not significantly less so in the 1940s.

The argument that valuation on the basis of Stock Market prices was 'unfair in principle' was put most fully by *The Economist*:

The Government contends that [share prices are fair], because these are the result of dealings in a free market between willing buyers and willing sellers. The flaw in this argument is that the commodity which can be bought in the market is not the commodity that the Government wants to buy; it is only a small fraction of it. Buyers 'for control' habitually negotiate outside the Stock Exchange; and, when the initiative comes from them, almost invariably have to pay substantially more than the market price.[35]

The Government's riposte amounted to a classic formulation of the efficient market hypothesis. As Sir Stafford Cripps put it,

Does anyone really imagine that, with all the highly skilled operators on the Stock Exchange, somehow or other, they all overlooked what are now thought to be the true factors of the financial position of certain steel companies, and so uniformly and consistently under-valued those shares that the sellers have been equally uniformly prepared to accept that under-valuation? . . . Any assumption such as that . . . makes, of course, complete nonsense of the Stock Exchange as a place to exchange stock.[36]

Judging by the complete failure of the Opposition to question this view, it appears that no-one really did imagine that the capital market was inefficient. On the contrary, '. . . an apparently bewildered Mr Churchill . . .'[37] admitted that he found it a '. . . brilliantly able argument . . . masterly in every way . . .'![38]

Given that the capital market was efficient it followed, as Sir Stafford pointed out, that valuation on the basis of earning power[39] would give the same value as share prices: 'It is the whole future probabilities as to the earning power that affects the price on the market, and that is why price is a fair criterion of the value of the share.'[40] Sir Stafford might also have pointed out that whether a seller is willing or not, if the value of a share is unbiasedly determined by earning power she or he will be fairly compensated by receiving its market value as this can be reinvested to produce an equivalent expected return. Finally, if share prices are an unbiased estimate of earning power, there is no need to revise this estimate merely because whole companies or a whole industry is being acquired on an outside initiative, as *The Economist* suggested. That company acquirers 'almost' invariably pay more than the Stock Market price of their target does not mean they 'invariably' do. 'Almost invariably', the share prices of takeover targets rise because the acquirer has plans, or reveals opportunities, for increasing their earning power. As we shall see later, the Opposition's major criticism of the Government was precisely that it had no such plans!

The Opposition's equivocation about the capital market's efficiency is again revealed by their argument that the threat of nationalization and voluntary dividend restraint had artificially depressed steel share prices. This implicitly accepted that the Stock Market usually did produce fair values, and merely asserted that in this case they did not. This assertion was difficult to sustain.

The fact that in 1947 all UK industrial companies had agreed to limit the increases in their dividends (they did not cut them) was unlikely to have significantly reduced share prices. In the economic circumstances after the war, with most companies investing heavily to make good war losses and to expand capacity, share prices would have been heavily influenced by the prospective future *growth* in dividends and not merely those currently being paid.[41] As the Government and their supporters implied, in an efficient capital market the future dividends which would flow in part from current investment should be impounded in share prices. There was no suggestion that dividend restraint would be permanent, as Sir Stafford reminded investors when he invited them '. . . to assess the likelihood of the continuance of . . . [the] . . . limitation of dividends'.[42] Thus, it seems unlikely that the prospect of a few years' 'restraint' of dividends in the context of an expansion of capacity and growing demand for steel would have seriously affected steel companies' share prices.

Finally, the claim that the threat of nationalization had depressed share prices was easily dealt with. The Stock Market was well aware that the Government had in its Election Manifesto '. . . solemnly promised that socialized industries would be 'taken over on a basis of fair compensation', and that this was likely to be based on Stock Market values.[43] That steel company share prices had in fact increased much faster than other industrial shares was clearly demonstrated by the

Table 5.2   Share price index

	31/12/38	30/10/47	29/2/48	30/5/48	22/10/48
Industrials	100.0	149.8	149.6	161.7	161.7
Iron and steel	100.0	142.6	151.8	166.9	173.0

Chancellor (Sir Stafford) who revealed the share price index compiled by the Ministry of Supply. See Table 5.2.

As Sir Stafford pointed out,

> This so-called threat . . . [of nationalization] . . . has hung over the industry since the last General Election so that, if it was a fact that the threat affected these shares in particular as distinct from the rest of the industrial shares, we should find that the steel shares had reacted less well to the improved industrial position than the other industrial shares. But that is not the case.[44]

Although steel shares had slightly underperformed Industrials up to October 1947, in the following year whereas Iron and Steel increased by 21 per cent Industrials increased by only 8 per cent. It seems unlikely that this scale of increase can be explained solely as a response to the rapid improvement in the production, consumption and export of steel as it implies that over this period the industry had a beta of some 2.6.[45] While this is possible, it seems more likely that some of this increase in steel share prices was caused by speculation on the terms of compensation. As the *Financial Times* of the 15th October 1948 put it, 'Yesterday's near-boom conditions in Iron and Steel shares reflected a gamble, pure and simple. Buyers are gambling on the contents of the coming Nationalisation Bill.'[46] The gamble was over what period the Government would allow investors to choose the highest quoted price. As Sir Stafford revealed, the gamble on whether prices in October 1948 were included was a close run thing: '. . . one of the matters that caused us to hesitate as to the propriety of taking October, 1948, figures was the admitted speculation that took place in steel shares, driving up their quotations in the middle of that month'.[47] Some thought the gambling had started earlier. As Mr R.H. Jenkins, Labour MP for Southwark Central (now Lord Jenkins), put it:

> . . . steel shares only began to catch up when the Prime Minister came to this House in October, 1947, and said that this Bill was definitely going to be introduced in the Parliament. Most of them gained sixpence on the strength of this dreadful piece of news alone, and, since then they have never looked back, and have gained strength as the date for the introduction of this Bill has come nearer and nearer.[48]

In any event, there are no grounds for believing that the share prices of steel companies did not reflect at least their expected earning power, and therefore every reason for concluding, as the Conservatives insisted, that the present value of steel was less than its replacement cost, and hence that investors wanted its managers to follow a 'holding' strategy. And this is what they did.

Industry investment planning

The very unsatisfactory financial returns in the 1920s and early 1930s did lead to some rationalization and the cartelization of the industry under the British Iron and Steel Federation (BISF), and its supervision by the Import Duties Advisory Committee (IDAC) in return for tariff protection. However, although profits improved, largely as a result of rearmament and an expansion of trade, most firms remained equipped with out of date plant, much of it poorly located.[49] The BISF's priorities were to control prices and investment. It replaced price rings with a system of maximum uniform prices designed to give every firm a 'reasonable' return on its capital. High cost plants were supported by a levy on the output of basic steel (ingots), and in 1937 the levy was also used to support those plants reliant on the increasingly costly imports of iron ore and scrap. This system inserted a clear bias against the removal of high-cost plants, and consequently few moves were made in the late 1930s to restructure the industry. Resource constraints inevitably continued this bias through the war, during which out of the £60m invested in the steel industry (half of it provided by public funds) only £6m was spent on bulk steelmaking.[50] Thus, unlike at the end of the First World War, the steel industry emerged from the Second with no surplus capacity and with an improved financial position.

In 1945 the BISF produced its first 5-year development plan. In outline, this proposed: (i) continuation of home market protection, price control ensuring subsidized supplies of scrap and imported ores, no price competition, and 'reasonable' returns on capital; (ii) increasing crude steelmaking capacity from 12m tons to 15m tons; (iii) reducing the consumption of home ores to prewar levels and increasing the consumption of imported ores; (iv) focusing capital investment on 'modernization'. Duncan Burn's work clearly shows that this plan was systematically biased against any radical restructuring of the industry, and the following summarizes some of its key elements:[51]

(i) State subsidies for high cost imported ore and scrap continued until 1949, when they were replaced by the prewar system of levy-subsidy whereby the extra costs of imported ore and scrap were averaged and spread over the whole industry. Both systems exerted a conservative bias into industry planning as (a) the state subsidy favoured the existing coastal plants using imported ores, and the levy-subsidy system favoured users of imported ores at the expense of users of home ores; (b) the low price of scrap, coupled with the low profit margins allowed for pig iron, favoured heavy users of scrap and discouraged investment in expanding iron smelting. At the same time, protection and the absence of price competition, by ensuring that all plants earned 'reasonable' profits, discouraged the closure of the less efficient plants. Many old small works were retained and renovated and the expansion of pig iron capacity was restricted.

(ii) The proposed increase in steelmaking capacity was based on a projection of home demand derived from a five-year moving average from 1910 to 1939. As Burn says, '. . . it was blandly assumed that history would, as it were, repeat itself'.[52] As this history included the depressed 1920s and 30s, the projection was considered by many as too conservative. Although the limited availability of new plant and raw materials may have meant that, initially, no further *capacity* could have been provided even if additional demand had been forecast, these facts could not justify the *demand* forecast as the plan implied. On the possibility of future expansion if raw materials and new plant became available, the plan made no explicit comments, merely noting that if demand exceeded 15m tons per annum, old plant could be retained. And this is what happened in practice.

(iii) In the plan new capacity based on home ores was explicity limited to 1 million tons. The reasons given were that (a) labour was scarce; (b) coastal areas were nearer to coal mines and scrap; (c) distribution costs were higher; (d) home ore was not suitable for a continuous strip-mill; (e) reserves of home ores were 'limited'. However, as critics pointed out, labour shortages would only have been temporary; some major coastal works were sited near expensive coal and had little local scrap; the plan provided no evidence that distribution costs from home ore sites were relatively high; home ore was suitable for all other products and could be suitable for continuous strip-mill production if the research effort was made; at projected usage rates there was sufficient ore in the Midlands alone for 150–200 years.[53] The fundamental reason for the plan's bias in favour of imported ores was its forecast that the cost of imported ore would fall to 30s. per ton. In Burn's view this forecast was 'very obscure' and deeply biased.[54] However, it was on this basis, and the fact that the cost of capital equipment had risen faster than most other costs and prices, that the BISF foresaw only a 'small' reduction in total costs (including capital charges) from using home ores. The 1m tons additional capacity based on home ores was never built because, 'The assumption . . . made in practice was not that radical change should be deferred till capital costs came into line, but that it should be to a large extent, abandoned in favour of lesser but more numerous scattered changes. . . .'[55]

(iv) The plan envisaged capital expenditure of £168m over 7.5 years, after which 40 per cent of the industry's equipment would be 'new'. However, as *The Economist* pointed out, 'The rate of expenditure proposed . . . however formidable in comparison with pre-war levels, is not greatly in excess of depreciation at current levels of replacement cost plus war-time arrears' (p 759). Modernization rather than expansion was to be the focus of capital expenditure. Plant sizes were deliberately limited to 500 000–800 000 tons compared with typical American practice of plants of 2 000 000 to 6 000 000 tons. As Burn concludes, 'The number of works at which the plan visualised expensive modernisation was such that it ruled out economies of large scale of the kind enjoyed not only in America but in north-west Europe'.[56] The size of British plant remained well below the internationally accepted technically efficient scale.[57]

Why was the plan biased against radical restructuring? Why, as Burn asks, '. . . should the firms not strain after . . . [this] . . . investment policy . . . if it offered lower costs and therefore greater strength in international competition and, one would suppose, *better profits*?'.[58] One answer, as we have seen, is that 'better' profits are not the same thing as the returns required by investors.[59] The BISF's own calculations showed that steel plants based on home ores would be *more* profitable than those based on imported ores, and they presumably realized that their biases had understated this advantage. By nevertheless rejecting investment in capacity based on home ores the BISF were accepting that for restructuring to have been justifiable to investors, it would have had to offer financial returns as good as those available from international competitors.[60] They had good reasons to believe that development on home ores would not provide these returns.

In the BISF's view the 'Costs of home ore were bound to "rise considerably" over the next 20 years whereas the present high prices of imported ore are more likely to fall than to rise'.[61] While this proved to be wishful thinking for some time, this was not necessarily crucial to the conclusion. The small margin in favour of home ores arose because the BISF used the *current* cost of coke based on national average costs, including many high-cost pits. Thus, the BISF was implicitly forecasting that British coke costs would not fall, and their recent knowledge of the coal industry may have suggested, correctly as it turned out, that they would rise.[62] Under this scenario, British plants based on domestic ores would *never* be as profitable as international plants using richer ores and cheaper coal and, therefore, if British steelmaking was *ever* to be sufficiently profitable to justify substantial reinvestment, retaining coastal sites would be necessary not simply to use 'cheaper' imported ores, but also to leave open the possibility of exploiting cheaper imported coal.

However, this did not mean that reinvestment was desirable to investors at that time.[63] As we saw earlier, they wanted managers to follow a 'holding' strategy, implying that although they did not want reinvestment, they did not want to divest either. Not surprisingly, in the world view of Accounting and Finance, their preference against restructuring was fully reflected in management's plans. Perhaps more surprisingly, Labour did nothing to effectively challenge them.

Labour, planning and nationalization

The Labour Party and its supporters were well aware of the need for restructuring, and were convinced that the industry would not do so if it remained in private hands. As The Iron and Steel Trades Confederation put it in their original statement of the need for nationalization,

. . . without doubt the crux of the whole position that now presents itself – is whether . . . the isolated efforts of individual firms to keep their plant up-to-date are sufficient to enable the industry to re-establish its position when compared with the progress made by its competitors in other countries. We submit that nothing short of national planning and conscious control of the industry will meet the situation.[64]

Labour's commitment in its 1945 Election Manifesto, *Let Us Face The Future*, was framed in the same terms. Nevertheless, nothing was done to correct the bias agaainst restructuring in the industry's plans, and lack of industry cooperation and fierce hostility from the Opposition were allowed to delay nationalization and to erode political support.

During the last years of the war several future Labour Ministers had close contacts with the steel industry as it prepared its postwar plans, yet the Labour Government had no plans for the industry when it came into office in 1945.[65] The Government remitted the BISF's plan to an interdepartmental committee which found it 'complete and adequate'.[66] Government concurred, its indifference to industry planning continuing throughout its periods in office. For example, the general consensus afer the first major Parliamentary debate on steel in May 1946, was that the Minister responsible 'Both in his speech and in his unqualified acceptance of the Federation's plan . . . demonstrated convincingly that he and the Government had nothing to contribute to the industry's conduct and future from either an economic or industrial point of view'.[67] Whether by default or design the Government's indifference gave the industry's managers a free hand to plan in investors' financial interests.

Although the nationalization of steel had been Labour Party policy since 1934, as the 1945 Election approached it became clear that 'Certain elements on the Executive, led by Herbert Morrison and Arthur Greenwood, wanted to forget about iron and steel nationalisation. . . .'[68] The reason, Dalton thought, was that Morrison '. . . had been lunching with some friends of ours in the City, who had told him that it was too ambitious to talk of any Public Board "owning" this complicated and troublesome industry'. It is of course impossible to know whether Morrison's consistent opposition to nationalization was influenced by City (that is, investors') interests, but the effect on them was clearly favourable. Ross even goes so far as to claim that 'The decisive factor in determining what can only be called the failure of steel nationalization was the three-year period of indecision and procrastination which preceded the introduction of the Iron and Steel Bill in 1948',[70] in which Mr Morrison took no small part.

The BISF's plan was received by the Government in December 1945. However, in early 1946 the Minister of Supply (Mr Wilmot) and his Permanent Secretary, both of whom had *governmental* experience of steel, drew the 'startling' conclusion that '. . . the Permanent Staff at Supply was not administratively equipped to deal with the nationalization of steel or, for that matter, with the questions of iron and steel policy in general'![71] Until this was remedied the Cabinet subcommittee, chaired by Morrison, took no decisions. Nationalization came to the full cabinet in March 1946 and, after lengthy arguments, with strong opposition from Morrison, but determination on the Left to proceed, in April the decision was made to go ahead. However, the seriousness with which the Government were pursuing nationalization was revealed when the Minister requested the industry, in effect, to draw up proposals for nationalizing itself, and withdrew it in August 1946 at the industry's refusal![72]

It took until April 1947 before even a 'skeleton plan had gone far enough to be brought before the Cabinet for consideration'.[73] Although an outline Bill was agreed, no decision was taken on the date of its introduction as the BISF had approached Prime Minister Attlee in search of a compromise avoiding public ownership. Morrison negotiated, and the Cabinet agreed to await the outcome. Towards the end of July 1947 the compromise was agreed. A new Iron and Steel Board would be established with more powers, and the industry would cooperate, but the industry would not be nationalized. In early August 1947 this compromise was discussed and rejected by the majority in the Cabinet who, in the face of widespread rebellion in the Party, succumbed to the view of Sir Stafford Cripps that '. . . the iron and steel issue was one which would test the Labour Government's Socialist convictions'.[74] However, again no date for nationalization was agreed and, whereas when the compromise scheme was agreed by Morrison and the BISF the Ministry was told to immediately begin preparing a Bill, no such instructions were issued for nationalization.

A Bill appeared in October 1948, with vesting day set for 1 May 1950. Although the Lords would undoubtedly object, an amendment to the Parliament Act 1911 had been passed during 1947 to reduce their delaying powers and allow the Iron and Steel Bill through. As no General Election was necessary until July 1950, all seemed set for the Labour Government to go to the country, either with its 1945 Election Manifesto promises fulfilled or, as the Left would have preferred, to go early over the issue of the power of the House of Commons to fulfil pledges to the electorate. However, when, as expected, the Lords amended the Bill to delay vesting until October 1950, the Government decided not to use the amended Parliament Act to force nationalization through. Their excuse was that 'The issue might well drag on well into 1950, severely limiting the Government's freedom to choose an election date'.[75] However, this neglects the fact that the original plans had only given the Government two months' leeway, and does not explain why the Government went *further* than the House of Lords by making 1 October 1950 the earliest date for appointing members to the new Corporation, and 1 January 1951 the earliest date for vesting! The Government's other excuse was that, as the Minister put it, '. . . we would have to rush (!) the preliminary steps required to make 1st May the take over date, so as seriously to jeopardise the successful launching of our scheme of public ownership'. However, he omitted to explain what, oother than the collection of securities and the payment of compensation, had

to await the Royal Assent.[76]

Although the industry finally came into public ownership in February 1951, its leaders stubbornly refused to cooperate, and the Government did not use its power to impose restructuring. As the Iron and Steel Act provided only for the transfer of securities and the establishment of a Board, nothing had been disturbed when the Conservatives turned to denationalization after their victory in October 1951.

As *The Financial Times* speculated,

> . . . ironically enough, the unique arrangement chosen by the Socialists for steel nationalization, whereby the identity of the industry's individual units is maintained and the Steel Corporation assumes physical ownership of all the industry's share certificates, *might* have been expressly designed to facilitate unscrambling.[77]

This type of thinking was not restricted to the financial press. Many on the Labour Left also saw design in the Government's management of steel. The mere fact that many Labour MPs and Labour supporters in the trade unions were '. . . prepared to make the nationalization of the iron and steel industry a test of the Government's regard for Socialist Principles'[78] suggests that they thought these principles were in danger of being abandoned.

Nevertheless, during the 1945–51 Labour Governments, 'Socialist Principles' were held widely enough and sincerely enough within the Labour Party and its leadership to force nationalization through. However, these principles were unable to prevent what '. . . was perhaps the most important political muddle of the post-war Labour Government. . . .'[79] The central weakness, Ross and others have concluded, was that neither the Labour Party nor the Labour Government devoted sufficient resources to planning for nationalization at an early enough stage to force the industry to submit to the Government's will, and then to cooperate. In Ross's view, '. . . it was obvious that if the Corporation had been granted more time, the Federation's resistance might have been overcome'.[80] However, this assumes that it was the *Federation's* resistance that was crucial, rather than *investors'*, as the world view of Accounting and Finance suggests. If the Federation were simply the agent of investors collectively, the test to which Socialist Principles were subjected by nationalization was not simply whether a Labour Government could subdue and gain the cooperation of an *element* of capital which, as we shall see, the Labour Left said it was, but whether it could subdue and gain the cooperation of capital as a *whole*. We shall see that this was a test for which the Socialist Principles of the Labour Left were not designed. Thus, its failure to 'replace private monopoly' in steel, as the 1945 Manifesto had promised, was not simply a question of insufficient planning. The failure to plan was itself a symptom of a failure to comprehend the challenge which nationalization posed to the 'private sector', and therefore the extent of the preparations that were required to make it successful.

The test of socialist principles

Sir Stafford Cripps explained the 'hard' nationalizers' view of the challenge posed to the private sector. In their view, opposition to steel nationalization came mainly from '. . . those who resent bitterly this attack upon the citadel of the power of the property owner. . . .' To the Left this opposition represented '. . . a challenge to the capacity of democracy to deal with the private industrial empires that have been built up under capitalism'. This, he declared, was '. . . a fundamental challenge which we accept. . . .'[81]

Note that the challenge was to 'private industrial empires' (and elsewhere to: 'deeply entrenched sectors of private enterprise', 'private interests', 'the owners of industrial property',[82] which had been 'built up under capitalism', and not to capitalism itself. As Mr Strauss, the Minister responsible for the Iron and Steel Bill said, '. . . it transfers to Parliament and the community that power to dominate the economic life of this country which *now resides with the steelmasters in Steel House*'.[83] The problem, in his view, was that it would be impossible to make the steel industry '. . . 100 per cent efficient as long as private owners with *sectional interests* remain in possession. . . . To rationalize the industry properly, and so to get maximum efficiency, a single owner must replace the many. . . .'[84] And Mr Morrison spoke plainly of the difficulties of coordinating 'a large number of separately owned undertakings' – *'The separate bodies of shareholders'*![85] Apparently, no-one in the Labour Party had heard of investors holding well-diversified portfolios.

Labour's characterizations of the challenge posed by nationalization suggests their acceptance of the 'pluralist elite' model of capitalism, because only in its terms can *sections* of capital be challenged without challenging capitalism as a *whole*. Presumably it is this possibility which provided the rationale for the Labour Party's concept of the 'mixed economy', part socialist and part capitalist, and its philosophy of gradual reform.[86] As Sir Stafford said, the complaint of the Labour Left was only that 'There has been *too much* . . . reliance upon the unrestrained operation of the law of supply and demand in association with the equally unrestrained operation of the profit motive'.[87] What was 'reasonable', he accepted, depended on the facts in '. . . any particular case'.[88] In the case of steel, of central importance was '. . . the present necessities of reconstituting the industry in large, up-to-date units. . . .' This meant, he concluded, that 'We cannot allow the steel industry to determine, from the point of view of nothing but its own profitability, the limits of its own expansion'.[89] In short, the view of the Labour Left was that

> Iron and steel was a central producing industry, the key to the economy in the post-war years to come. Not only did it supply raw materials for most of Britain's manufacturing industry, it had vast ramifications of its own in the manufacturing side as well. . . . Iron and steel was a crucial centre of economic power, perhaps *the* most crucial centre of economic power in Britain.[90]

Although Labour argued that steel was an *isolated* centre of economic power which could be taken into public ownership without challenging capitalism as a whole, the Conservative Opposition were wholly unconvinced. Moving the Opposition amendment, Mr Oliver Lyttleton, complained that '. . . the only object of this Bill . . . [is] . . . to pull down every form of private enterprise'; '. . . if the nationalization of steel is carried out, a revolution, not evolution, will have taken place'.[91] Churchill declared the Iron and Steel Bill was '. . . not a plan to help our patient struggling people, but a burglar's jemmy to crack the capitalist crib . . .',[92] and Anthony Eden even asked Mr Morrison whether, if the Conservatives denationalized the industry, he would '. . . regard that as a provocative act justifying revolutionary action'!⁹³ The Opposition were apparently convinced that this

> . . . attack on one of the central bastions of economic power could only be seen as an attack on the position of the ruling class itself . . . [T]he nationalization of iron and steel might be a major advance in the direction of a Socialist Britain.[94]

Thus, Mr Henry Strauss (Combined English Universities) pointed to the disturbing precedent that would be set:

> . . . if it is right in the present circumstances to nationalise this extremely efficient industry, which is doing so well at present, there is no industry in the country which will feel any security that it may not be the next in the list to be nationalised.[95]

Significantly, Mr Eden, winding up for the Opposition, received considerable theatrical support from the Government's backbenchers to the proposition that '. . . this will lead to wholesale nationalization and to the steady reduction to a negligible proportion of the remaining free sections of our national economy', but little from the Government frontbench, the exception being Aneurin Bevan.[96]

In the terminology of Accounting and Finance Mr Strauss and Mr Eden appeared to be asking, if the profitable and 'efficient' steel industry could be acquired by the State, what was to stop it acquiring the market portfolio?[97] That the Opposition saw nationalization of steel as a challenge on this scale is suggested by Mr Henry Strauss's acceptance that 'On Marxist principles it is absolutely right',[98] an inference supported by Mr Marples who '. . . look[ed] up the Principles of the Socialist Party, which are the common ownership of the means of production, distribution and exchange'.[99]

However, not only did the nationalization of steel set a precedent for the advance of socialism. Even if this advance were resisted, from investors' point of view the restructuring of steel would represent a significant distortion in the allocation of capital. The Labour Left's view was that along with the restructuring of steel should come a major expansion of capacity. However, in the context of a major expansion of steel capacity in the USA during the war, and the prospect of the recovery of Germany and Japan as steel producers, the current sellers' market in steel was not expected to last more than a few years,[100] and therefore the restructuring and expansion implied an equally significant expansion and modernization of UK manufacturing industry. This did not appear to be desired by investors, nor did it happen.[101]

Conclusion

The unique political controversy over the first nationalization of the steel industry makes it an interesting test of the Labour Left's Socialist Principles during this period. An application of the concepts of Accounting and Finance suggests that nationalization at that time, and for some time to come, was directly against investors' interests, and yet a self-styled Socialist Government made it the test of its commitment to those Principles. While this commitment was sufficient to eventually secure nationalization in the face of fierce opposition, the principles themselves were an inadequate representation of the threat which nationalization posed to private interests, and therefore greatly underestimated the task involved. Apparently disarmed by the belief that it posed a threat to only an element of capital, the Labour Left failed to plan and prepare to engage their real adversary, capital as a whole. To this weakness in Socialist Principles must be laid at least some of the responsibility for the failure of the first nationalization of steel.

Appendix

The well-known trade off between risk and return demanded by investors provides the cornerstone of the Modern Theory of Finance.[102] A widely accepted model of the relationship between the returns required by investors for different levels of risk is the Capital Asset Pricing Model which postulates that $r = rf + B(rm - rf)$

where r = the return required by investors for this investment
       rf = the riskless rate of interest (e.g. from investment in government securities)
      rm = the return available on the stock market as a whole
       B = 'beta', the sensitivity of the returns on this investment with the returns on the market as a whole

If the returns on an investment move in perfect harmony with the returns on the whole market its beta is measured as one. If, as a merely visual inspection of Figure 5.1 (below) suggests is the case with investment in steel, the returns increase faster

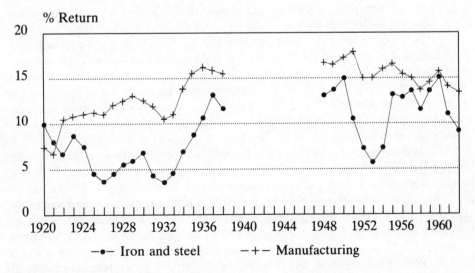

Figure 5.1   Current rates of return on capital.

than the market when the market is rising, and fall faster when the market is falling, its beta is greater than one.[103] A beta greater than one implies that the return on capital should be greater than the return on capital on the market as a whole, or any asset with a lower beta. To show this we need only express a generally accepted share valuation formula in terms of the rate of return earned on capital.

As the steel industry's dividends and share prices increased virtually continuously over this period an appropriate share valuation model is:

$$P = \frac{d}{r - g}$$

where P = share price, d = the expected dividend, r = the required return and g = the expected dividend growth rate.

Thus, $r = \frac{d}{P} + g$. From the $CAPM$ $r = rf + B(rm - rf)$

Thus, $B = \dfrac{\dfrac{d}{P} + g - rf}{rm - rf}$, where

$rm = \dfrac{dm}{Pm} + gm$, with all the terms being market equivalents.

As $d = ROC\left[\dfrac{E}{E + D}\right] BV.b$, where

ROC = return on capital, E = the book value of total equity, D = the book value of debt, BV = the book value of equity per share and b = the payout ratio (the proportion of the disposable income paid out as dividends), and the same expression can be formed for the market as a whole.

Thus, it is clear that if the steel industry had an average expected growth rate in dividends, an average ratio of equity to total capital, an average book value of equity per share, and an average payout ratio, with a beta greater than 1, it would need to have a higher than average return on capital to earn the required return on the replacement cost of its assets. This certainly seems to have been the case around the time of the first nationalization, although note that ex post data can never provide conclusive evidence for what are strictly expectational variables. NIESR data for 1949 to 1953 shows that whereas steel companies had broadly average (compared with the top 100 companies) proportions of total capital represented by equity (64 per cent compared with 62 per cent) and book values per share (£2.6 compared with £2.4), the payout ratio of the steel companies was significantly lower than average (28 per cent compared with 37 per cent). Also, up to 1954 dividends from steel had not grown as fast as those from all other companies – although from then on those from steel grew faster (Foldes and Wilson, 1961, Table 3). With the other variables broadly equivalent between steel and industry generally, steel's significantly lower than average payout ratio reinforces the suggestion that it should have earned a significantly greater than average rate of return on replacement cost to earn its required return – assuming it had a beta greater than one.

Indirect evidence that the steel industry's beta was greater than one is that with (i) a riskless interest rate in 1948 of some 4 per cent per annum, (ii) a long-run excess return on the UK stock market of around 9 per cent per annum (Dimson and Brealey, 1978), (iii) a dividend yield of around 4–7 per cent (Hansard, 15 November 1948, col. 135), and (iv) an expected dividend growth of 11 per cent per annum,[104] the implied beta is:

$$B = \frac{4\% + 11\% - 4\%}{9\%} = 1.22, \text{ or}$$

$$B = \frac{7\% + 11\% - 4\%}{9\%} = 1.55.$$

Notes

1. Henceforth, the 'steel' industry
2. 31 August 1946
3. This had seemed obvious to repeated inquiries since the Board of Trade recommended radical restructuring in 1916 (Burn, 1961, p 281)
4. By the Ministry of Supply and the Iron and Steel Board. The iron and steel industry was publicly owned for only eight months
5. Miliband, 1972, p 301
6. *The New Statesman and Nation*, ibid.
7. Cf. Ross, 1965, particularly his Epilogue
8. Miliband, 1973
9. Op. cit., p 34
10. Op. cit., p 32
11. Op. cit., p 29
12. Op. cit., pp 44–5, my emphases
13. Edwards, 1980 p 7
14. See Jeffreys, 1938, who points out that the popular aphorism of the day was 'hold 30 stocks in 10 countries'
15. Markowitz, 1952
16. That is, no other portfolio gives as great a return per unit of risk. In practice, a stock market index is used as a surrogate for the market portfolio
17. For a classic statement of the Efficient Market Hypothesis and a review of the evidence see: Fama, 1970
18. Op. cit., p 34
19. Brealey and Myers, 1984, p 21. The 'present value' of an expected future cash receipt is the amount that would have to be invested now at the prevailing rate of interest (or required return) to produce the expected future cash flow. Thus, for example, the present value of £1 to be received in one year if the

rate of interest is 10 per cent is £0.909 – if this is invested for one year at 10 per cent it will produce £1. If the investment to secure the £1 was £0.9, the 'net' present value is £0.1. The value of the iron and steel industry *to investors* was represented by the value of their shares – the present value of the dividends which they were expected to pay, or the net present value of the *firm*

20. The key output of financial reporting is, of course, net profit, but it is not widely appreciated that this is the accounting model's estimate of an enterprise's 'earning power', its long-run sustainable dividends

21. The determination of the required return by the widely accepted 'Capital Asset Pricing Model' is outlined in the Appendix

22. Hart, 1965, Tables 18.A.1, 18.A.2. The ratio measured is gross profit before depreciation, taxation and interest divided by capital employed before depreciation in *current* prices – that is, the current cost of replacing the capital employed. The importance of measuring capital employed at current replacement costs is discussed later

23. For diversified investors, the risk of an investment is determined by the sensitivity of its returns to those on the market portfolio. Thus, firms with high fixed costs and cyclical demand are relatively risky. Although steel was cartelized and protected by import tariffs, so was much of manufacturing industry

24. For a formal demonstration see the Appendix

25. For example, in 1928 a report by Lord Weir to Prime Minister Stanley Baldwin concluded that 'no solution can achieve success unless we visualise our industry on an adequate scale – a scale comparable at least with that of other countries whose production costs have been lowered by the magnitude and completeness of their equipment and organisations' (quoted by Vaizey, 1974, p 51)

26. That is, $\dfrac{i}{RC} < r$, where i = current income and r = the required return.

As $r = \dfrac{i}{PV}$, substituting this in the above gives $\dfrac{i}{RC} < \dfrac{i}{PV}$, and

therefore $\dfrac{PV}{RC} < 1$.

Although Hart only provides the *gross* rates of return for the iron and steel industry, because of its relative capital intensity and the rapid increase in the replacement cost of its fixed assets, there is little likelihood that the relationship between steel industry and average *net* rates of return on capital is materially altered. Foldes and Wilson show that in eight of the twelve years 1948 to 1959 the 55 major iron and steel companies, accounting for 95 per cent of the UK production of crude steel, earned a lower ratio of *historical* cost profit before interest and tax as a percentage of closing net assets than the average of all other industries. This suggests that the returns from these iron and steel companies would have been significantly worse on a *current* cost basis. Certainly, iron and steel industry net returns on current replacement cost were consistently and significantly lower than manufacturing industry from 1960 onwards (*British Business*, 28 September 1979, Table 2)

27. Recall that the present value of the iron and steel industry *to investors* was represented by the value of their shares – the present value of the dividends which they were expected to pay over the remainder of their lifetime

28. As Clarke put it in 1936, 'The official Labour Party policy is, in general, to compensate on the basis of "net maintainable revenue" ' (p 137). As we shall see, for the iron and steel industry this was equivalent to the market values of its companies' share prices

29. Hansard, op. cit., cols 272–3

30. As the replacement cost of iron and steel plant had risen steeply in the previous years, and much of the equipment was old, if Sir John was providing historical cost figures, as he appears to be, this implies that the current cost valuation ratio was considerably smaller than his figures suggest

31. *The Economist*, 6 November, 1948, p 757

32. *The Economist*, 13 November, 1948, p 804

33. *The Economist*, 13 November, 1948, p 804

34. See, for example, Keane, 1983

35. 20 November, 1948, p 845, my insertion

36. Hansard, 16 November 1948, col. 316

37. *The Economist*, 20 November, 1948, p 845

38. Hansard, 16 November 1948, col. 316

39. 'Earning power' is the accounting estimate of the long-run distributable cash flow based on net maintainable operating income

40. Hansard, 16 November 1948, col. 313

41. Any funds in excess of investment needs and the restrained dividends would be invested outside the firm and accumulate for future dividends

42. Hansard, 16 November 1948, col. 312

43. Jay, 1950, p 538. Jay shows that based on their experience to 1948 investors could have had no fears that the Government would drive a hard bargain over steel. Compensation on the basis of share values was the *worst* they could expect

44. Hansard, 16 November 1948, col. 313

45. Beta measures the responsiveness of the expected returns of a share to changes in the expected returns on the market as a whole. A beta of 2.6 implies that for every 1 per cent change in the expected returns on the market, the expected returns from the iron and steel industry changed by 2.6 per cent. Assuming that Industrials had a beta of around one, iron and steel increased $21\%/8\% = 2.6$ times as much

46. Hansard, 16 November 1948, col. 314

47. Hansard, 16 November 1948, col. 314

48. Hansard, 15 November 1948, col. 134

49. Rostas (1943) estimated that the relative productivities of the USA, Germany

and the UK at the start of the war were 361:115:100 for blast furnaces and 168:114:100 for steel melting and rolling

50. Burn, op. cit., p 13
51. Burn, op. cit.
52. Burn, op. cit., p 187
53. Burn, op. cit., pp 179–82
54. Burn, op. cit., p 76
55. Burn, op. cit., p 268
56. Burn, op. cit., pp 185–6
57. Even when allowance was made for British conditions. See: Anglo-American Council on Productivity, *Iron and Steel Productivity Team Report*, 1952
58. Burn, op. cit., p 280, my emphasis
59. Burn's answer was that it was the product of administrative and organizational 'inertia'. Thus, he asks, rhetorically, 'Was the degree of cost reduction which could be enjoyed by more radical change worth the extra effort – primarily intellectual and administrative – which would be needed?' (p 289)
60. As UK investors have traditionally held internationally diversified portfolios, the required return on UK iron and steel should have reflected the availability of investment opportunities in overseas (particularly North American) steel companies
61. Burn, op. cit., pp 255–6
62. The major steel companies were large colliery owners prior to the nationalization of the coal industry in 1945
63. Or, of course, that they should finance it when it was
64. 1931, p 8. See also Clarke, 1936
65. Mr Wilmot, who became Minister of Supply in the 1945 Labour Government was in 1944 Parliamentary Secretary at the Ministry of Supply with responsibilities for iron and steel, under Sir Andrew Duncan, the Minister of Supply, who subsequently became Chairman of the BISF. Burn describes Herbert Morrison as '. . . one of the Labour Ministers in the coalition who had had the closest contacts with the steel industry' (op. cit., p 124). Hugh Dalton also had an interest in the steel industry as President of the Board of Trade (op. cit., p 82)
66. Hansard, 28 May 1946, col. 1026
67. Ross, op. cit., p 52
68. Ross, op. cit., p 39
69. Quoted by Ross, ibid.
70. Op. cit., p 155
71. Ross, ibid.
72. Cf. Ross, op. cit., p 58
73. Ross, op. cit., p 61
74. Ross, op. cit., p 67. The nationalization of iron and steel was a resigning issue for Aneurin Bevan; 19 Labour MPs published an open letter in August 1947 which proclaimed 'Steel [a]s the real test of power in this Parliament', and

200 backbenchers signed a petition calling for 'quick and decisive action' (Ross, op. cit., pp 70–1)

75. Ross, op. cit., p 114. One reason for choosing a late Election date was that the economy was improving

76. Hansard, 16 November 1949, col. 2041. Particularly galling for Labour supporters must have been the thought that the time taken to pass the amendment to the Parliament Act could have been used to pass the Iron and Steel Bill (Ross, op. cit., p 83)

77. 14 November 1950, p 4, my emphasis

78. *The Times*, 12 August 1947, p 4

79. Op. cit., p 154

80. Op. cit., p 147. This argument was used by proponents of nationalization when the Government sanctioned the industry plan in May 1946: 'The longer nationalization was put off, they claimed, the more difficult it would be to obtain the technical support needed for its success from leading professionals in the iron and steel industry. The sooner nationalization occurred, they argued, the more time the industry would have to adjust itself under public ownership before the next General Election in 1950' (op. cit., pp 45–6)

81. Hansard, 16 November 1948, col. 325

82. Hansard, 16 November 1948, cols 325–6

83. Hansard, 15 November 1948, col. 78, my emphasis. Mr Lyttleton for the Opposition strongly hinted at the category mistake involved with this designation: 'The case which the Socialists wish to make is that . . . power over a basic industry is concentrated into a mere 2,000 firms, into only a few hundred thousand shareholders *who are described by the right hon. Gentleman as steel masters . . .*', col. 85, my emphasis

84. Hansard, 15 November 1948, col. 59, my emphasis

85. Hansard, 17 November 1948, col. 490, my emphases

86. Eatwell, 1979. Examples of this philosophy applied by Labour MPs to steel nationalization are: Mr Jenkins, who saw nationalization as merely '. . . the natural next step', and Mr Evans, who appealed to the '. . . good sense and patriotism of those who at the end of the present Parliament will still own 85 per cent of the means of production in this country' to make the '. . . transitional period between finance capitalism and collectivism . . . short and sanguinary . . .' (Hansard, 15 November 1948, cols 98, 137). Aneurin Bevan justified paying compensation to the 'modern private barons' in steel on the grounds that 'It was no use to carry out reforms in a revolutionary way; they had to take the tiger claw by claw' (quoted by Burn, op. cit., p 308)

87. Hansard, 16 November 1948, col. 325, my emphasis

88. Hansard, 16 November 1948, col. 318

89. Hansard, 16 November 1948, col. 321

90. Ross, op. cit., p 27

91. Hansard, 15 November 1948, cols 79–80

92. Hansard, 16 November 1948, col. 228

93. Hansard, 17 November 1948, col. 480

94. Ross, op. cit., p 27. Although it may be tempting to dismiss the Opposition's language as hyperbole, to do so it must be explained why it was generated only by the nationalization of steel
95. Hansard, 15 November 1948, cols 122–3
96. Hansard, 17 November 1948, cols 477–8. A man whom Viscount Hinching-brooke, and many others, thought so 'dangerous' that he should be '. . . out of public life altogether' (Hansard, 15 November 1948, col. 111)
97. In principle, all assets at their market values
98. Hansard, 15 November 1948, col. 130
99. Hansard, 17 November 1948, col. 428
100. Between 1941 and 1944 the USA had built over 20 million tons of new integrated steel-making capacity, and although 'It could be foreseen that the post-war period would begin as a seller's market, . . . it had been visualised that there would be a day of reckoning, not long to be deferred, when British steel would have to meet either American or Continental competition . . .' (Burn, op. cit., p 129). In the Second Reading Debate on the Iron and Steel Bill, Viscount Hinchingbrooke did not '. . . believe that hon. Gentlemen opposite have sufficiently appreciated what a plight our country may be in when manufacturing countries who are more primitive and more ruthless than ourselves have made up their accumulated war deficiencies . . .' (Hansard, 15 November 1948, col. 111). Germany's output began to grow fast from 1948
101. From the mid-1950s important parts of UK manufacturing industry (autos, engineering, textiles) consistently earned much lower rates of return on replacement cost than those of the major Western economies (Trade and Industry, 17 August 1979). The UK experienced the lowest rate of investment in manufacturing industry over this period, even though it was widely agreed that major restructuring was technically necessary (Bryer, Brignall and Maunders, 1984)
102. Sharpe, 1985
103. To my knowledge no-one has calculated UK betas for the postwar period
104. Between 1949 and 1959 dividends from the 55 largest iron and steel companies grew by some 11 per cent per annum compound (Foldes and Wilson, 1961, Table 3). In an efficient market we should expect that investors' expectations are on average realized

References

Brealey, R.A., Myers, S. *The Principles of Corporate Finance*, Second Edition, McGraw-Hill, London 1984

Bryer, R.A., Brignall, T.J., Maunders, A.M. 'The origins of plant closures' in Levie, H. et al., eds, *Fighting Closures*, Spokesman Books, Nottingham 1984

Burn, D. *The Steel Industry 1939–1959*, Cambridge University Press, Cambridge 1961

Clarke, R.W.B. *The Socialisation of Iron and Steel by 'Ingot'*, Victor Gollancz, London 1936

Dimson, E., Brealey, R.A. 'The risk premium on UK equities', *The Investment Analyst*, December 1978

Eatwell, R. *The 1945–51 Labour Governments*, Batsford Academic, London 1979

Edwards, J.R., ed. *British Company Legislation and Company Accounts, 1844–1976*, Arno Press, New York 1980

Fama, E. 'Efficient capital markets: a review of theory and empirical work', *Journal of Finance*, May 1970

Fienburgh, W., Evely, R. *Steel Is Power, The Case For Nationalisation*, Victor Gollancz, London 1948

Foldes, L.P., Wilson, S.S. '55 iron and steel companies, 1948–59', *London and Cambridge Bulletin No. 37, The Times Review of Industry*, March 1961

Hart, P.E. 'A long-run analysis of the rate of return on capital in manufacturing industry, United Kingdom, 1920–62' in Hart, P.E., ed., *Studies in Profit, Business Saving and Investment in the United Kingdom, 1920–1962*, vol. II, George Allen & Unwin Ltd, London 1965

Jay, N.V. 'Fair compensation under the British Labour government', *Political Science Quarterly*, December 1950

Jeffreys, J.B. *Trends in Business Organisation in Great Britain Since 1856*, PhD, University of London, June 1938

Keane, S.M. *Stock Market Efficiency, Theory, Evidence, Implications*, Phillip Allan, Oxford 1983

Markowitz, H.M. 'Portfolio selection', *Journal of Finance*, March 1952

Miliband, R. *Parliamentary Socialism, A Study in The Politics of Labour*, Second Edition, Merlin Press, London 1972

Miliband, R. *The State in Capitalist Society, The Analysis of the Western System of Power*, Quartet Books, London 1973

NIESR. *Company Income and Finance*, 1949–53

Ross, G.W. *The Nationalization of Steel, One Step Forward, Two Steps Back?*, Macgibbon & Kee, London 1965

Rostas, L. 'Industrial production, productivity and distribution in Britain, Germany and the United States', *The Economic Journal*, April 1943

Sharpe, W.F. *Investments*, Third Edition, Prentice-Hall, Englewood Cliffs, New Jersey 1985

Vaizey, J. *The History of British Steel*, Weidenfeld & Nicholson, London 1974

6 Marginal cost pricing and the peak-hour demand for electricity, 1945–51

Martin Chick

This paper is a study of frustrated reform. The frustration is that of ministers and civil servants whose efforts to reform electricity tariff structures were successfully obstructed by electricity managers. The study addresses two main questions. Firstly, to what extent did marginal cost pricing offer a relevant and practical solution to the 'peak-hour problem'? Secondly, why were the obstructionist tactics of the electricity industry successful? How could a nationalized industry effectively destroy the best-laid plans of its minister and sponsoring department? If the nationalizing Labour Government could not influence decisions on such funda-mental issues as pricing policy, then what were the implications for future relations between governments and nationalized industries in general? The outcome of the battles over electricity pricing policy was to have consequences not just for electricity pricing and resource allocation decisions in the 1950s, but also for the long-term development of relations between ministers and nationalized indus-tries.

The problem

In the years immediately following World War II, the total demand for electricity was high and the peak-hour demand was often in excess of available capacity. Such demand placed considerable strain upon scarce coal and capital investment resources. The general rise in demand for electricity was not surprising. Not only was industry becoming increasingly mechanized and electricity being extended to more households, but the attraction of electricity compared with other potential substitute power sources had increased since the interwar period. Electricity was much less amenable than coal to central physical rationing and its price to domestic consumers had fallen, not only in relation to coal and gas, but also in real terms. While wartime increases in the pithead price and freight costs of coal had been passed on automatically to the industrial consumers of electricity who had 'coal clauses' in their contracts, this had not applied to non-industrial and domestic consumers. Thus, while the average price per unit for power units had risen by 0.22d., the average price per unit sold for lighting, heating and cooking had gone down by 0.138d.[1] On average, domestic electricity supplies were cheaper in January 1948 than they had been in 1938.

The increased total demand for electricity placed considerable pressure on national coal supplies. During the immediate postwar period, the electricity industry's coal-burn consistently exceeded deliveries of coal to power stations, forcing the electricity industry to burn steadily into its reserve stocks of coal. A severe winter, the freezing of railway tracks and the intense demand for electricity combined to produce the 'fuel crisis' of 1947. Yet, dramatic though the fuel crisis was, it was peak-hour demand rather than total demand for electricity which was of more long-term concern to officials within the Ministry of Fuel and Power. Not only did peak-hour demand stretch existing capacity, but, if unchecked, it was likely to make a considerable call upon current and future capital investment resources. It was the peak-hour demand which determined the capacity requirements of the industry, and there were time-lags of 3–4 years in adjusting capacity. Load-shedding in response to excess peak-hour demand was commonplace during the Attlee Government's period in office. Even in the 1950s, admittedly with the added burden of the Korean War rearmament programme, load was shed on nine out of ten working days between November 1950 and February 1951. On occasions the estimated load shed was 2 million kilowatts (16 per cent of available capacity) and over 1 million kilowatts on 23 days.[2] Given power station construction times of 3–4 years, the main scope for easing immediate supply problems, as well as pressure on capital investment resources, lay in acting so as to reduce peak-hour demand.

What made the size of peak-hour demand so important in the electricity industry was the technical impossibility of storing electricity. Other industries, such as gas, had daily demand curves which contained peak periods, but the ability to store gas produced in off-peak periods meant that peak-hour demand did not have such a direct impact on capacity requirements in gas as it did in the electricity industry. With the electricity industry's capacity requirements being set by peak-hour or simultaneous maximum demand (SMD), the most desirable demand structure was one which minimized the gap between peak and average demand, by reducing peak-hour demand and thereby improving the industry's load factor. Daily winter[3] peak-hour demand fell between 7.45–9.00 a.m. and 4.30–6.00 p.m.[4] Half of this peak-load was accounted for by industrial users, with domestic and commercial users accounting for 25 per cent and 20 per cent, respectively.[5] The predominant peak-hour use of electricity was for lighting, this lighting-load being responsible for between one-quarter and one-third of the winter peak-loads. Yet while industry was the largest user, and lighting the largest use, deterring either user or use was neither desirable nor practicable. Rather than reducing industrial use and thereby endangering production, civil servants within the Ministry of Fuel and Power pointed to the domestic use of peak-hour electricity as being a suitable target for deterrent measures. Given that the domestic lighting load was likely to prove difficult to shift, the peak-hour use of electricity by domestic consumers for such purposes as space heating became an obvious area for their attention. The task of targeting and reducing such demand confronted postwar planners with a fundamental task of economic planning; that of devising the most suitable mix of bureaucratic and market mechanisms with which to achieve their main objectives.

The administrative response

There were two leading 'physical' or bureaucratic approaches to the peak-load problem. One was to place controls on the availability of electrical appliances, in particular electric fires. The other was to use load limiters to restrict the load being consumed by households at particular times of day (see next section). Proposals to control the supply and availability of electric fires were not seriously considered until the beginning of 1947. It was only in the face of the emerging fuel crisis that the Cabinet Coal Committee established a Working Party on Domestic Gas and Electricity Restriction. Prior to this, the extending of British Summer Time into winter and the early close-down of BBC night-time television transmission had been some of the few measures taken to reduce the national use of electricity. Such measures did not address the peak-hour problem.

At its first meeting on 29 January 1947, the Working Party on Domestic Gas and Electricity Restriction[6] did consider the peak-hour problem, calling for measures to restrict the availability of electric fires. Yet, effecting such a restriction was neither administratively easy nor likely to restrict the current use of electric fires. The ostensibly powerful system of licences and direct controls available to planners was incapable of targeting the production of a single product such as the electric fire. Even as late as 1952, officials were still struggling to devise a mix of controls which could limit the supply of electric fires. While the Ministry of Works could and did reduce the issue of licences for the manufacture of electric fires to 5 per cent of each firm's productive capacity, it recognized that these licences, although usually respected and honoured by large, highly visible firms such as Ferranti, were very largely ignored by many of the smaller manufacturers.[7] Nor was the use of direct controls such as steel any more successful. Many firms did not in fact use steel in the production of electric fires and even where they did, alternative materials such as aluminium and copper were available. Seeking to target the allocation system more precisely, the Minstry of Works persistently sought to persuade the Ministry of Supply to control the allocation of nichrome wire, this being the one essential material used in the manufacture of electric fires. It was only after lengthy negotiations between the two departments that the Ministry of Supply persuaded the Ministry of Works that such control was unlikely to be effective since nichrome wire was used for a number of purposes besides the manufacture of electric fires and often by the same firms producing electric fires. It was thought to be administratively impracticable, for example, to prevent a firm which had been allocated nichrome wire for the production of electric cookers from using part or all of its allocation in the production of electric fires.[8] Nor could such measures prevent the 1–2 million electric fires currently in the pipeline from emerging onto the market, or do anything to reduce the existing stock of electric fires being used.[9] Wartime investment in the light engineering industries and the early conversion of these industries to peace-time production had produced a somewhat bizarre postwar world in which, amid shortages of clothes, bread and potatoes, electric fires were comparatively freely available. Given the rationing of coal, mainly middle-class householders with electricity in their homes were not slow to purchase electric fires.

The increased use of electric fires was not simply due to private initiative. Public encouragement also came from harassed local Fuel Officers who, often as local authority employees, were responsible for administering coal and coke rationing schemes. Encouraging the use of electric fires was just one strategy adopted by Fuel Officers in their efforts to reduce the pressure on coal and coke supplies, as well as on themselves. Elsewhere within local authorities, other solutions to different problems also indirectly increased the use of electric fires and other appliances. Faced with the task of housing the homeless, many local authorities placed people in 'pre-fabs', most of which were all-electric structures. To the central planners, it must have seemed at times that local officials were conspiring to try to make their task of controlling the total and peak-hour demand for electricity ever more difficult. Certainly, within the Ministry of Fuel and Power, the civil servant, Philip Chantler, who was at the centre of efforts to ease the peak-hour problem, was withering in his observations;

> That such household equipment was ever installed with the prospect of a huge deficiency in generating capacity before us seems to me monstrously bad planning. If indeed the householders who find their bills substantially increased pour such coals of fire as they can get on the heads of their local councillors, it may check similar faults in the future and help us to ease our problem of the squeeze on electricity supply.[10]

A role for pricing?

Chantler's own preferred solution to the peak-hour problem was to make greater use of pricing mechanisms and tariff structures by providing consumers with 2-dialled meters which would record on- and off-peak use. Appropriate on- and off-peak differentials would also be introduced. At peak hours a tell-tale light would glow. The switching between the two dials would be centrally controlled by means of a simple pair of dog clutches between the meter gear train and the dials, ripple control,[11] for example, being used to operate the dog clutches from a central point.[12] Chantler regarded this as a more liberal and flexible approach to the problem than the heavy-handed use of load limiters favoured by the electricity authorities. Under the load limiter scheme, by applying a system of clock controls to particular appliances or by the central switching on and off of particular appliances on special circuits, the consumer would simply opt to have current for certain purposes during the off-peak hours to which an off-peak rate would apply. Under this scheme the problem of peak and off-peak use was settled by the electricity authorities and was not left as in Philip Chantler's proposals as a matter for the consumers' vigilance. Moreover, it allowed the electricity industry too much ability to influence both the size and structure of demand. Decentralized decision-making by consumers responding to differential tariffs was far more to Chantler's liking. Moreover, if the price and tariff structure could reflect the marginal costs of supply, then Chantler believed that a rational long-term basis for monopoly utility pricing decisions and internal and external resource allocation would have been established. Chantler was not backward in stressing the virtues of marginal cost pricing:

> a real effort should be made to vary the charge for electricity supplied to domestic consumers as between peak and off-peak hours. If the consumer insists on switching on 2 kilowatts or more of electric fire during the peak hours, he should be made to pay the marginal costs of that supply. If he confines his consumption to off-peak hours, he has a right to a rate corresponding to off-peak costs.[13]

and

> The economic ideal is that the tariff structure should closely mirror the costs of actual supply to particular types of consumer and, as far as possible, to particular consumers. . . . The closer one comes to this ideal, the nearer one gets to the best distribution of economic resources and – what is of vast importance to us at the present time – the closer to an economic solution of peak load problem.[14]

Whatever the appeal of marginal cost pricing to economists like Philip Chantler, such advocacy of the greater use of price mechanisms encountered fierce opposition from the electricity industry itself. Although the high and often excess demand created supply problems for the industry, electricity managers were disinclined to accept proposals for using the price mechanism to dampen demand. The predominant interest within the industry was in increasing sales and thereby expanding the industry. This commitment to expansion was in part a continuation of the prewar experience of growth and the continuing public sector ethos of many managers. Also, as monopolists enjoined simply to cover costs taking one year with another, the pursuit of growth rather than of profits rapidly became one of the main aims of management. During the postwar house construction programmes, the electricity managers were keen to present electricity as both more modern and cheaper than its main rival gas, and, by persuading as many people as possible to opt for all-electric homes, to increase its share of the domestic power market. Clearly, price increases would not assist such a strategy. Moreover, so long as excess peak demand for electricity continued, the more the industry felt able to lobby the Treasury, the Investment Programmes Committee and other economic planning authorities for additional capital investment resources with which to increase the capacity of the industry. That the industry should refrain from attempting to ease the excess demand problem by acting purely on the supply side was repeatedly made clear to the industry by the Treasury. Clearly, if it could be shown that demand was likely to be resistant to either bureaucratic or market efforts to change its shape and structure, then the supply side solutions of the industry would be strengthened. It was with such thinking that electricity managers approached the issue of tariff reform.

The main arguments raised by the electricity industry against the extension of time-of-day meters in domestic households were that their introduction would take too long and that the cost/benefits of such an exercise were unknown. Not only would there be long lags before sufficient meters were installed, but there would also be further lags before consumers became responsive, if at all, to the new tariffs. The obvious response to the complaint that such reforms would take time to introduce was that the sooner a start was made the better. Such was the blunt response from the Ministry of Fuel and Power to Walter Citrine, Chairman of the British Electricity Authority, in 1950:

> We agree with him that this could only be a long-term measure. *That is a very good reason for starting now* and if a start is made now, and publicized, one part of their immediate task (and ours) will be made much easier.[15]

More problematic was the issue of the likely cost/benefits of such a scheme. The small point of how much it was likely to cost to produce and install the necessary meters was unknown but Philip Chantler thought that a two-dialled meter and a pair of dog clutches, operated by ripple control, could be mass-produced comparatively cheaply.[16] Whatever the nominal cost, Chantler was quite certain that it was less than the cost of providing additional capacity to meet peak-hour demand. However, what would not become clear until the reformed tariffs had been applied for a reasonable period was the extent of any peak-hour price elasticity of demand. Not surprisingly, the industry held stubbornly to its self-interested view that any such elasticity was low. More worryingly for Chantler was the fact that by 1950 officials within the Ministry of Fuel and Power were also expressing doubts about the size of the benefits likely to be gained from the operation of reformed tariffs. Many of these doubts were brought to the surface with the circulation within the Ministry in 1950 of a paper by H.S. Houthakker, who at the time was working under J.R. Stone at the Department of Applied Economics at Cambridge University. His draft paper on 'Electricity Tariffs and the Peak Load Problem: A Preliminary Report'[17] was broadly in accord with Chantler's own thinking, but as it made its way around the department dissenting marginal comments and appended memoranda began to question the faith of Chantler and Houthakker in the ability of price mechanisms to ease the peak-hour problem. One of the main objections raised was that precisely because peak-hour loads occurred on cold winter days, it was unlikely that consumers would reduce their use of electricity on such days. In short, sheer necessity would cause electric fires to be switched on, irrespective of any peak-hour tariff structure. Many of the civil servants' doubts began to echo some of the arguments made by the electricity industry.[18] The civil servant, A.G.F. Farquhar's comment that:

> since electricity is used most at the actual peak because it is most needed then, any system of differential charges based on the time-of-day will improve the load factor, not by reducing the peak, but by filling in the valleys[19]

was a familiar incantation at the BEA. Similarly, many of the doubts expressed by the electricity industry concerning the time needed for any reforms to have any effect also began to be voiced within the Ministry. As Chantler noted of the divisions within the Ministry of Fuel and Power in 1950:

> I should say that the main cause of the difference of view between Electricity Division and myself on the significance of improving load factor . . . is that the Electricity Division are considering prospects over a shorter period of time than I had in mind. If, for instance, it is agreed that tariffs and control devices can improve load factor to the extent of 1.5% *annually*, then in the long run they do seem to offer possibilities of quite significant reductions in the average cost of electricity.[20]

'In the long run', the establishment of marginal cost pricing within the electricity industry was seen by many both inside and outside the Ministry of Fuel and Power as being desirable.[21] However, what many came to question was the contribution which marginal cost pricing could make to easing the 'short-term' and immediate problem of peak-load demand. What was at issue was not simply the question of how long it would take consumers to become aware of a new reformed tariff structure. Rather, it was whether cost-based pricing had any relevance in conditions of excess demand. Of more relevance were prices related to demand, rather than to cost, but political concern for the inflationary and redistributive consequences of market pricing and the political and statutory requirement that nationalized industries should not earn high book profits, constrained this option. In time, cost-based pricing and market-based pricing might come to approximate more closely. What was clear in the 1945–51 period was that a significant gap existed between the prices resulting from the use of each criterion. In the longer term, the calls of Chantler for nationalized industries' prices to be based on marginal cost principles, would appear to have been broadly correct. Certainly, they were fundamental to any successful coordination of resource use within sectors like fuel and power and transport and communications. In the short term, however, Chantler was left to explain the extent to which a cost-based price for electricity would help to tackle a problem of excess demand. Similar pricing and demand problems existed in the coal industry, and the tension between the determination of some to provide a cost-based pricing system for the coal industry and the need to resolve the problem of excess demand for coal at the prices being charged bedevilled the Ridley Committee's discussions on fuel policy.[22] As Denys Munby noted in a perceptive critique of the Committee's discussions and final report, at times even the proponents of marginal cost pricing confused prices reflecting costs with prices reflecting demand.[23] This became particularly apparent when discussions turned to the short- and long-term applications of marginal cost pricing to coal. While making all the usual case for marginal cost pricing in the long term, the supporters of marginal cost pricing argued that

> On a strict interpretation of marginal cost pricing, there would in present conditions have to be a very sharp increase in the price of coal – say £3 a ton at the pithead – to equate 'unrationed' demand with available supplies.[24]

116

Since the £3 a ton increase is considered as a price to equate supply and demand, it is essentially a market demand price rather than a marginal cost price, however 'short-run marginal costs' are construed. Ian Little, in *The Price of Fuel*[25] was much clearer in drawing a distinction between market (demand) and marginal cost (supply) prices, but even he had little hard quantitative evidence to contribute on the question of the price elasticity of demand for scarce fuel and power output. The call for a greater use of market prices which Little makes in *The Price of Fuel* is posited on the assumption that the price elasticity of demand for coal is reasonably high, but, as with similar discussions on the pricing of peak-hour electricity, in the end this seemed to reflect individuals' faith in the influence of market mechanisms, rather than any new information.[26] Given the mixture of proposals for marginal cost pricing, average cost pricing, market price and the variations in the short- and long-term applicability of each (not to mention the issue of fuel demand substitutability which few ever did) and the varying views on the price elasticities of the various fuel demands, it was perhaps not surprising that discussions of fuel policy and electricity (and coal) pricing at times exhibited a certain confusion.

Consulting the public corporation

The differences of opinion within the Ministry of Fuel and Power on the likely impact on demand of any reformed pricing structure certainly did not strengthen the hands of would-be reformers like Gaitskell and Chantler in their battles with the electricity industry. However, although the lack of a clear consensus within government on the appropriate pricing principles was important, it was by no means the only factor enabling the industry to resist major changes to the level and structure of electricity prices. Certainly as important, was the statutorily defined structure of the relationship between the industry and the minister.

As a public corporation, the electricity was to be supervised by government 'at an arm's length'. The intention was to allow management to organize the day-to-day business of the industry free from government supervision, while requiring management to be accountable to government for the broader policies of the enterprise.[27] This assumed that policy, in major matters at least, could be distinguished from matters of management or administration.[28] Whatever the imprecision of the statutory division of responsibilities and power between the Minister and the public corporation, it was widely hoped that the common concern of government and public corporation to act together 'in the public interest' would provide the basis for the succcessful operation of the relationship. Indeed, Morrison urged that the 'board and its officers must regard themselves as the high custodians of the public interest'.[29] What should happen if and when the board and the minister held different views of the 'public interest' was not made clear. Yet, there were also practical reasons why the minister might wish to consult with the industry before any 'policy' changes were introduced. Often, in considering the likely effects of proposed changes, the monopoly industry was the sole source of the information and technical expertise needed for such exercises in estimation. Moreover, since any changes or reforms would have to be implemented by the industry, then it was desirable that the broad agreement of the industry to such change should have been secured. The traditional way of securing such agreement was through consultation and negotiation. This was precisely what Gaitskell attempted in establishing a Committee in February 1948 under the Chairmanship of Sir Alexander Clow to examine and report on the scope for reducing peak-hour demand by using a mixture of meters, limiters and/or alterations in the tariff for domestic and non-industrial consumers.[30] However, what both Clow and Gaitskell underestimated was the extent to which the electricity managers were unprepared to depart from their stubborn commitment to expansion and hence from their opposition to price reform. While Clow had some sympathy for some of the criticism of proposed tariff reforms, he also clearly saw the main purpose of the managers' objections:

> Those who argued that certain possibilities were not really related to the 'peak' problem had some ground on their side. At the same time, they tended to reflect a rather stereotyped position which, to me at least, seemed to have too little elasticity of mind or relation to present conditions. None of them would defend the present chaotic tariff system as needing no revision; but I doubt if they would agree that the whole basis of the system (as distinct from its details) calls for a full examination in the light of modern development. The system exhibits ingenuity and a multitudinous variety, but there seems to have been little internal study of the general principles or deliberate exchange of economic experience, and I get the impression that the technical leaders of the industry are inspired by few ideas except the value of expansion.[31]

The intransigence of the managers was to anger Gaitskell and to frustrate Clow. Crucially, the need to consult with the industry as a public corporation provided the industry with an opportunity effectively to hijack and stall the Committee's proceedings. Days were consumed in repetitive restatements of the industry's opposition to tariff reform and their technical objections to schemes for metering. Even in its final days, the Committee's discussions were slow and rancorous:

> Yesterday they discussed a mainly technical page of the draft with constant objections (expressing no consistent view) on statements of facts. It was the most unfruitful meeting we have had and any repetition of this mode of discussion might delay conclusions indefinitely. I am inclined, therefore, to ask the Committee at the next meeting to reach conclusions, because it seems likely that if decisions have not been reached, there will be a continuous struggle by individuals to modify the draft in such a way that its descriptive method leads to conclusions which they themselves favour.[32]

Nor were matters helped by erratic attendance at committee meetings, with only 2 of the 23 meetings being fully attended. Clow was unhappy with his Committee's final report, complaining to Gaitskell that it was:

not the type of document I would have preferred. It is in fact a mixture (but not always a blend) of different outlooks . . . the report does not embark adequately on various issues of tariff policy.

and that:

There is rather more stress on the short-term indicated by this year's *Economic Survey* than I would have liked, and there was a tendency to treat the issues before us as issues of much shorter concern than I (or Mr. Edwards) believe.[33]

To be disappointed, one must have had hopes. To a seasoned civil servant, not only did the Report 'pull its punches', but:

This Report illustrates the truth of the maxim 'Blessed are they who expect nothing, for they shall not be disappointed'.[34]

The end result of this process was a recommendation that a differential be introduced between the winter quarter and the three (summer) quarters of the year. This seasonal differential was almost the very least that the Committee could recommend without becoming silent. Clearly, the seasonal differential failed to address, except extremely indirectly, the issue of peak-hour demand. All that such a differential was attempting to signal to consumers was that the resource costs of using electricity in winter were higher than in summer. Yet, even the details of this differential were successfully contested by the electricity industry. While Gaitskell wanted what he referred to as a 'substantial' differential, with winter unit charges being increased from 0.75d. to 1.25d. and summer unit charges being reduced to 0.5d., the industry pushed for a winter-summer differential of 1.0d. to 0.7d. Gaitskell and the industry implicity agreed that to be effective any differential had to be substantial. Indeed, this was the very reason for the industry's efforts to reduce the size of the differential. If even on a seasonal basis, price movements could be shown to influence demand, then the existence of some price elasticity of demand for electricity might have to be acknowledged. However, if the differential could be narrowed so as to be insubstantial and therefore ineffective, the industry could then begin to argue that clearly such price adjustments were of very limited use in reducing demand. The objections raised by the electricity industry against Gaitskell's proposed seasonal differential continued their general argument that the price elasticity of demand in general was low, and that the price elasticity of peak-hour demand was non-existent. Hence extrapolating out of the likely effects of a seasonal differential, they argued that any time of day differential was at best only likely to improve the load factor by increasing off-peak use rather than by reducing peak demand. Moreover, given the traditional withdrawal of plant for repair and maintenance during the summer months,[35] the net effect of inflating summer demand could well be to extend capacity problems throughout the year. However, the managers simultaneously urged that the seasonal differential should not be too large lest it lead to a reduction in the industry's revenue. While not necessarily inconsistent with their argument on the distribution of any price elasticities, it did seem that either winter demand had to fall to such a point that winter revenue fell or that the increase in summer use would not be large enough to generate significantly larger revenue, or both. Given this implicit admission that some price elasticity of demand was likely to be present, the only argument which could be employed to limit the impact of such an admission was that while winter demand in general might be price sensitive to an extent, peak-hour demand was not. Hence, the argument returned full circle to the industry's contention that winter peak demand, being 'necessitous', was completely insensitive to any use of the price mechanism.

The final outcome, after stormy meetings between the Minister and the Area Board chairman and private talks between Gaitskell and Citrine was a compromise differential of 1.1d. in winter and 0.65d. in summer, a differential closer to the industry's proposals than to Gaitskell's. The differential, grudgingly implemented by the industry, managed to attract public criticism without having a significant effect on peak-hour demand. Many consumers only learnt of the extra-winter charge as they received their bills at the end of the winter quarter, and as the 'summer' differential charge was about to be implemented. Convinced that he had been right in principle, but beaten in practice, Gaitskell announced in the House of Commons on 11 July 1949 that the Clow differential would not be continued in the forthcoming winter.

Taxing consumption

The apparent ability of the electricity industry to obstruct attempts to reform pricing and tariff structures by exploiting the consultative process in particular, and the relationship between the Minister and a public corporation in general, encouraged aspirant reforming civil servants to consider whether other mechanisms outside the industry's influence could be used to achieve their main objectives. One obvious means of increasing electricity prices without requiring the cooperation or approval of the industry was to introduce an electricity consumption tax. Not surprisingly, Philip Chantler was a keen advocate of such a tax, seeing it as an opportunity to pursue a policy:

> urged all round by economists of making the market forces work with and not against the Government's economic policy.[36]

Proposals for a tax on electricity consumption became particularly prominent during 1947 and 1951 when capacity shortages and load-shedding were particularly serious. Their added attraction was that in addition to any impact which they had on demand, taxes would free the industry from the consequence of earning inflated (book) profits, namely ferocious public criticism and accusations that the industry was earning monopoly financial profits.[37] Yet, whatever their appeal to some economists and civil servants, the proposals for an electricity tax proved to be politically unacceptable. The principal objection raised by politicians was that any such tax was likely to be unequal in its incidence, and that it was also likely to prove most burdensome to low income households.[38] Clearly, low income households required electricity for basic heating and cooking purposes, and yet because of their low incomes the poorest sections of society may never have been able to afford to use electric fires extravagantly, or indeed to buy them at all. Thus, a consumption tax might not only be missing its target, but also punishing the poorest for the sins of the richer. One proposed method of easing this problem was to make the consumption of the first 300 units tax exempt, but subsequently to operate a progressive rate of taxation starting at a flat rate of 1.0d. per unit.[39] However, these exemption rates would also have to be apportioned between households according to the proportionate gas and electricity composition of the household's fuel use, and some attempt would also have to be made to distinguish between the end-use of electricity within each household. Proposals to make variations in the quantity of current to be exempt from tax on such a basis as whether a cooker was used or not, opened up a complex of issues and value judgements. If cookers, then why not baby's bath water. 'Is not a baby's bath water as important as father's dinner, and so on'[40]. Moreover, particular groups of the poor, such as those living in the all-electric pre-fabs, were likely to be heavily caught by any such tax.[41] Concern was also expressed among ministers and mandarins at the inflationary effects of any such tax, the length of the delay between its implementation and its impact on consumption, and the general problems of administering such a tax.[42] Moreover, once again this was a tax on general consumption, not on time-of-day use. Yet, whatever the attractions of such a tax in circumventing the government-public corporation relationship, it was a political non-starter. The general view within the Ministry of Fuel and Power was that 'the inequities and unfairness' of such tax schemes made them 'politically unmanageable',[43] with even the reform-minded Gaitskell emphasizing to Cripps that

political objections rule out anything in the nature of a tax on consumption.[44]

New governments, old problems

By 1951, frustration characterized the attitude of many Ministry of Fuel and Power officials towards the electricity industry. Frustration above all at the industry's ability to exploit the structure of the Minister-public corporation relationship for its own expansive ends. Relations between the industry and the Ministry were not good. The Ministry accused the industry of 'dragging its feet'[45] on the peak load problem and spoke of the need to 'bludgeon the electricity people into agreeing . . . [with the necessary reforms]'.[46] Legislatively and practically prohibited from forcing price increases upon the industry, civil servants, like M.P. Murray, began to search for loopholes whereby the tariff structures, rather than the price level, might be adjusted on the government's orders.

> The time has come when an important matter of principle and policy must be decided in regard to the Minister's powers and responsibilities relating to the tariffs of the Electricity Boards. We have hitherto maintained that the

Minister has no responsibility for the prices charged for electricity which, under Section 37 of the Act of 1947 'shall be in accordance with such tariffs as may be fixed from time to time' by the Central Authority or the Area Boards. I consider that this view is correct but it is now necessary to examine what are the Minister's responsibilities in regard to the tariff structures of the boards as opposed to the prices charged under these tariffs.[47]

One possible means of breaking the impasse might have lain in the creation of an independent Tariffs Advisory Committee which would advise and report on pricing policies in nationalized industries such as electricity. Indeed, the Ridley Committee proposed that just such an independent Committee should be established to advise and report on pricing polices in all of the nationalized fuel and power industries in the hope of securing a greater degree of coordination within the sector as a whole.[48] The proposal was considered by the Conservative Government, which had been elected in 1951, but rejected, the Government preferring to continue to rely on 'regular weekly meetings between the Minister and the chairmen of the Boards'.[49] Nor was the Churchill Government prepared to accept the proposal of the Ridley Committee that a Joint Planning Board be established as a means of bringing together managers and civil servants from the fuel and power sector under an independent chairman, supported by a Permanent staff. Significantly the Government doubted whether it could find sufficient experts outside of the nationalized fuel and power industries to staff such a Committee. Moreover, given their previous experiences of dealing with managers in these industries, civil servants within the Ministry of Fuel and Power were not convinced that bringing representatives of each industry together on a single committee would necessarily bring forth sweetness and light.

Indeed, as its staff would require experts – already far too scarce – drawn from the nationalised fuel industries themselves, the result in the end might be less rather than more effective co-operation.[50]

Even when Treasury officials like Sir Bernard Gilbert began to suggest that greater control over the nationalized fuel and power industries might be secured by exerting tighter control over their borrowing activity, it was recognized that personalities and power structures might well hamper such efforts.

The only solution I can see of these problems is a more intrusive administration by the Ministry of Fuel and Power than there has been hitherto and a more harmonious co-operation in the execution of such policy as may be agreed. But this is easier asked for than secured. Given personalities in electricity and a very awkward distribution of responsibility in gas, a good deal of perseverance will be required.[51]

The problem of how government could establish greater influence over the activities of the nationalized industries, which had begun to emerge during the Attlee government's period in office, came increasingly to concern Conservative Governments throughout the 1950s. Where pricing had been the specific subject of discussion in the late 1940s, in the 1950s it was the subject of fuel policy which provided the government maypole around which the industries could dance and cavort, albeit with thoughts of infertility and prevention in mind. The subjects and topics under discussion may have changed but the fundamental issues had not. Nor had the aims and tactics of such industries as electricity. For his sins, Philip Chantler moved from arguing over pricing policies in the 1940s to despairing over fuel policy in the 1950s. Appropriately, the last words should be his:

> The subject [fuel policy] is immensely complex and the whole discussion has been bedeviled by prejudice and half truths. It is sometimes difficult to assign any particular view to any one of the protagonists, because it sometimes seems as though there is a stock of ideas which go round and round, and one or other of these ideas is from time to time advanced by one or another.[52]

Time and topic might have changed, but the tale sounded very familiar.

Acknowledgement

I wish to thank Sir Alec Cairncross and Leslie Hannah for their comments on this chapter.

Notes

1. PRO T228/308 Memorandum on 'Electricity policy', by Hugh Gaitskell (Minister of Fuel and Power) to Stafford Cripps (Chancellor of the Exchequer), 23 January 1948
2. PRO POWE 14/357 O.C.C.(51)16 Cabinet Official Coal Committee, Report on 'The load limiter electricity tariff', 5 May 1951
3. Winter being defined as 1 December–1 March
4. Little, I.M.D. *The Price of Fuel*, Oxford 1953, p 57
5. PRO POWE 14/110 Paper by Philip Chantler on 'Improving electricity load factor'. Date of covering letter to Kelf-Cohen, 15 October 1946. Also see PRO POWE 14/113 'BEA: the electricity supply position'
6. PRO T228/308 D.E.R.1 Working Party on Domestic Gas and Electricity Restriction, 25 January 1947
7. PRO T228/308 Note on 'Electric fires', A.M. Jenkins to Mr Shillito, 31 January 1952
8. PRO T228/308 Note on 'Electric fires', A.M. Jenkins to Mr Shillito by A.M. Jenkins, 31 January 1952
9. PRO T228/308 Memorandum on 'Electricity policy', by Gaitskell to Cripps, 23 January 1948
10. PRO POWE 14/320 Note from Philip Chantler to Mr Watkinson, 13 October 1947

11. Ripple control is achieved by super-imposed high-frequency signals being sent out by the power station along the distribution cables

12. PRO POWE 14/110 Paper by Philip Chantler on 'Improving electricity load factor'. Date of covering letter to Kelf-Cohen, 15 October 1946

13. PRO POWE 14/110 Paper by Philip Chantler on 'Improving electricity load factor'. Date of covering letter to Kelf-Cohen, 15 October 1946. Tariff reform offered particular possibilities for relating domestic consumption more directly to costs, as industrial and large commercial user's tariffs already contained a maximum demand component, which encouraged them to keep down their maximum demand and to develop an even load. The worse their individual load factor, the higher the average charge they were to pay for the current

14. PRO POWE 14/319 'Electricity tariff policy and the ministry', Philip Chantler, Economics Branch, 18 April 1950

15. PRO POWE 14/328 Murray to Minister of Fuel and Power, 17 October 1950, 'Briefing notes and points for Minister's lunch meeting with Citrine'

16. PRO POWE 14/110 Paper by Philip Chantler on 'Improving electricity load factor'. Date of covering letter to Kelf-Cohen, 15 October 1946. During the Ridley discussions, Professor Lewis also tried to calculate the cost/benefits of load-limiters. He reckoned that the cost of manufacturing and installing a meter time switch was around £10 which was very much less than the cost of supplying 1 kW of supply capacity. However, he still lacked and sought information on how many kilowatts were likely to be saved at peak hours by the introduction of a given number of time switches

17. POWE 14/370 'Electricity tariffs and the peak load problem: a preliminary report', by H.S. Houthakker, March 1950. The final version of this paper was published in the *Economic Journal*. See H.S. Houthakker, 'Electricity tariffs in theory and practice', *Economic Journal*, March 1951, 61, 1–25

18. PRO POWE 14/365 Letter from Citrine to Gaitskell, 13 September 1949

19. PRO POWE 14/370 'Comments by A.G.F. Farquhar on Houthakker's paper', 5 May 1950

20. PRO POWE 14/319 Note by Chantler on 'Future trends of electricity prices', 2 August 1950

21. PRO POWE 14/707 M.C.C.(SG2)6 Ministry of Fuel and Power's Coordinating Committee: Joint Study Group on General Principles of Pricing. 'Principles of pricing. Some problems', Explanatory Note by Ministry of Fuel and Power representatives, 30 April 1953. 'There is a wide acceptance of the general principle that to avoid the dangers of wrong pricing methods which their monopolistic position would admit, the nationalised industry should adopt as the criterion of their pricing policy the rule that prices should correspond with the relevant cost'

22. The Ridley Committee agreed (para 59) that prices should not be less than cost. They divided (para 60) on what the relevant cost was. Professor Hawthorne, Professor Lewis, Mrs McIntosh and Miss Schofield thought it should be marginal cost. Lord Ridley, Mr Lincoln Evans, Mr Gardiner and

Sir Claude Gibb thought it should be average. *Report of the Committee on National Policy for the Use of Fuel and Power Resources*, September 1952, Cmd. 8647

23. Munby, D.L. 'The price of fuel', *Oxford Economic Papers*, 1954, N.S.6, pp 226–42
24. Ridley Report, para 62
25. Little, I.M.D. *The Price of Fuel*, Oxford 1953
26. For some preliminary estimates of price elasticity of demand for coal, see K.S. Lomax, 'The demand for coal in Great Britain', *Oxford Economic Papers*, February 1952
27. Vickers, J., Yarrow, G. *Privatisation: An Economic Analysis*, MIT Press, London 1988, p 126
28. Robson, W.A. *Nationalised Industry and Public Ownership*, George Allen & Unwin, London 1960. Quoted in Vickers and Yarrow, *Privatisation*, p 126
29. Quoted in Vickers and Yarrow, *Privatisation*, p 127
30. For the official conclusions and thinking of the Committee, see *Report of the (Clow) Committee to Study the Peak Load Problem in Relation to Non-Industrial Consumers*, Cmd. 7464, July 1948
31. PRO POWE 14/365 'Sir Alexander Clow's Confidential Memo'
32. PRO POWE 14/362 G.E.615/48 Note by Clow, 24 April 1948
33. PRO POWE 14/365 'Sir Alexander Clow's confidential memorandum on the Clow Report'. At that time, Ronald Edwards was lecturing at the London School of Economics
34. PRO POWE 14/365 Note by W.G. Nott-Bower, 3 June 1948
35. PRO POWE 14/365 'Draft notes of a meeting in Minister's room', 27 July 1948
36. PRO POWE 14/320 Note from Philip Chantler to Mr Watkinson, 13 October 1947
37. Hannah, L. *Engineers, Managers and Politicians*, Macmillan, London 1982
38. PRO POWE 14/320 'Draft memorandum on restriction of domestic gas and electricity consumption', Ministry of Fuel and Power, 7 October 1947
39. PRO POWE 14/320 'Draft memorandum on restriction of domestic gas and electricity consumption', Ministry of Fuel and Power, 7 October 1947
40. PRO POWE 14/320 Note from Philip Chantler to Mr Watkinson, 13 October 1947
41. PRO T228/308 Memorandum on 'Electricity policy', Hugh Gaitskell to Cripps, 23 January 1948
42. PRO POWE 14/529 'Draft memorandum for official Coal Committee. An emergency tax on gas and electricity consumption', 10 January 1951
43. PRO POWE 14/529 'Paper by R.N. Quirk on emergency tax on gas and electricity consumption; Mr Chantler's draft memorandum', 10 January 1951
44. PRO T228/308 Memorandum on 'Electricity policy', by Gaitskell to Cripps, 23 January 1948
45. PRO POWE 14/328 M.30/4/29 'Draft personal letter for Minister to send to Citrine', 31 October 1950

46. PRO POWE 14/362 Comment of 27 April 1948 by Murphy on Clow's note of 24 April 1948
47. PRO POWE 14/319 Note by M.P. Murray (Electricity Division) on Minister and Tariffs, 6 April 1950
48. Ridley Report, paras 62–3
49. Minister of Fuel and Power, in debate on 28 October 1952, Hansard, col. 1753. See also debate in House of Lords, 19 November 1952. See Munby, *Oxford Economic Papers*, 1954, p 242, footnote 4
50. PRO POWE 14/557 'Meeting of NPACI Emergency Committee, 4 December 1952; draft outline for Minister's introductory statement', 25 November 1952
51. PRO T229/483 Extract from Sir Bernard Gilbert's minute to the Chancellor of the Exchequer on 'price policy in the nationalised industries', 18 February 1953
52. PRO POWE 14/552 'Ideas about national fuel policy', note by Philip Chantler to Sir L. Watkinson, 4 June 1952

7 The evolving regulatory framework in British banking

Forrest Capie

'In each advanced industrialised country with a well developed banking system, the central bank regulates both banking institutions and the flow of credit. The extent to which banks are supervised is greater than for any other sub-sector of the economy. It has gradually been recognised that, while competition and the operation of a free market generally may be desirable objectives, banking is somehow or other different' (Grady and Weale 1985, p 35). That recent view is an interesting one and perhaps the first question to ask of it is: is it true? Does it hold for all (or any) developed economies? The argument of Grady and Weale (and of course many others) is that while competition may be good for most industries, removing the inefficient, that does not hold in banking where 'the social costs of failure outweigh any advantages that untrammelled competition might bring' (ibid.). British banking has been and is being increasingly regulated but whether interference has been greater in this sphere than any other sector of industry must surely be open to doubt. The comparison, by virtue of the nature of different types of arrangements, is not always an easy one to make, though the papers in this volume may allow some to be made.

This paper sets out in section I the case for intervention in modern banking but shows in sections II and III that, in the British case, for most of the twentieth century the industry has been allowed to take its own actions to control its members though there has usually been an ultimate powerful threat from the state hanging over it. There have been costs, some of them measurable, and some are presented in section IV. At the same time it should be recognized that whatever the constraints imposed, be they self or government, British banking has remained less controlled than many and even most other industrial countries. This relative freedom has resulted in some gains and these are the subject of section V.

I The argument for regulation

The economic argument for regulation in banking derives in the main from the fact that there is asymmetrical information. That is, the banks know more about the

127

quality of their loans and the security of their assets than do, or can, prospective depositors. Theory shows that markets of this kind do not work as well as they might and can gain from intervention. (Whether the benefits of intervention exceed the costs is another question.) One approach to intervention would be to monitor bank solvency and not simply publish but publicize the gathered information. A difficulty with this is that if the information is unfavourable then the publicizing of it will have the effect of hastening the demise of the institution. The regulators made responsible for the monitoring will therefore wish to avoid such a result and to do so will find that their regulatory powers will need to extend over a range of banks' activities, and also cover entry to the industry.

The problem associated with solvency is that of bank runs. The fundamental concern in banking is not the risk of an individual bank failure but with the stability of the banking system. If a bank's net worth is zero and it closes, then, as with any firm, the shareholders bear the loss. But in the bank's case the depositors also lose. When therefore depositors in other banks see such a failure they may withdraw their funds from their own bank and so precipitate the failure of what was a fundamentally sound bank. If this continues we describe it as a contagious run. Such a series of withdrawals need not lead to the collapse of the system, though. Liquidity problems would be created for the banks losing funds, but if depositors were placing their funds in institutions they regarded as sound then the system would survive. Only in the extreme, and very rare, case of a flight to currency would the system fail.

One means of allaying the fear of depositors and preventing overhasty withdrawal has been to provide deposit insurance. So long as there is confidence in the insurance system there will be no need for depositors to withdraw. If, nevertheless they do, then the authorities can come to the rescue of an otherwise sound group of banks by providing liquidity. This would be the central bank or monetary authority acting in its role of lender of last resort. It is important to note that such a role does not involve bailing out insolvent institutions. Some commentators have suggested that a difficulty lies in distinguishing between insolvent and illiquid institutions. But this is clearly not the case if bail-outs are not countenanced. The lender of last resort simply provides funds on the evidence of good commercial paper, or good collateral, and has no need to investigate an individual institution. The sound ones will survive just so long as there is sufficient liquidity in the system.

Another solution to the problem in banking is to allow the system to restrict entry and regulate itself and for society to suffer the welfare loss involved. As we shall see, the evolution of the British system produced something quite close to a self-regulatory system with the support of a practised lender of last resort, the Bank of England.

II The evolution of the system

The British banking system that was in place in 1920 and remained virtually unchanged in its major aspects until 1970, had evolved in the nineteenth century.

What had grown up in the industrial revolution was a system of many hundred individual small banks that had a centre firmly established in the City of London. The small banks were susceptible to failure – sometimes scores at a time. What had developed by the end of the nineteenth century was a growing concentration of banking activity in the hands of fewer and fewer large joint stock banks with thousands of branches. Many of the branches were formerly small private banks that had been taken over by a large joint stock enterprise (Capie and Rodrik-Bali).

The shape of the system was influenced by several pieces of legislation that dictated the extent of joint stock banking: its geographical location, its rights of note issue, details of disclosure and so on. But much of the shape was due simply to responding to the desire to find stability and to the needs of a growing economy in a climate of laissez-faire. In the eighteenth century the commercial banks had established their own clearing house. By 1819 40 clearing banks belonged. In 1854 the joint stock banks were admitted. The Bank of England joined this house in 1860, and membership was ultimately essential to successful retail banking. Access to the clearing house was in fact one of the reasons for merger or acquisition.

Mergers had of course always taken place and the nineteenth century witnessed the same sort of activity in banking as went on in the rest of the economy. But the pace of the activity increased after 1870 and then accelerated markedly in the 1890s. By 1900 there were 188 banks with 5922 branches. Some further activity took place so that by 1920 there were 75 banks with 9668 branches (Capie and Webber).

Parallel with the growth and change in structure of the banking system came changes in the Bank of England. The central concern in the nineteenth century was how the Bank should behave in a crisis – the issue of lender of last resort. It was clear that the Bank had, almost since its inception, provided the market with liquidity in times of need. It had done this in the eighteenth century as Clapham showed. It continued to do so in the nineteenth century. But it never declared in advance that it would. Bagehot's advice (1873) was that given the circumstances, it should declare in advance its intentions to behave like this; and from the 1870s the Bank accepted this role. Attention settled more and more on the Bank's discount rate (called Bank Rate) since it was variations in this rate that reflected the Bank's view of the City's needs. High rates indicated penalty prices when crises threatened. This rate had, therefore, to be effective. Prior to about 1880 Bank Rate seems to have lagged behind the market, suggesting that the Bank came into line with market needs. But after the 1880s and particularly the 1890s Bank Rate can be said to have led the market. For it to achieve this it helped for the Bank to have influence over the major participants and encourage them to behave in a way that would assist it in its desired intentions. This is sometimes called moral suasion, though whether or not it worked as such we leave aside here. What is of interest is that it was this need of the Bank to influence the market that explains why the Bank did nothing to discourage the emerging oligopolistic banking structure. With just a few chairmen close at hand to talk to, the Bank felt it was more able to implement monetary policy.

Thus by the opening years of the twentieth century there was a highly concentrated banking system, dominated by the Big Five clearers, acting in cooperation with the Bank (unthinkable at the beginning of the nineteenth century), with stability resting on a branching system and a responsible lender of last resort. With such a proven system in place it is hardly surprising that the government kept a distance. At the same time it is important to remember that for the years prior to 1945 that was quite generally true in the economy, apart from the experience in the two wars.

III The system in the twentieth century

The system that we have described as having evolved was to remain more or less unchanged in its essential form from 1900 to 1970. We have noted how, and the main reasons why, it took this form. We will return to say something of the costs of such an oligopoly later; suffice for the moment to say that by 1970 that cost was regarded as being too high. The pressures were then for a more competitive system, hence the introduction of 'Competition and Credit Control' at that point.

The banking structure after the First World War was that of an oligopoly with its own clearing house all supported by the central bank (Capie 1988). The essence was that retail banking was distinct and separate from wholesale banking and of discount market business, and it was encouraged to look after itself, as were the other parts of the financial sector. Thus the Accepting Houses Committee looked after the affairs of the 'wholesale' banking sector, the merchant banks; and the London Discount Market Association attended to that part of the market; and for retail banking the Committee of the London and Scottish Clearing Bankers took responsibility.

These 'clubs' generally worked to restrict entry and therefore limit competition and of course the public paid a higher price for the product as a result. There was no formal restriction on entry into banking but without access to the clearing house it was impossible for a new entrant to provide the same service as existing banks.

There is certainly a case to be made for such arrangements. There is an argument that such groupings are better equipped for regulation, for only they can assess accurately the quality of the appropriate information and place that alongside their better knowledge of the industry – capital needs and so on (Goodhart 1987). Also, their taking responsibility for themselves makes life easier for the authorities. Secondly, the self-regulatory club benefits from the greater security of monopoly profits and is better placed than otherwise to support an ailing but deserving member and to discipline an errant member.

These essentially self-regulatory clubs left the consumer worse off. The arrangements in banking were not quite those that prevailed in the insurance market. Lloyds has a central place in the British insurance industry, though it is not necessary to be a member to transact insurance business. However, this club subjects members to a variety of rules and inspections, while the reputation of the institution allows members to attract business they would not otherwise have attracted. The consumer does not suffer under this system in the same way as he does in banking, since he is free to go elsewhere. This arrangement has been described as competition in regulation, providing the advantages of both (Kay).

When we look at banking in Britain in the twentieth century however, the term self-regulation is something of an exaggeration and became increasingly so as decades passed. The following paragraphs will indicate the role that government played in relation to banking.

The Treasury was the department responsible for banking. In 1919 a Treasury committee (the Colwyn Committee) reported with a number of suggestions. One recommendation was that legislation should be passed specifically in relation to further amalgamation. However, the proposed Bill was dropped and replaced by a private undertaking between governments and the banks. A Special Advisory Committee was set up to consider any proposals.

An example of the clearing banks operating on their own was the agreement they made in 1919 to publish standardized monthly balance sheets. This was intended to decrease the amount of window dressing – the practice of fudging cash holdings and their relation to liabilities. In fact, all the banks did was collude to regularize the system. Publicly, the intention was to show reduced window dressing, for the banks were to provide a monthly average balance as the average of a day in each week for each month. However, the banks worked together so that they each prepared their balance sheets for a different day in each week; Barclays (with £347m of deposits in December 1920) on Monday, Lloyds (with £345m) on Tuesday, the Midland and National Provincial (with £649m) together on Wednesday, and Westminster (with £305m) on Thursday (alphabetical order!). The heaviest demand for liquidity was on Wednesday, the Bank of England balance sheet day, and that which was avoided was Friday, when wages were paid and the discount market and the banks required cash to purchase Treasury bills at auction. The system was thus regularized and made easier the window-dressing of accounts; and many contemporaries remained unimpressed (Capie and Webber).

There followed many examples of collusion, particularly on price, and the relationship between Bank Rate and the rate banks paid on deposits.

The striking example of self concern and support in the 1930s was the agreement struck between the Bank, the banks and the discount houses to preserve the discount houses. The collapse in interest rates in the 1930s had left the discount houses with losses – the minimum lending rate to the discount houses had for some time been the rate the banks themselves paid for deposits. In the agreement the banks reduced their minimum lending rate, agreed to stop tendering for Treasury bills on their own account, and to refrain from buying bills of less than one week to maturity. All of this reduced competition at the tender and allowed the discount houses a return above the rate at which they borrowed (Griffiths 1973).

At the end of the interwar period, whatever competition that remained in banking came to an end. Agreements were made to abolish competition for the course of the war. After the war the banks were acting even more as one unit.

The nationalization of the Bank of England in 1946 was the major piece of regulation in the post-World War period. There was a radical Labour government in power and there had been growing dissatisfaction with the Governship of Montagu Norman. In the world of the 1940s the power that the Bank had and Norman had seemed to have was unacceptable. The Act was:

> to bring the capital stock of the Bank of England under public control, to make provision with respect to the relations between the Treasury, the Bank of England and other banks and for purposes connected with [these matters] . . .

The Act gave the Treasury power to direct the Bank, and the Bank power, with Treasury consent, to give direction to the banks. But in practice informality prevailed. The world had apparently changed greatly and yet the Bank and the banks were in effect still to be left largely free to sort out their own affairs. There was, however, one important instruction to the commercial banks and that was on the precise size of their reserve (or cash) ratio – a minimum value of 8 per cent was set. That ratio remained there from the 1940s to 1971. In addition a liquid assets ratio of 28–32 per cent was prescribed. (In 1957 the latter was given a minimum value of 30 per cent and was later reduced to 25 per cent.)

Through the 1950s and 1960s there were further instructions issued to banks guided by the dictates of monetary policy. Bank advances were restrained, then freed, later restrained again; special deposits were required; penalties exacted for deviation; and so on. The banks found many of the measures irksome and resisted them up to a point. They certainly regarded the cash and liquidity ratios as being far too high in relation to prevailing banking requirements. It was clear by the 1960s that self regulation was a considerably exaggerated description of the system even if the old forms remained and the cartel had hardened. On the fringes new ways around the restrictions were being explored and exploited.

In relation to special deposits, the failure of the banks to reduce their advances sufficiently in 1969 led the Bank to impose for the first time what has been described as a 'fine' in the form of a halving of the interest paid on special deposits (*BEQB*, June 1969, p 145) which lasted until the Chancellor announced its removal in the 1970 budget (*Hansard*, 1969–70, vol. 799, 14 April, c. 1235). This was an unprecedented step, being taken on neither a traditional nor a statutory basis, and was not well received by the clearing banks. When they accepted the scheme of special deposits in the 1950s it was regarded as one of a series of monetary controls realized to be necessary and so accepted. The halving of the rate paid (Treasury bill rate) represented a loss of income to the banks on the £224.1m (2 per cent of available funds) of special deposits outstanding in December 1969 of about £8.5 million, the Treasury bill allotment rate then being 7.65 per cent. The banks thought it a very unfair criticism of the efforts that they had been making to comply with the Chancellor's request of 28 per cent. Also, there was no consultation with the banks on the matter, the Governor only asked whether it was agreed that the penalty already having been decided upon, that it should be imposed on all banks irrespective of the relation of a particular bank's lending to its own ceiling and this was agreed on 3 June (*S.C. Nationalised Industries, First Report*, 1970, Q 643–58).

While the Bank of England Act (1946) provided powers for the Bank, with

Treasury consent, to enforce compliance with its policies no sanction was written into the Act. Parliament intended the Act should be the ultimate deterrent, where mere existence would insure that no financial institution would so act as to invite its actual use in prescribing policy. Lord Radcliffe supposed that resort would be had to the courts. In the 1960s the banks were clear that statutory controls could not secure better results than the existing arrangements. Instead of resorting to the Bank Act the Governor would 'read the Riot Act' to a recalcitrant banker. Whilst the Bank operated the system of 'moral suasion' there were sanctions available to it in the ordinary course of its business. No responsible financial institution would carelessly incur the Bank's displeasure. The Bank might withhold re-discount facilities from discount houses it considered weak (as it did in the 1930s to encourage consolidation into stronger units). The Bank's willingness to discount the bills of the accepting houses, and at the finest rates, was both valued *cachet* and a potential sanction, since it could be withdrawn. For the clearing banks the ultimate sanction was the threat to withdraw their right to hold a balance with the Bank, but they were also anxious to be recognized as authorized dealers under the Exchange Control Act, a privilege which could also be withdrawn even though they are the largest currency dealers (*S.C. Nationalised Industries*, 1970, paras 76–7, pp xxvi–xxvii).

IV Some costs of regulation

The banking sector was the subject of some self-imposed restraints and was also subject to government regulation. The various restrictive practices, ranging from prices charged to hours of business, had adverse effects on efficiency. The misallocation of resources was of the kind always found when monopoly power is used to restrict output and raise prices. There was dissatisfaction with this in some quarters in the 1950s and the rumblings grew to outright condemnation by the 1960s. The fact that there were 'parallel markets' appearing in the 1950s and 1960s, made up of the clearing banks' subsidiaries that were not subject to many of the restrictions, including the cash and liquidity ratios, was evidence of the kind of escape the banks were seeking. Though of course they hung on to the benefits of the cartel where they could.

In the early 1960s the then Governor of the Bank of England, Lord Cromer, expressed doubts in public about the rigidity of prices and lack of service and competition (*The Banker*, 1963). By 1967 there was widespread dissatisfaction and the Prices and Incomes Board report (Bank Charges Rept No. 35, Cmnd. 3292) was highly critical of the cartel and all its restrictions.

Various costs then resulted from the collusion. One was that borne by the Treasury as a consequence of the uncompetitive bill tender system. More centrally was that resulting from the imposition on the clearing banks, of a cash/deposit ratio of 8 per cent. Such forced holding of cash leaves the banks subject to an implicit tax, for it involves an interest free loan to the monetary authorities – this is split between the Bank of England and the Treasury depending on how much was held in bankers deposits at the Bank and how much in notes and coin. If the banks had chosen to hold a ratio of 0.5 per cent (as recent experience shows to be the case) rather than the enforced 8 per cent, then the annual cost of the tax can be calculated by taking the proportion of the actual reserves considered excess, and multiplying that by the prevailing short term market rate of interest, representing the opportunity cost of the funds. This is what is attempted in a rough fashion in Table 7.1. The actual calculation is to multiply the reserves held by 0.925 to arrive at the 'excess' figure. This is then multiplied by the market rate of interest – in this case the Treasury Bill rate is selected as a reasonable proxy. These calculations must be regarded as rough orders of magnitude. But it can be seen from Table 7.1 that over the twenty years from 1950 to 1970, moving from the tail end of the 'cheap money' period to the period of rising interest rates, that the cost of this regulation rose steeply. As to how these numbers divided between the Bank and Treasury, one calculation for 1969 showed that the split between was 20 per cent and 80 per cent (Griffiths 1970, p 31).

From the figures in the Table something would have to be subtracted for the cost of the services performed by the Bank for the banks. But there is an additional cost that should be added, for the system of special deposits in operation in the 1960s was an attempt to raise the cash ratio but not pay a market rate of interest on the funds. In other words there is a further tax on the banks equal to the difference between the rate earned on advances (assumed to be the highest yielding bank asset) and the rate paid by the Bank of England on special deposits. Table 7.1 gives the figures for special deposits in the 1960s, but the data on the differential interest rates would be too fragile to make precise calculation sensible.

Finally, the quantitative restriction on advances that were in force forced bankers to increase their holdings of government debt. Government debt earns a lower return than preferred investments and the difference between the two could be calculated and added to the other costs. Again data prevent precision and it seems advisable simply to make some upward mental adjustment to the the total.

In summary, the banks could not have been producing efficiently and the Monopolies Commission felt:

> Because the banks have been permitted to conceal their true profits and their true reserves they have escaped the stimulus to efficiency and competitiveness that informed comparison of performance and profitability might have been expected to produce. Indeed the bankers when questioned by us made no satisfactory suggestions for measuring their own efficiency, let alone for comparing with that of their rivals. (Monop. Comm. Report, p 219)

There were substantial costs borne by society but such is the nature of the data that it would be imprudent to attach a precise figure to these. What would be needed would be a comparison of the counterfactual economy with a competitive system with the actual economy and non-competitive system.

Table 7.1   Some costs of regulation

	1 Bank reserves £m (annual average)	2 Treasury bill rate	3 Special deposits £m (annual average)	4 Costs £m
1950	507	0.51		2.4
1951	522	0.58		2.8
1952	525	2.18		10.6
1953	531	2.30		11.3
1954	551	1.80		9.2
1955	553	3.83		19.6
1956	540	4.96		24.8
1957	550	4.88		24.8
1958	569	4.46		24.6
1959	591	3.35		18.3
1960	619	4.86	79	27.8
1961	639	5.14	183	30.4
1962	662	4.09	167	25.0
1963	682	3.62	–	22.8
1964	735	4.70	–	32.0
1965	781	5.82	59	42.0
1966	812	6.07	144	46.0
1967	839	5.79	204	45.0
1968	895	7.07	219	58.5
1969	922	7.76	225	66.2
1970	868	7.04	270	56.5

Sources: Col. 1 Capie and Webber 11(2), p 154
Col. 2 Capie and Webber 111(1), p 495
Col. 3 Capie and Webber 111(2), p 399
Calculation: Col. 4: Col. 1 × 0.925 × Col. 2

V   Some gains from relative freedom

There were costs then in the British system but there were also undoubtedly gains from the relative freedom British banks enjoyed compared with other countries. The principal gain originated in the restrictive climate that American banks had to operate in and the natural second home that London offered by virtue of language and commercial association.

One of the benefits of the sound banking system was that London had emerged as the world's foremost international financial centre before 1914. Situated (in the nineteenth century) in the world's largest industrial economy, Britain's economic strength and political power gave her enormous influence and placed London at the heart of the world's monetary system. New York was in the ascendant at this time but for the period up to 1914 no one seriously questions London's position. After World War I however there were changes, and there are differing views on London's relative position. In the late 1980s London is still one of the two leading financial centres in the world, and an important part of the explanation for that undoubtedly lies in some fortuitous events but with the distinct impetus that came from relative regulatory freedom.

At the end of the First World War relative economic strengths had clearly changed. The US was then undeniably the biggest economy in the world. Indeed this had been true for some years prior to the war. The war had also been more expensive for, and much more damaging to, the British economy, and the financial strength of London had been severely shaken. The war had been even more damaging to Germany and to France, and Berlin and Paris both of which had been growing financial centres in the late nineteenth century, were effectively finished.

New York too had been growing as a national financial centre in the decades prior to the war, and given the strength of the US economy after the war New York was clearly poised to take over the role as the leading centre. Alibur (1966) regards the First World War as the critical turning point and the date for which transference of dominance moves to New York, but the reason for this is far from clear. The US economy had been growing rapidly and had long since overtaken the British economy, though that is insufficient reason. (Take, for example, the similar experience of post-World War II West Germany and Japan.) There are several reasons for being wary of this story. The US banking system (and more generally the US economy) had always been much more volatile than the British, and those of other industrial economies, and there was far from widespread acceptance of New York. Secondly, the US had only just acquired a central bank – the Federal Reserve was born in 1912 – and its mature operation was obviously still some way off. Time was needed to develop the techniques necessary for smooth cooperation with its own peculiar banking system – peculiar in comparison with Britain and Europe in that it was a unit system with thousands of very small banks without a concentration of headquarters. Even the large New York banks did not have the resources of London's leading joint stock banks. Further, although it is not imperative that a financial centre be the home of a nation's central bank, the probability is that such an arrangement would facilitate the growth of a centre. (Frankfurt is said to have prospered in recent years partly because the Deutsche Bundesbank made its home there.) Washington was the real home of the Fed. even if power rested in New York in the 1920s. Power certainly shifted to Washington in 1928 after the death of the New York governor Benjamin Strong, and the replacement of the Open Market Investment Committee (that was dominated by New York) by the Open Market Committee that had all twelve banks participating.

But these are not the chief reasons for doubting the assumption of the leading role by New York immediately after the war. The main point is that after 1918 the

US in several ways set out to distance itself from European and World affairs. Such a posture was hardly conducive to the promotion of New York as the world's leading financial centre. It is true that the US lent massively (especially to Germany) in the course of the 1920s but this overseas lending was not of the same character as British lending had been before 1914. International economic relations were in disarray after 1920 and widespread uncertainty and new obstacles greatly reduced trade and capital flows. Some central bankers such as Strong and Norman promoted a certain amount of cooperation in the financial community but this could not prevent the rather abrupt halt to American overseas investment in 1928. Outflows stopped and funds abroad were repatriated in order to participate in the great boom that was underway on Wall Street.

Kindleberger's view that the important date for the switch from London to New York is 1929 is open to the same objection. The eminent French historian Braudel has also adopted this position; '. . . in 1929 after some hesitation the centre of the world unquestionably shifted from London to New York'. Apart from the objections raised above, that apply to the whole interwar period, the reason that his date is a poor advance on 1919 is that the Fed. was in that year (1929) carrying through a severely damaging monetary policy, one that resulted in the failure of thousands of commercial banks. The subsequent depression in the US saw output fall by over 35 per cent in three years – amongst the worst in the world – and the whole system was exposed as fragile. The US was therefore a long way from being regarded as an automatic haven for the world's funds, and certainly not as a source of borrowing.

Britain suffered very much less in the world depression. And London banks suffered only slight setbacks in profitability; not one failed, which contrasts sharply with the widespread collapse in Europe and North America. And while the British economy had difficulties in the 1920s it was nevertheless experiencing its fastest rate of growth for thirty years and outstripping its European neighbours. It also suffered much less in the depression years of 1929–32 (or any peak to trough comparison). Britain was still at the centre of a large and still developing Empire whose trade was growing at rates faster than any other blocs. London's position was under pressure but very far from doomed. When we recall that the British economy grew faster than most others in the 1930s and that sterling was as strong as it had ever been it is not surprising to find London still a leading and even the leading centre.

In other words, although American economic power had clearly taken over from Britain, and New York had most of the necessary attributes of an international financial centre, it is not so clear that New York had taken over from London before World War II. The volume of international business transacted around the world after 1919 was greatly reduced but we would need to know much more about respective market shares before any claim on New York's dominance could be supported with confidence. London and New York were the leading financial centres but respective size is difficult to measure.

At the beginning of the post-World War II era, the British and American economies were by far the strongest in the world; indeed they were the only major industrial nations in any position to take up their former roles. Once again Britain had suffered in several ways (loss of foreign assets, depletion of capital stock and so on) but other industrial rivals had suffered much more. No European economy was in any position to compete and Japan was in an even worse state.

In short, the outcome of World War I and the course of events in the interwar years meant that London was not seriously under threat before 1939. And again the consequences of World War II meant that London was at least in a position to re-establish itself. Two other related developments followed that help explain the continued and even accelerating growth of British banking after the immediate postwar adjustment. These are financial regulation and the emergence of the euro-markets.

After World War II there was an enormous flow of dollars to Europe that began with the Marshall plan but persisted long after that. (Even the Soviet Union and some East European countries built up dollar balances from trade.) These and other dollars continued to be held and traded outside the US. There was also an enormous shortage of capital in Europe, and the US was the only economy, and New York the centre, that was able to supply the capital required. In these elements lie the origins of the euro-currency and euro-bond markets.

But an important factor behind the flow of dollars from the US after World War II was the prevailing US regulatory framework. The McFadden Act of 1927 was an early piece of legislation that limited the geographic expansion of a bank to its home state. Branching was ruled on by individual states. But the origins of even important legislation lie in American experience in the Great Depression of 1929–32; it was this that produced both state and federal laws that left deposit institutions subject to an array of complex requirements and under the control of various supervisory agencies. All of this of course was in stark contrast to the British experience if not the European. The large British banks did not suffer greatly in the great depression. In the first place the British depression was mild in comparison but even in 1931 when the liquidity crisis spread across Europe, London remained sound. Some merchant banks were badly shaken, but the commercial banks suffered only a dent to their profits and consequently no need was seen for a change in the regulatory framework. If anything, this experience served to strengthen London's reputation.

In the US the first shock was the stock market crash of October 1929 that prompted the distinction to be made between commercial banks and investment banks – something that has persisted as a basic feature of US banking. Of great direct importance for banking was the fact that between 1929 and 1933 thousands of banks failed (20 per cent of the total and holding nearly 10 per cent of deposits) and the whole sector was left in a state of shock. In 1933 Congress passed the Glass–Steagall Banking Act in order to help restore confidence and bring stability to the banking system. This Act brought improved protection for depositors and strengthened the hand of the Federal Reserve. One of the provisions of the Act that is of importance for later developments was that the Federal Reserve was authorized to prescribe interest ceilings for various kinds of deposits. In addition, a Federal Deposit Insurance Scheme was introduced.

Much of the regulation had no profound effect in banking until after World War II. But by the 1950s and 1960s the flow of dollars abroad was encouraged by the restrictions suffered under regulation. Regulation Q restricting the interest American bankers could pay on deposits meant that as soon as the ceiling was reached there was an incentive for depositors to send funds to higher-yielding eurodollar accounts. Another piece of legislation was Regulation M. That governed the reserve ratio of US banks but prior to 1969 it did not cover deposits in foreign branches. Further, since eurodollar accounts had no reserve requirements the banks were able to pursue different lending behaviour. Perhaps differential reserve requirements have been the most important incentive in bank establishment. The influence is lessened of course if interest is paid on compulsory reserves. But other things being equal, the lower the reserve requirement the lower the cost of banking and the higher the returns that can be offered to investors. The cost advantage is a function of both the reserve requirement ratio and the level of nominal rates. And higher rates from the late 1960s onwards are undoubtedly part of the explanation for the great growth of off-shore centres since that time.

Regulations also affected capital outflows and were usually designed to improve the US balance of payments. For example the interest equalization tax introduced in 1963 effectively closed the New York market to foreign borrowers. In 1965 the US introduced a voluntary foreign investment restraint and in so doing encouraged US companies to find funds abroad for financing investment abroad. In 1968 the controls were made mandatory. Against all this and other regulations the Euro-markets are characterized by an absence of restriction on entry and expansion.

The result was that the volume of business in London soared through the 1960s and after a hiccup in 1969/70 set new records in 1971 and 1972. The OPEC surpluses of 1973/74 onwards gave another fillip to the London banks for they provided the outlet and source for the surplus and deficit countries respectively. London, by virtue of the position it was in during the 1950s, was ideally placed to capture the bulk of this new business, and it quickly became the most important centre.

Summary

Government/industry relations in banking in the twentieth century have been conducted essentially at arm's length, though in the last decade or so a closer relationship has been pursued by the authorities. For most of the twentieth century British banks have been left very largely to keep their own house in order and the British, relative to other industrial countries, have placed a very low reliance on statutory rules. The structure of the commercial banking system minimized the likelihood of a bank failure and stability was achieved by the means and at the costs we have indicated.

However, the secondary banking problems of 1974 and associated problems of a major London clearing bank, together with a European Community directive on the coordination of banking law, all worked to bring about the passage of the 1979

Banking Act. That Act – ironically passed in a year that is now taken as a turning point on the road to greater economic freedom, and deregulation – introduced a number of extensions to the responsibility of the Bank as supervisor/regulator of the system. The Bank of England was made responsible for authorizing all new banks and for supervising all institutions that called themselves banks. There is now a veritable army of supervisors in the Bank offering advice and guidance and even demanding conformity on such basic banking business as lending policy. Thus a system that was essentially free and self disciplined has become much more directly supervised and controlled.

References

Alibur, R. *The Future of the Dollar as an International Currency*, Praeger, New York 1966

Bagehot, W. *Lombard Street, A Description of the Money Market*, John Murray, London 1873

Bankers Almanac. Annual from 1900

Bank of England. *The Development and Operation of Monetary Policy*, 1984

Bank of England Quarterly Bulletins

Capie, F. 'Structure and competition in British banking' in Moggridge and Cottrell, eds, *Money and Empire*, Macmillan, 1988

Capie, F., Rodrik-Bali, G. 'Concentrations in British banking, 1880–1920' in *Business History*, 1982

Capie, F., Webber, A. *A Monetary History of the United Kingdom*, Allen & Unwin, 1985

Goodhart, C.A.E. 'The economics of Big Bang' in *Midland Bank Review*, Winter 1987

Grady, J., Weale, M. *British Banking 1960–1985*, Macmillan, 1986

Griffiths, B. *Competition in Banking 1970*, Hobart Paper IEA, 1971

Griffiths, B. 'The development of restrictive practices in the UK monetary system' in *Manchester School*, 41 (1), 1973

Hansard. Various

Kay, J. 'Comment on Baltensperger and Dermine, "Banking Deregulation" ' in *Economic Policy*, April 1987

Kindleberger, C.P. *A Financial History of Western Europe*, George Allen & Unwin, 1983

Kindleberger, C.P. *The Formation of Financial Centres, A Study of Comparative Economic History*, Princeton Studies in International Finance, 1974

King, W.T.C. *History of the London Discount Market*, Routledge & Sons, London 1936

Nevin, E., Davis, E.W. *The London Clearing Banks*, London 1970

Prochew, H.V., ed. *The Eurodollar Market*, Rand McNally, Chicago 1970

Reed, H.C. *The Pre-eminence of International Financial Centres*, Praeger, New York 1981

Sykes, J. *The Amalgamation Movement in English Banking*, P.S. King & Sons, London 1926

Parliamentary papers

Banking Act (1979)
Bank of England Act (HMSO, 1946)
Colwyn Committee Cmd. (HMSO, 1919)
Committee to Review the Functioning of Financial Institutions, Cmnd. 1937 (HMSO, 1980)
National Board for Prices and Incomes, *Bank Charges*, Cmnd. 3292 (HMSO, 1967)
Select Committee on Nationalised Industries Final Report

8 Government-industry relations in the British chemical industry

Wyn Grant

Although this chapter is primarily concerned with government-industry relations since 1945, it is necessary to say something about events between 1914 and 1939 as they shaped the rather special relationship that developed between the chemical industry and government in the postwar period. In a country where government-industry relations have been fraught with difficulty, those between government and the chemical industry have been relatively harmonious and mutually satisfactory, although new strains have developed since 1979. Whether this is because chemicals has been a relatively 'problem free' industry from government's point of view, or for other reasons, is a question that will be returned to later in the analysis.

In the 1980s the chemical industry would be categorized (in terms of such measures as contribution to the balance of payments) as one of Britain's more successful industries. At one time, however, it was an area of major failure. From having the world's largest chemical industry, Britain's position had gone into decline, largely because of a failure to replace the Leblanc process for soda ash production by the more economical Solvay process. At the time of the outbreak of the First World War, Britain was so dependent on supplies of chemicals from overseas, particularly Germany, that there was real concern that it would not be possible to supply khaki dye for the uniforms of the army. This particular problem was solved, and a number of dye firms were merged into a publicly funded body called British Dyes, later amalgamated with another group to form the British Dyestuffs Corporation. With the victory over Germany, a so-called 'Chemicals Mission' was sent to Germany with the object being, as the instigator put it, 'to pinch everything they've got' (Kennedy 1986, p 16). The Germans tried to conceal as much as they could by painting out dials, and removing stairs between floors, and the plans that were drawn by the British group from memory were stolen by persons who broke into the guarded railway truck they were being transported in by cutting from underneath. However, notes kept in a kitbag by one member of the party, and the recollections of the others, were sufficient to provide a basis for building a nitrogen plant at Billingham using the Haber–Bosch method, on land made available by the Ministry of Munitions.

The significant event in the postwar period was, however, the formation of Imperial Chemical Industries (ICI) in 1926 from a merger of Brunner, Mond; the

United Alkali Company; the British Dyestuffs Corporation; and Nobel Industries. The formation of ICI was seen as a British counter move to Germany's creation of IG Farben in the preceding year. ICI's establishment took place against a background of discreet government encouragement. In January 1926, Reginald McKenna, a former chancellor and by then chairman of the Midland Bank, lunched with Sir Harry McGowan of Nobel Industries and suggested 'that it would be acceptable in the highest circles of government if a coalition of the British chemical companies were to rescue British Dyestuffs' (Kennedy 1986, p 22). What happened in essence was that Brunner, Mond and Nobel took over the two weaker companies (United Alkali and British Dyestuffs) who only had part-time members of the board of the new company.

Government thus chose indirect rather than direct involvement in the problems of the British chemical industry. Rather than create a state owned chemical company, the preference was for a 'chosen instrument' that would have a special relationship with government. The relationship between ICI and government became even closer as war approached, although 'government' in this context meant departments connected with defence after the Committee of Imperial Defence started to examine wartime preparations in 1934. In the years leading up to the war, contacts were mainly with the War Office and Air Ministry, during the war with Supply and Aircraft Production (see Reader 1975). Kennedy claims (1986, p 78) that ICI was 'the government's largest industrial agent in the Second World War'. Certainly, ICI had a 'good war' in terms of the expansion of its business, the development of new products and processes, and an increase in profits (even if eaten into by wartime taxation). The contribution of the chemical industry to the war effort compared very favourably with the difficulties encountered during the First World War. A severe critic of British industrial performance during the Second World War, Corelli Barnett, has remarked, 'Only the chemical industry (really ICI) came up to scratch in wartime; and the chemical industry has remained Britain's most solid performer ever since, though even so falling behind Germany and the United States in scale and mix of products.' (Barnett 1987, p 33)

Why had government become involved in the affairs of the industry at all? A primary motivation was that it was evident from the experience of the First World War that success in a science based industry such as chemicals was essential to the effective conduct of modern warfare. Britain could not rely again on the First World War expedient of buying German supplies from German companies, or using the talents of German émigrés. Although the solution that was adopted, the encouragement of the formation of ICI, was in many ways an *ad hoc* and pragmatic reaction to particular events, it was also remarkably far sighted. It created a private enterprise company with something of a public service perspective to spearhead the task of 'catching up' with Germany; in France and Italy, after the Second World War, state owned companies played a much more important role in similar strategies than had been the case in Britain. Indeed, after the Second World War, ministers in the new Labour Government were to state that they had better cooperation from ICI than from some of the newly nationalized industries (see Williams 1982, p 133). It may, of course, be that the threat of nationalization was a factor in ICI's behaviour, encouraging it to be cooperative with government, although ICI's 'public service' conception of itself led it in the direction of a partnership with government. Certainly, ICI considered itself to be a candidate for any widened programme of nationalization, and if Labour had won the 1951 elections, the industry could well have ended up in public ownership.

One particular area of cooperation between the industry and government in the reconstruction process was regional aid. As a growing industry, chemicals appeared to be a promising area for action to offset some of the persistent regional imbalances in the economy. Dalton, at the Board of Trade, was particularly concerned with regional policy and the then ICI Chairman assured him that he 'regarded it as a national duty to help in starting up new enterprises in what would otherwise be postwar depressed areas' (Pimlott, ed. 1985, p 624). ICI was willing to expand in the depressed areas because they calculated that such areas would receive priority when buildings and materials licences were being allocated. They were correct in this assumption, but then had to embark on fortnightly meetings with government to coordinate the forward ordering of materials.

One practical consequence was the enlargement of the proposed North-East Development Area to encompass ICI's new Wilton works, which had an employment target of five thousand (Pimlott, ed, 1985, p 746). The actual number employed was significantly smaller, and the general value of the chemical industry as an instrument of regional policy was somewhat offset by its capital intensive character. Indeed, it has been argued that the generous regional assistance provided to the industry in the postwar period served to enhance its capital intensive character, and led to net job losses rather than to job gains (although without such assistance, losses might have been even greater). (For a discussion of these issues, see Robinson and Storey 1980.)

The postwar relationship with ICI

In many respects, the postwar relationship between government and the chemical industry has to be seen in terms of the relationship between government and ICI. ICI remained the dominant company in the chemical industry and had a broader significance as the flagship of the British industrial economy. This picture has to be qualified in one respect, however. The postwar development of the petrochemicals industry involved the oil companies in the industry in a significant way. In the 1980s, there are four ethylene producers in Britain (ethylene is the basic building block of the petrochemicals industry): ICI; BP Chemicals; Shell Chemicals; and Esso Chemicals. However, even BP Chemicals had a turnover in 1985 of less than one-fifth of that of ICI (£1922 million as against £10 725 million). What the three oil majors shared with ICI was the sophistication of their government relations operations, although ICI was a pioneer in this field.

What was characteristic of the relationship throughout the postwar period was the desire of both government and ICI to keep it in good repair. This is illustrated by an incident which happened when Peter Walker was Secretary of State for Trade and Industry under the Heath Government. Sir Jack Callard, chairman of ICI, expressed the view that there was insufficient communication between the Government and ICI. As a result, a system was agreed whereby Callard wrote a personal letter to Walker each month listing any complaints or problems which the Government could help to remedy. Walker undertook to reply immediately and in detail to the letter. 'The moment the letter came in the various problems were relayed to the relevant sections of government and within a short time a full and detailed reply was prepared' (Walker 1977, p 87).

ICI's relationship with government occurs at a number of levels and in relation to a variety of departments. Thus, for example, ICI's Agriculture Division has close links with the Ministry of Agriculture, whilst the pharmaceuticals division relates primarily to the Department of Health and Social Security. A number of divisions have links with the Department of Energy. However, the company's principal point of contact within government has been with the Department of Trade and Industry which has housed the sponsorship division for the industry. Contacts have not, of course, been exclusively with the sponsoring division within the department. There has, for example, been a tradition of bi-annual meetings involving the department's permanent secretary, the ICI Chairman and perhaps one other board member. The agenda at these half-day meetings might include ICI's investment plans, and the Department's assessment of general economic trends. However, it is the sponsorship division (Chemicals and Textiles) which has been the principal contact, the people that ICI's government relations manager has turned to when ICI has encountered problems with other ministries, or has not been getting what it wanted out of the system. It is therefore interesting to speculate how ICI will cope with the abolition of the sponsorship function by Lord Young in 1988. Of course, it should be recalled that the sponsorship function declined in importance after the Second World War, and was only revived again in the early to mid-1960s when government started to take a more active role in relation to industry.

ICI's relations with the Treasury have probably been less good than with other government departments. This reflects the Treasury's macroeconomic concerns, and a feeling on the industry side that it does not really understand industry in the way that the DTI does. Indeed, one reason for the closeness of the ICI–DTI relationship may be that ICI has been able to supply the DTI with information on such subjects as the effects of sterling fluctuations on their operations, information which could be utilized by the DTI in its discussions with the Treasury.

The relationship since 1979

Since 1979 there has been something of a deterioration in the relationship between ICI (and the chemical industry generally) and government. This change should not be exaggerated. Working relationships between ICI staff and civil servants remain good. ICI's headquarters organization is somewhat bureaucratic in terms of its own operations. On the positive side, it can have a dialogue with the civil servant based on a recognition on ICI's part of the importance of economically worded, analytically rigorous papers to support its position. ICI still enjoys access to the very highest political levels of government in a way that few other firms do. Moreover, ICI staff have continued to provide assistance to government, notably the secondment of an executive director, Sir Robin Ibbs, to the Cabinet Office for two years as Head of the Central Policy Review Staff (during this period he relinquished his ICI directorship). Following his return to ICI, he was given a part-time appointment as the Prime Minister's Adviser on Efficiency and Effectiveness in Government.

Although in many respects the relationship conforms to the general pattern of the postwar period, there has been some deterioration. One point to be borne in mind is that the chemical industry (as distinct from the pharmaceutical industry) is not a major donor to the Conservative Party. For example, ICI has a policy of not making political donations. There has also been a perception on the part of some individuals associated with the Thatcher Government that ICI is a paternalistic company with a liking for what are regarded as old-fashioned types of government–industry relationship. Thus, when ICI encountered a period of difficulty at the beginning of the 1980s, the reaction of monetarists was 'Oh, ICI – they're just as bureaucratic as the Civil Service' (Keegan 1984, p 148).

From the point of view of ICI and other chemical firms, there were a number of factors which had introduced new difficulties into the relationship with government. As the Chemical Industries Association somewhat acidly remarked in its evidence to the House of Lords Committee on Overseas Trade:

The Government's policies aim to create the conditions for profitable and non-inflationary growth and for the encouragement of enterprise. From the chemical industry's point of view this is epitomized by very high energy prices, the removal of regional grants, and the changes in the regulations on the collection of VAT on imports, etc. (Chemical Industries Association 1985, p 329)

ICI's chairman from 1981 to 1986, Sir John Harvey-Jones, was a Social Democrat in his personal life. He was more flamboyant and outspoken than was customary for ICI chairmen. Some of his remarks caused offence in Downing Street, as on the occasion when, asked at a Brussels press conference why the recession had bitten so much harder in the UK than elsewhere, he replied, 'We've got Thatcher' (*Financial Times*, 1 April 1982). His Dimbleby lecture was a classic example of his ability to make a carefully constructed and persuasive case for the continued significance of manufacturing industry (Harvey-Jones 1986). In his evidence to the House of Lords Committee on Overseas Trade, Harvey-Jones commented, 'I do not believe that the Japanese Government would do some of the slightly thoughtless things that seem to happen in this country which have had a significant effect on our ability to compete internationally' (Harvey-Jones 1985, p 463). He continued, 'it is true that Governments cannot make industrial successes but they sure as hell can make it a lot more difficult to achieve' (Harvey-Jones 1985, p 463).

The chemical industry is often characterized as 'industry's industry'. In other words, the core industrial chemicals sector of the industry (as distinct from the more peripheral subsectors such as soap and detergents) is selling intermediate products to industrial users. It therefore relies on a strong industrial base to sustain domestic demand. The Conservative Government's reluctance to attempt to limit the appreciation of sterling between 1979 and 1981 contributed to a substantial erosion of the UK manufacturing base. ICI estimate that 'we lost about 20 per cent of our customer base in our petrochemicals and general chemicals business. As a result of this, together with the development of petrochemicals plant based on cheap feedstocks in the Middle East, ICI moved out of the production in the United Kingdom of several commodity products' (Harvey-Jones 1985, p 452).

Apart from its concern about the conduct of general macroeconomic policy, the chemical industry also saw itself as adversely affected by particular aspects of Government policy. Along with other energy intensive industries, the chemical industry was concerned about higher energy prices for industrial users compared with competitor countries. Although it was able to win concessions on electricity and gas prices, the prospect of further substantial industrial electricity price increases in 1988 led to renewed concern about whether the Government appreciated the competitive impact of energy prices on an industry such as chemicals.

Cutbacks in regional aid which particularly affected capital intensive industries such as chemicals also met with opposition from the industry. The Chemical Industries Association noted in its 1984 annual report, 'It is . . . a matter of great concern that the industry stands to lose considerable investment support as a result of the Government's new Regional Policy legislation'. The amounts involved could be quite substantial for individual companies. In the case of ICI, government grants not yet credited to profit amounted to £183m in 1980; £211m in 1981; and £203m in 1982.

The deterioration in ICI's relations with government would appear to be reflected in a four year court battle which finally ended when the House of Lords refused in 1986 to give leave to the Government to challenge a Court of Appeal ruling in ICI's favour over claims that unfair tax advantages had been given to its oil company rivals. Shell and Esso built a new petrochemicals plant at Mossmorran in Scotland which used ethane as a feedstock, whilst BP converted its Grangemouth plant from a naphtha cracker to a mixed methane and ethane feedstock. ICI continued to use a naphtha feedstock at Wilton. The 1982 Finance Act introduced a new fiscal regime for the valuation of ethane for petroleum revenue tax purposes. ICI claimed that they would be the only UK ethylene producer unable to take advantage of the new regime. Ironically, while the case was being fought throughout the courts, the fall in oil prices removed ICI's problems at Wilton, whilst compounding the competitive problems faced by Mossmorran.

The details of the case are not relevant here. What is of interest is the light it throws on the conduct of government-industry relations in the chemical industry. It is 'reasonably clear that by mid-1981 Esso and Shell were not prepared to go on with the Mossmorran cracker project unless they received some form of financial assistance from the Government' (*Common Market Law Reports*, 26 March 1985, p 592). ICI used traditional lobbying techniques to prevent this, holding 'a series of meetings with the Government at the very highest level. Meetings took place between the Chairman of ICI and the then Chancellor of the Exchequer, the Chief Secretary of the Treasury and other ministers and senior officials of the Revenue' (*Common Market Law Reports*, 26 March 1985, p 592). It is clear that the Government continued to view ICI as a highly regarded company which should be consulted on matters affecting its operations. As the responsible minister told the House of Commons committee considering the 1982 Finance Bill, 'Of course, a company as highly respected and responsible as ICI deserves to have its queries properly considered by the Government' (House of Commons Standing Committee A, 24 June 1982, col. 975). The difficulty that ICI faced was that other chemical companies, such as BP, were also putting forward their particular point of view. Hence, ICI was forced to resort to the unusual step of taking the Government to court.

Although it is apparent that difficulties have appeared in the relationship between the Government and ICI since 1979, they should not be overstated. Successive governments and the chemical industry have generally had a harmonious relationship, particularly if one places the relationship in the context of the difficulties that have afflicted government's relations with industries such as steel. A more long-term pressure on the relationship is the internationalization of the industry, a topic which will be returned to later in this chapter.

Tripartism and the National Economic Development Council

One other aspect of the relationship between government and industry needs to be discussed. The National Economic Development Office (NEDO) is not part of the government machine as such, but economic development committees and sector working groups have provided a forum for discussion between employers, unions and government of the problems facing the chemical industry. The chemical industry has had both a Chemicals Economic Development Committee and sector working groups for petrochemicals and specialized organics. These committees have produced a number of analytically rigorous and timely reports on such subjects as research and development in the industry, or the overcapacity problem in petrochemicals. The problem, as with other such committees, has been ensuring that the reports lead to some 'follow through' in terms of changes in policy. Even under the Labour Government's 'industrial strategy' of 1975–79, which gave an enhanced importance to the economic development committees and sector working parties, the impact of their reports on Government policy often seemed to be limited. One factor may have been that the DTI did not wish to see NEDO emerging as a separate source of policy initiation and advice. In any event, the downgrading of the National Economic Development Council and its committees by the Thatcher Government after the 1987 election further reduced the significance of these committees. In the case of chemicals, only the specialized organics committee seemed likely to survive.

The tripartite committees were most valued by the unions as a mechanism for securing some input (however indirect) to the governmental policy-making process, and for discussing issues with the employers that could not readily be raised within the normal processes of collective bargaining (such as future investment plans). The employers had a much more limited view of the value of these committees. One manager commented in interview, 'Since the concept of EDCs exists, most people see them as a necessary evil. Most people in industry don't think they do all that much good on a consistent basis, but unless industry participates you get an unbalanced structure of government and trade union representatives. People see them as something they have to participate in.'

One other tripartite structure which has disappeared in the 1980s is the training board for the industry, the Chemical and Allied Products Industry Training Board (CAPITB). Employers in the industry took the view 'that the Board was too inspectorial and interventionist, and that consultancy and advisory work had not been effective in encouraging training in key skill areas' (Rainbird and Grant 1985, p 35). The training board was replaced by a number of non-statutory training organizations (NSTOs). The largest of the new NSTOs, that of the Chemical Industries Association (CIA) and the Association of the British Pharmaceutical Industry (ABPI) set up a review body, the Chemical and Allied Industries' Training Review Council (CAITREC). This organization coordinates and disseminates information about training through its constituent NSTOs which include bodies other than the original founders such as the Proprietary Association of Great Britain (PAGB). In terms of the coordinating role performed by CAITREC, and the level of activity of the individual NSTOs, such as that of the CIA, the chemical industry is relatively well served compared to other industries.

Government relations divisions and industry associations

The British chemical industry is characterized by the existence of specialized government relations divisions in all the leading firms, but also by a number of well resourced and sophisticated industry associations, notably the Chemical Industries Association (CIA). Chemical industry firms are also actively involved in the work of the Confederation of British Industry (CBI). It should be noted that for firms such as ICI, having a government relations division, and being actively involved in business associations, are not 'either or' choices. They devote considerable resources to both types of activity.

Firms such as ICI, BP and Shell have among the most sophisticated government relations operations of any British company. Typically, the government relations unit in such a firm is small, but is placed high up the organization with access to senior staff. The seriousness with which public affairs work is taken is indicated by the fact that it was one of two corporate functions which Sir John Harvey-Jones concentrated on during his tenure as ICI chairman (the other was corporate planning). The staff in government relations units are either high flying executives in mid-career, who spend a few years in a function, or more senior staff with considerable experience of all facets of the company's activities.

Clearly, there are sometimes commercial issues when the interests of one chemical company are at variance with those of another (as in the case of the taxation dispute referred to earlier). However, government relations work is not confined simply to matters in which the company has a distinctive commercial interest. Companies see it as important to maintain an effective dialogue with civil servants and politicians. One government relations manager defined the objective of his unit as 'being to ensure that politicians have a good understanding of what we're doing and that our managers have a good understanding of what politicians think'.

The managers interviewed saw the role of industry associations as being particularly important in more technical areas where the industry needed to take a concerted view. Abvove all, the role of associations was stressed in relation to the development of an industry response to proposals for extending environmental and health and safety regulation of the industry. It is really in this area that the chemical industry has its most intensive relationship with government, rather than in relation to more conventional forms of industrial policy. As one government relations manager commented in interview, 'Industrial policy hasn't been a central plank of British governments, government lifetimes are short, they want results on a short-term horizon, our investments are longer term. We have a feeling that industrial policy has been more consistent in France, Germany [and] Italy.'

Although ICI is active in all the industry associations, it is careful not to dominate them. Indeed, an analysis of major committees of the CIA shows that it has reduced its presence over the years. A government relations manager in another company commented, 'ICI takes less of [a] high profile than it once did, urging other companies to play a more prominent role in speaking for industry'. It must be emphasized, however, that this is a relatively highly concentrated industry in which a small number of large companies play a key political role. As one government relations manager commented in interview, 'CIA Council is very powerful, meets once a month. Once you've taken out ICI, there are ten or twelve very big ones. My impression is that there are fairly close links between senior bosses in the chemical industry because they're a sufficiently small number, [CIA Council] acts as an informal policy-making forum.'

The CIA, which combines the functions of a trade association and an employers' organization negotiating 'framework' agreements, is highly respected by civil servants as one of the better organized and more effective British business associations. In 1986, the CIA's income was just under £3 million and it had a staff (in terms of the weekly average number) of 79. There are a number of associations which serve particular subsectors or products within the industry. Some of these are affiliated to the CIA (e.g. National Sulphuric Acid Association); others (e.g. Paintmakers' Association) are not.

Some disquiet has been expressed by some of the larger chemical companies about the cost effectiveness of the overall system of business associations in the chemical industry. This concern led to the establishment of a working party headed by Sir John Harvey-Jones in 1982 to look at the effort effectiveness of the associational system of the industry, but, despite the seniority of the chairman, this investigation led to no organizational changes. As the CIA President commented in the organization's 1982 report:

> There is still the same proliferation of Trade Associations and Employers Organisations in our sector . . . as when Lord Devlin commented so unfavourably in his 1982 report. Wherever possible we continue to work in a pragmatic way with other Associations having common cause within the industry, but this is no alternative to a properly structured deployment of our total representational resources. We have only to look over the Channel to such countries as Germany and France to see the benefits that come from a more rational approach.

The chemical industry is very active in the CBI, both through the CIA and through the contribution of individual companies such as ICI and BP. ICI has provided two CBI presidents since the organization's inception, and it makes a significant contribution to the work of the organization. However, the breadth of the CBI's membership means that it cannot always adequately represent the views of the chemical industry. This was evident in relation to the industry's concern about what it viewed as excessive energy prices. The CBI has to represent both energy producers and energy consumers. Hence, the CIA largely worked through an informal grouping of trade associations representing energy intensive industries known as 'the energetic seven'.

The importance of the European dimension

Government-industry relations in the chemical industry cannot properly be understood without an appreciation of the importance of the European dimension. This manifests itself in three ways. First, Western Europe is of central importance in the global chemical industry. Four of the five leading world chemical companies are West European, and the region is heavily involved in world trade in chemicals. Second, companies such as ICI and BP which operate throughout Western Europe treat the region as an integrated market. Third, the actions of the European Community have a considerable impact on the industry, in many cases greater than that of national governments. This particularly applies in two areas of vital importance to the industry: trade policy, where the emergence of new producers in the Middle East and elsewhere is disturbing traditional patterns of supply; and environmental regulation, where the EC is taking the leading role in developing new regulations.

Leading firms in the industry have their own public affairs representatives in Brussels, but interviews confirmed that associative action was regarded as more important at the European than the domestic level. The principal organization representing the industry is a well resourced body, CEFIC (the European Council of Chemical Manufacturers' Federations), although there are also distinct bodies for subsectors such as agrochemicals. The importance with which CEFIC is regarded is indicated by the fact that individuals such as Sir John Harvey-Jones have fulfilled the demanding role of president for a two year term. Changes in the internal organization of CEFIC in 1985 gave greater influence to the large firms operating in more than one European company. The CEFIC building also houses the Association of Petrochemical Producers in Europe which has as direct members the large firms which produce petrochemicals. The industry is thus very well organized to defend its interests at the European level.

Access to information

Information is a key resource in dealing with a technologically advanced industry such as chemicals. A government wishing to generate a policy for the future development of the industry would require considerable amounts of information about future supply and demand trends, company performance, investment plans etc. Of course, governments in Britain have not attempted to develop such a policy. If they had wished to do so, they would have found the sources of information available to them within government would have been relatively limited. The sponsorship division (when it existed) was staffed by generalist civil servants who relied on the files inherited from their predecessors, and the knowledge they could accumulate from informal contacts with the industry (admittedly well developed). (By way of contrast, the comparable division in the US Department of Commerce, which remains in existence unlike its former British counterpart, includes individuals with extensive experience of the industry.) Some accumulated expertise existed within the National Economic Development Office; the various reports issued by the Chemicals EDC and the sectoral groups provided good analytical accounts of the problems facing the industry. However, the best sources of information on the industry lie outside government, particularly among securities analysts such as Stuart Wamsley of Morgan Stanley International, consultants such as Chem Systems International, and the editor of a specialist newsletter, Michael Hyde of *Chemical Insight*. Wamsley in particular has built up a substantial data base which allows him to monitor developments in the world chemical industry. His analyses of likely future developments are essential reading for individuals interested in the industry. (The contrast with the US is again interesting, where the Department of Commerce produces 'competitive assessments' of the performance of the US industry in particular product areas.)

As was stressed earlier, government involvement in the industry is more evident in areas such as environmental and workplace regulation. However, the resources available to bodies such as the Health and Safety Commission and Executive are limited, particularly compared with countries such as West Germany (see Grant, Paterson and Whitston, forthcoming). The Health and Safety Executive does have a specialist National Industry Group for chemicals. However, its resources are limited and in relation to such matters as guidelines for the bulk storage of chlorine, much of the necessary expertise has been provided by specialist CIA working parties.

Conclusions

The view one takes of this asymmetrical distribution of information between the industry and government will depend on a judgement on what government's role in relation to the industry ought to be. In many respects, the industry has been able to solve its own problems, notably in responding to the overcapacity crisis of the early 1980s in the West European petrochemical industry through inter-company agreements. In Britain, the ICI model of a private enterprise 'chosen instrument' seems to have worked well if one compares the economic performance of the chemical industry with other British industries. As Reader has commented, 'ICI's foundations were laid both in public policy and in sound business practice, and in this aspect of ICI's history, perhaps, we may find a good deal that is relevant today to the practice, if not the theory, of handling economic affairs' (Reader 1977, p 242).

In considering what government's role *ought* to be in relation to the chemical industry, one has to bear in mind that chemicals is one of the most internationalized industries. For example, 25 per cent of ICI's sales in 1987 were in the UK, 25 per cent in Continental Europe, 27 per cent in the Americas, and 23 per cent in other markets. ICI's board includes American, German and Japanese directors. The company has been substantially increasing its presence in the US through a programme of acquisitions. It is quoted on the New York Stock Exchange, and, in an important symbolic move, it has even held board meetings in New York. In ICI's view, one consequence of its 'ever increasing internationalism' is 'that we are not unduly dependent on a particular economy or product' (ICI Annual Report 1987, p 3). Another consequence is that ICI has had to develop its political capabilities on a worldwide basis. Thus, ICI Americas has five executive staff in its Washington office, a far higher level of government relations staffing than in London, although in part this reflects the more unpredictable character of the American political system, leading most major companies to invest considerable resources in their 'Washington offices'.

From ICI's perspective, an internationalization strategy undoubtedly makes good commercial sense. However, the growing internationalization of the chemical industry does mean that there are limits to the impact that a single national government can have on the operations of chemical companies. Of course, a national government may choose to take no action on matters relating to its chemical industry. The US Government has stood by while its chemical industry has been 'Europeanized'; six of the top twenty chemical firms in the US are now European owned. This lack of reaction is perhaps less surprising when it is apparent that executives in the industry do not know how to react to the change of ownership. A poll of 298 managers on the foreign investment issue found that 33 per cent were not sure whether it was good or bad, and 18 per cent had no opinion (*Chem Week*, 29 April 1987).

One implication of internationalization is that intergovernmental agencies will become increasingly involved in regulating the industry. This has already happened, with the European Community taking important decisions in such areas as competition policy, trade policy and environmental policy. The completion of the internal market should accelerate this transfer of responsibility for the industry from the national to the European level. However, the industry operates on a global level, and if Community regulations were in conflict with those of the US, there could be a highly distorting impact on trade flows. This creates a coordinating role for organizations such as the OECD which has a Chemicals Programme within which work 'has been directed towards harmonization of chemicals control measures so as to protect health and environment and to avoid unnecessary disruptions to trade' (OECD 1983, p 89). A number of specialized UN agencies are also involved in the regulation of the international chemical industry in areas such as the transport of potentially hazardous chemicals by sea (the International Maritime Organization) or by air (the International Civil Aviation Organization).

Nevertheless, this does not mean that there is no scope for national policy in relation to the chemical industry. Even within a social market industrial policy, it is acknowledged that government has a responsibility for setting a framework within which companies can act in an enterprising and innovative fashion. Such features of national policy as relatively high energy prices can discourage domestic production. Government does need some internal mechanism for understanding the problems of the industry and communicating with it. Although such communications will necessarily take place right across the government machine, a central focus can ensure that the particular needs of the industry are not overlooked when general policies are being formulated. It is therefore to be regretted that the British Government has decided that the concept of sponsorship is outmoded. Other major western countries (e.g. the US, Canada, West Germany) continue to maintain specialist industry divisions with responsibility for the chemical industry.

The expertise available on the industry in international bodies such as the European Commission is limited. Within the directorate-general responsible for industrial questions there has been one person responsible for the entire European chemical industry, admittedly with some assistance. There are chemical industry experts in directorates dealing with competition policy and with the environment, but they are very hard pressed, particularly in dealing with the large number of environmental initiatives taken by the Commission.

In the interwar period, chemicals was regarded as a 'problem' industry in terms of its performance. Government encouraged the formation of ICI which 'succeeded in its major objective: to make sure that the British chemical industry could stand up for itself, or alongside, the American and German heavyweights' (Reader 1977, p 230). The major objective was to secure the wartime supply of essential chemicals, and hence tensions between employment and improving efficiency did not come to the surface in the way that they did in other industries. The close relationship between ICI and government continued in the postwar period, with ICI standing 'midway between a company in private business, properly so-called, and a public corporation of the kind that has been established, since ICI was founded, for running nationalized industries' (Reader 1975, p 476). Concentration was only a background factor in facilitating good relations between government and the industry.

In the 1980s a number of factors have led to some changes in the relationship. ICI went through a difficult commercial period which required major changes in its management and operations, changes brought about through the appointment of a somewhat unorthodox individual as chairman (see Pettigrew 1985). ICI and other companies in the chemical industry became more internationalized in their outlook and operations. The Thatcher Government was less interested in a partnership relationship with industry than its predecessors.

Much of the writing on government-industry relations is dominated by the analysis of problem industries such as steel. Examining an industry such as chemicals where relationships have been more harmonious and effective is therefore a useful corrective. The fact that they were not always effective (in terms of producing an efficient British industry) suggests that the interventions made in the interwar period had a long-term beneficial effect. Although the industry has faced less pressing problems than some others, it now faces substantial challenges to its successful export record through the emergence of new producers in the Middle East, South East Asia and Latin America. These challenges can best be met by developing the government-industry relationship at the European Community level.

Acknowledgement

This chapter is based on research supported by the Economic and Social Research Council (Reference number E0525004). I am grateful to the editor for a number of helpful comments which assisted me in revising the chapter.

References

Barnett, C. 'Reply to criticisms on the thesis of the *Audit of War, Contemporary Record*, 1987, vol. 1(3), p 33

Chemical Industries Association. 'Memorandum submitted by the Chemical Industries Association', House of Lords Select Committee on Overseas Trade, HMSO, London 1985

Grant, W., Paterson, W., Whitston, C. (in press). *Government and the Chemical Industry: a Comparative Study of Britain and West Germany*, Oxford University Press, Oxford

Harvey-Jones, J. 'Memorandum submitted by Mr Harvey-Jones and Examination of Witness', House of Lords Select Committee on Overseas Trade, HMSO, London 1985

Harvey-Jones, Sir J. *The Listener*, 10 April 1986, pp 12–15

Keegan, W. *Mrs Thatcher's Economic Experiment*, Penguin, Harmondsworth 1984

Kennedy, C. *ICI: The Company That Changed Our Lives*, Hutchinson, London 1986

OECD. *Economic Aspects of International Chemicals Control*, OECD, Paris 1983

Pettigrew, A. *The Awakening Giant: Continuity and Change in ICI*, Blackwell, Oxford 1985

Pimlott, B., ed. *The Dalton War Diary*, Jonathan Cape, London 1985

Rainbird, H., Grant, W. 'Employers' associations and training policy', University of Warwick Institute for Employment Research, Coventry 1985

Reader, W.J. *Imperial Chemical Industries: a History, Volume II, The First Quarter Century 1926–1952*, Oxford University Press, London 1975

Reader, W.J. 'Imperial Chemical Industries and the state, 1926–1945' in B. Supple, ed., *Essays in British Business History*, Clarendon Press, Oxford 1977, pp 227–43

Robinson, J.F.F., Storey, D.J. 'Employment change in manufacturing industry in Cleveland 1965–76', typescript, County of Cleveland Planning Department Report No. 176, 1980

Walker, P. *The Ascent of Britain*, Sidgwick and Jackson, London 1977

Williams, P.M. *Hugh Gaitskell*, Oxford University Press, Oxford 1982

9 Institutional insularity: government and the British motor industry since 1945

Stephen Wilks

Generalizations about government-industry relations in Britain are easy to make but hard to sustain. Virtually every generalization can be contradicted or falsified by producing contrary examples, questioning its causes or disputing its effects. The Government-industry relationship varies with the industry, the time period, the type of policy involved and the particular issue in question. The objective of this chapter is to draw conclusions from a more limited experience of one industry and specified time periods. Such conclusions draw on previous analyses, not all of which can be marshalled here (Wilks 1988) and are therefore relatively well grounded in empirical examination of the industry. At the same time, it is likely that conclusions may have a more general validity in other sectors of manufacturing and service industry. Such generalizations would need to be undertaken with care because, if one lesson emerges from recent research into government-industry relations, it is that sectoral patterns of relationships vary widely and persistently (see Wilks and Wright, eds 1987; Wilks 1989).

To anticipate the argument, it will be suggested that government-industry relations in the British motor industry are marked by elite insularity and an associated underdevelopment of institutional linkages. These general problems reflect, in turn, four abiding features of the British political economy, namely: respect for the autonomy of the firm; a 'weak state' tradition of public authority; an internationalization of industrial capital; and a lack of an adequate movement of industrial modernization.

In order to sustain this argument and to illustrate its effects the following discussion proceeds in six sections. First the motor industry is presented as a 'strategic' industry which demands attention from government; second, the argument of insularity is posed in a comparative context; third, a chronological section presents a survey of the orthodox view on what has gone wrong with relationships and with policy towards the industry since 1945. The fourth and fifth sections risk dichotomizing the relationship by looking, respectively, at weaknesses on the government side, and then on the industry side. The sixth section presents a concluding summary.

A strategic industry

Defined widely to include trucks and components, the motor industry has some claim to being the most important sector of manufacturing industry. Its importance is partly due to size. In 1984 it directly employed over 600 000 people and accounted for 5 per cent of GDP and 11 per cent of manufacturing exports (Rhys 1988, p 167). Just as important, however, is its integration into the industrial economy. It incorporates a myriad small and large factories across the country producing items as varied as glass, carpeting, steel and plastics. Several excellent studies have established the acccelerator and decelerator effects of changes in the level of economic activity in the industry (Rhys 1972; CPRS 1975; TISC 1975; Altshuler et al 1984). Hence the industry has been an essential component of economic growth, a component that has also been recognized in the policies of countries such as West Germany, Spain, Japan and South Korea.

What must also be emphasized is that the motor industry is a 'new', high tech, high value-added industry. The smokestack/sunrise distinction often made between mature and new industries can be seriously misleading and it would be gross error to consign the motor industry to the declining category. In areas such as automated production, the development of innovative labour utilization techniques, use of industrial robots, silicon chips, new materials and computer aided design the motor industry is at the forefront. In Rhys' (1988, p 178) terms it is a 'new infant industry', in the words of Jones and his colleagues it is 'dematuring' (Altshuler et al 1984).

The motor industry is important in yet another sense. It is an innovator and a model in the field of industrial organization. It is highly unionized and a pacesetter in labour settlements. It was the testbed for the age of mass production and for the associated managerial strategies that have appropriately been labelled 'Fordism'. It is becoming an equivalent model for the dissemination of Japanese production techniques such as 'just-in-time', 'total quality', and egalitarian factories (see Wickens 1987). Similarly, the multi-divisional company and associated management philosophies owe much to the experience of Alfred Sloan at General Motors. These dimensions feed in to the industrial culture and the policy making process. The influence could be symbolized by the interaction of Terence Beckett as Director General of the CBI in the mid-1980s with Moss Evans, General Secretary of the TGWU. The former had made his career with Ford, the latter came up through the union as the motor industry negotiator. Their attitudes and priorities reflected their motor industry experience.

This salience of the motor industry creates difficulties for government. The success or failure of the industry is extremely important for many interests and many areas of the country. Moreover, the car industry produces a consumer product with relatively volatile demand, characteristics which are easily understood and overtones of national prestige. Everyone is an expert on the motor industry and many are also chauvinistic.

It could not be said either that government's dealings with the industry, or the industry itself, represents a postwar success story. Indeed, the decline and collapse of the British-owned motor industry since 1945 is both grotesque and scandalous.

Here again, study of the motor industry is instructive since it helps to illuminate some of the wider causes of the relative postwar decline of British industry. The statistics in Table 9.1 perhaps tell their own story but the figures are by now fairly familiar and are dulled by repetition. The decline is nevertheless so dramatic, the opportunities missed so attractive, that they deserve constant emphasis. In Wood's (1988, pp 1–2) words, 'Britain had Europe's second largest motor industry until 1932 when she overtook France and remained in this pole position until 1955. In 1950 Britain moved ahead of America to become the world's largest exporter of motor vehicles and when, in 1968, the indigenous industry combined to form the British Leyland Motor Corporation, it was fifth in world terms behind the American big three and Volkswagen.' Yet by 1988 the UK had slipped to seventh in the world production league table. On the trade front, car trade went into deficit in 1973, commercial vehicles in 1977 and total motor trade (including components) in 1982. The House of Lords (1985) identified the motor industry as having the worst deterioration in its trade balance of any sector of industry and the 1986 deficit stood at £3.9 billion. Until very recently optimists could point to a strong truck industry to compensate for decline in cars. Here the decline is more recent and equally spectacular. To quote Rhys (1988, p 167) 'over a relatively short period between 1974 and 1987 the UK heavy commercial vehicle industry went from a position of strength to the verge of near extinction'.

It is usual, consciously or not, to analyse relations between government and industry in a normative context of the most suitable conditions for industrial competitiveness. Before conforming entirely to that approach it is worth making a

Table 9.1   Postwar performance of the British Motor Industry

	UK production of cars '000	% world total	UK production of CVs '000	% world total	UK exports % world total	
					cars	CVs
1947	287	7.0	155	9.6		
1951	476	8.2	258	12.2	44	30
1957	861	9.0	288	14.2	29	26
1960	1354	11.4	458	18.6	24	26
1967	1552	9.4	385	9.1	16	26
1974	1534	7.5	403	6.1	8.8	10.6
1977	1328	5.0	386	4.5	5.9	9.0
1981	955	4.1	230	3.0	4.1	3.3
1984	909	3.5	225	2.4	2.5	2.9
1986	1019	3.6	229	2.2	2.1	1.7

Source: SMMT, *The Motor Industry of Great Britain*, various issues. Note: figures include the main producing countries only

corrective sociological and normative diversion. One can detect a vein of ambivalence about the motor industry within British society. If British culture is imbued with an 'anti-industrial spirit' then the combination of images which the motor industry has presented could be expected to invoke that spirit. From its origins in bicycle repair workshops, its association with greasy-handed mechanics, with shifty car salesmen and brash overpaid workers the industry has appeared less than respectable. Historically the companies were profoundly anti-intellectual. Morris, Lord Nuffield, 'even went so far as positively to discriminate against graduates' and when Ford introduced their graduate recruitment policy in 1948 it was considered revolutionary (and was not emulated) (Wood 1988, pp 94, 113). Neither Birmingham nor Oxford (God forbid!) ever became 'Motown', Coventry was perhaps the nearest British equivalent and David Lodge nicely encapsulates the image of Midlands vulgarity in his cameo of 'the cocktail bar of the Ritz, Rummidge's best hotel, on a Saturday night, when the car-workers gathered with their wives and girl friends for the conspicuous consumption of alcohol. However high the hotel pegged its prices in an effort to maintain a classy atmosphere, the car workers could match them' (Lodge 1975, p 202). The point has also been made that between the wars 'engineering was not a proper occupation for a gentleman' (Wood 1988, p 89) but on the other side of the political and social divide there was some question about whether making cars was a proper occupation for a socialist.

On the left of the Labour Party and among the more radical elements of the workforce there has always been an awareness that as a product cars are both inegalitarian and harmful. The motif of production for need rather than profit inspired a series of 'alternative plans' for vehicle companies in the mid-1970s. The ideological critique of the industry was bolstered by revelations of the dismal life on the shop floor as portrayed in Beynon's (1973) brilliant *Working for Ford*, which encouraged a more critical and adversarial stance among union activists.

This British ambivalence about the worth of the modern motor industry might be expected to resurface in the environmental context over the next decade. The contemporary motor car is expensive and absurdly oversophisticated. Its mass use generates serious pollution, impossible congestion and an horrific toll of death and injury. The industry as a whole is irresponsibly profligate with scarce raw materials and the car itself has become in Hirsch's (1977) terms a 'positional good' – the more you have the less use they are. As a means of transport in an urban environment the private car is simply unsuitable. Nevertheless, after the post oil-shock disillusionment of the mid-1970s the motor industry is again in optimistic mood. Industry studies anticipate that the industry will develop relatively unchanged into the twenty-first century (see Altshuler et al 1984) and it is not at present apparent that any serious studies in government or the industry anticipate moves towards a more utilitarian, environmentally conscious industry within the next 50 years. This could be a strategic mistake. It is evident that short-term conservatism on such issues as pollution control might save money but hinders the longer term competitiveness of the industry. The motor industry will have to adapt to increased environmental concern. The sentiments expressed by Mishan in 1967 to the effect that 'the invention of the private automobile is one of the greatest disasters to have befallen the human race' (in Dunnett 1980, p 115) may begin in the 1990s to impact upon the industry.

It can be argued, then, that the motor industry is strategic. It affects the longer term development of the economy and the society and will have a material effect on governmental and societal aspirations. This is as a result of its size, its integration into the economy, its use of new human and material technologies and its salience in public debate. Hence its serious decline is, or should be, a cause for universal concern.

Discussion of government-industry relations thus takes place against a backdrop of decline. Many factors have been identified as contributing to that decline but in general the emphasis has moved from blaming unions to blaming management. As far as government is concerned some studies have come close to identifying adverse government action as the major culprit. Thus Dunnett (1980, p 13) argues that 'government contributed to the decline', while Bhaskar (1979, p 15) impetuously states that 'it has been successive and consistent government action which is primarily to blame for the poor state of the industry as a whole'. It is also argued by Conservative ministers that government has no role to play in reversing decline. Companies should provide their own solutions and government should strictly refrain from interference and contact. Both arguments, that government is to blame, and that government can do nothing, are equally fatuous. In contrast, the position taken in this chapter is that the institutions and culture of government made it impossible to define suitable policies for dealing constructively with the motor industry. The problem has not so much been the policies themselves but the government-industry relationship which produced them.

Insularity in comparative context

It is important not to be myopic when examining government-industry relations in Britain. In a number of ways Britain is exceptional but, since we are used to them, the peculiarities and occasional absurdities of British practices only become apparent when we consciously compare foreign experience. In the case of the motor industry foreign comparison emphasizes three important realities.

Firstly, it is clear that all countries with a motor industry experience regular and significant contact between government and the industry. Only in Britain does it seem necessary constantly to reaffirm that the policies and actions of government affect the motor industry at a variety of levels. To a Japanese or a German it is obvious that the existence and activities of government are constitutive of the conditions within which the industry operates. In Britain the view persists that government either is, or can be, detached from the requirements for industrial success. The problem then is to structure relationships so that government and industry communicate, and have some understanding of respective needs and interests. In Japan, France and Korea these contacts are routine, regular, informal and involve personnel movements so that it can become difficult to see where the state ends and the company begins. In Italy and the USA businessmen move into government, lobby, and present industrial demands with a weight that cannot be ignored. In the Federal Republic of Germany (FRG) relationships are more formal but entirely routinized (Streeck 1984; Wilks 1989b). It is difficult to judge how successful such relationships have been, but what is clear is that close governmental involvement has not inhibited the growth of such overseas motor industries.

The second point to be made from comparison is that every other major industrialized country has a motor industry of considerable economic importance. The Japanese growth is familiar and is being repeated by South Korea, whose car production is forecast to overtake the UK in 1990 (DRI forecast, *Financial Times*, 20 October 1988). For Europe, the figures are given in Table 9.2.

Table 9.2   The importance of the Motor Industry in Europe

	Automobile sector % of gross mfg value added, 1982	Car production 1988 forecast '000
West Germany	12.4	4 348
France	9.8	3 172
Belgium	8.2	292
Italy	7.1	1 858
Spain	5.8	1 464
UK	5.5	1 194
Total EC	8.7	12 454

Sources: *Eurostat A Series; Financial Times*, 20 October 1988

This introduces the third lesson from comparison. It is no longer possible to analyse government-industry relations in the motor industry in a strictly national framework. Analysis of the industry and its economics can be undertaken on a European basis but should properly include global factors. Supply, demand and competition need to be evaluated on a European scale. Model strategies and market shares are determined by reference to an increasingly homogeneous European market. Specific company strategies are also in Britain constructed by reference to global trends. Nissan and Rover/Honda are self-evidently influenced by Japan. Ford, General Motors/Vauxhall by the United States. Analysis of government and of policy can still be related to national concerns, and to this extent this chapter remains valid. But it also needs to be borne in mind that policy for trade and for the granting of state aid is becoming dominated by the European Commission while the proposed 1992 reforms will similarly equalize technical regulations and the fiscal environment.

The striking contrast between government-industry relations in Britain and the other countries discussed above lies in the profusion and regularity of contact abroad – in the *intensity* of the relationship; and in the absence of regular contact in Britain – the *sporadic* nature of the relationship. Each country has distinctive mechanisms or institutions of contact and information flow. Briefly to enumerate them, we can observe a grands-corps network in France where a former senior civil servant, Jaques Calvet (who was Giscard d'Estaing's directeur de cabinet when he was Finance Minister) can move to head not the nationalized Renault, but the private sector Peugeot/Citroen. In Japan there is a constant dialogue between companies and officials in the process that has been labelled 'consensus genera-tion'. In the USA businessmen move in and out of government with ease and there is plentiful access to government agencies through the so-called 'iron triangles' whose Congressional pole is open to industrial lobbying. In the FRG ministers are accessible to corporate executives while motor companies can also find open access through Land governments (such as Bavaria's sponsorship of BMW) and can enter the capitalist network through the big three universal banks. Also worth emphasiz-ing is the loyalty of the giant metalworkers union, IG Metall, which can be relied upon to represent the interests of the industry in the councils of the SPD (see Markovits 1986). Italy is different again but there can be no doubt about the influence of FIAT within the state or the willingness of ministers to consult with its senior management. FIAT has, of course, been represented as a second, and periodically more powerful, government of Italy to whom ministers defer (see the 'exposé' by Friedman 1988, chapters 6, 8, 10).

The brief comments above are unavoidably superficial but they present a picture of intense contact seen overseas which contrasts with a relationship in Britain of distance punctuated by crisis engagements. Various institutional devices have been introduced to establish a regular, structured contact: in particular the National Advisory Council (1946–47); the Economic Development Committee (Motor Manufacturing EDC, 1967–71); the Industrial Reorganisation Corporation (IRC, 1964–70); the Motor Industry Tripartite Group (1976–80); and the National Enterprise Board (NEB, 1974–84). All the indications are that such groups have met erratically and commanded a low level of commitment from officials and the companies. Their existence has been symbolic of a recognition of the need to communicate without answering that need. Similarly leaders of companies do of course talk, on a bilateral basis, to ministers and senior officials. The frequency and content of such meetings are rarely revealed but again the available evidence indicates that they are infrequent, exceptional, uninfluential and almost 'diplo-matic' in their caution. One of the few worthwhile insights is provided by Michael Edwardes' autobiography. He carefully and professionally cultivated relations with Whitehall. Ministerial contact included a dinner between the BL Board and a ministerial team at Number Ten in October 1980 which 'became the focus of the Prime Minister's resentment, it was probably counter-productive and was not repeated'. More interesting was Edwardes' unique innovation in securing the secondment of a DoI Principal to BL in 1979. He makes clear how useful this was. 'Information could be exchanged or draft letters cleared informally without establishing precedents or commitments. It also contributed to establishing rela-tionships with other departments' (Edwardes 1983, pp 230, 218). Edwardes' links with government were exceptional. The usual model has been a polite, distant formality attended by mutual incomprehension.

The striking feature of institutional structure and behaviour in Britain is therefore their insularity. This operates at many levels and goes well beyond government and industry. Three examples are illustrated. The relationship between financial institutions and industrial corporations is cautious, instrumental and arm's-length. Banks and the City are disinterested lenders and shareholders with minimal involvement in management and investment decisions. This general syndrome is widely accepted and its origins and effects have recently been analysed by Ingham (1984). In the motor industry the situation may have been a little different between the wars. For instance, the Manchester and Liverpool District Banking Company reorganized the Leyland Board in 1922 (Turner 1971, p 17), and the Midland Bank put a receiver into Austin in 1921 and two men on the Board in 1922 (Wood 1988, pp 45, 47). Postwar, however, the industry has been consistently under-capitalized and there has been no similar experience of involvement by the clearing banks. Indeed, their appearance on the scene has chiefly been to precipitate crises through withdrawal of overdraft facilities (as with BLMC in 1974 and Chrysler UK in 1975), and to demand loan guarantees.

A second example is provided by the relationship between companies and unions. The motor industry unions have consistently regarded the employers with intense suspicion, which has been amply reciprocated. The 'us and them' mentality so widely deprecated as an expression of the British class system has meant that management and unions have fought over the distribution of the existing cake without, as happens in the FRG, Japan, and even the USA, orienting themselves to increasing the size of the cake. Opportunities for a more conciliatory or constructive union posture have been reduced by the proliferation of competitor unions. Rhys (1972, p 445) cites 36 unions in BLMC, 22 in Ford. Discipline within the big unions has been weak. In the motor industry the shop floor has always had great independence and during the 1960s and 1970s the shop steward movement exerted that independence, sometimes in defiance of their national leadership. The inability of the unions to 'deliver' the cooperation of their members is notable and is, of course, inconsistent with corporatist interpretations. Thus the TGWU was all in favour of the Ryder Plan for BL and its Deputy General Secretary was a member of the Ryder team, but the union found it impossible to secure the labour peace which the plan required.

The roots of union intransigence should not be misunderstood. It has not been due to simple bloody-mindedness on the part of management or workers but has been built into the very system of industrial organization. In this respect Britain remained the 'workshop of the world' rather than the 'factory' of the world. Workers, individually and in groups, were allowed considerable autonomy over the work process in respect of work rate, short-term planning, work methods and work allocation. To take an exaggerated comparison one could draw a parallel with the 'putting out' system employed in the early days of the textile industry where work was subcontracted to individuals or groups outside the employer's premises. Such workers would do the job in their own way and in their own time. It was almost as if a similar system had been perpetuated within the car factories from the twenties and onwards. The system rested upon craft unionism, 'mutuality' in the introduction of changes on the shop floor and the 'piece work' method of payment which continued in parts of BL until 1974. The resulting system of factory organization could be termed 'self-regulation', which is the term used by Lewchuck (1987, p 110) in his excellent study of the industry. The system worked relatively well in periods of growth and labour cooperation during and immediately after the war but it created a crisis in the philosophy and competence of management by the 1960s. Ford had always paid fixed rates and operated an assertive American-style management system. John Barber, who joined Leyland from Ford in 1967, recalls that piecework 'enabled management to abdicate . . . once a man is paid piecework he is going to earn enough money to live on so you don't have to "manage" him, it's a sort of self-managing but, inevitably, if he'd finished his quota by three o'clock in the afternoon, he would go home' (Barber quoted in Wood 1988, p 179). Thus we have the paradox that unions were actually performing a managerial task at the factory floor level but were persistently excluded from management at middle or higher levels. British industry has strenuously resisted worker participation or a works council system on the German model.

A third area of insularity lies in the relationships between the firms themselves. As far as defining common interests goes, and representing such interests to government, British industry is typically weak. Leys (1985, p 14) has argued that 'for more than a century and a half British capital has been weakly represented both politically and bureaucratically'. The argument has been developed by Grant with Sargent (1987), who emphasize the fragmentation of collective organization of capital, the difficulty of reconciling diverse interests and the hesitancy of the CBI. The motor industry is represented by the Society of Motor Manufacturers and Traders (SMMT) which is a large, relatively well resourced and well regarded lobbying organization. But the SMMT is essentially a clearing house. Its ability to articulate the interests of the British industry is restricted by the fact that it represents importers as well as manufacturers and by its adamant refusal to discuss individual companies. In practice, the large companies all deal bilaterally with government which is to be expected considering their ownership structure. The industry is now owned by American, Japanese, Dutch, Swedish and French companies. Their interests are defined by an extra-national company network and there is a reduced incentive for them to organize on a British basis.

Elsewhere, the argument has been developed that the government shares this syndrome of insularity (Wilks 1986, 1988). The combination of 'elite insularity', the *immobiliste* effect of frequent changes in party government, and the secretive, essentially liberal traditions of the British civil service have produced a government machine which has been broadly disinterested in the fortunes of the British motor industry. 'Government policies have at times imposed additional burdens on the motor industry and government had failed in the more important task of providing leadership and reform. But the main indictment is that government as a system has lacked awareness, has pursued policies which almost accidentally have harmed the industry and has operated irresponsibly where a real responsibility for the national interest existed' (Wilks 1988, p 273). We can go on to review the experience of government-industry relations since 1945 to illustrate the origins, forms and effects of this insularity.

The relationship in practice

An orthodox critique has developed of the form and inadequacies of policy for the British motor industry since 1945. An elaborate exegesis is not possible in the space available but an indicative summary can be undertaken. The substance of the critique is important in its own right but it is also important to appreciate that the level and style of government-industry relations has changed quite drastically, and that policy issues have similarly altered. Only by appreciating the discontinuities can we properly identify any underlying continuities. Rather than take a complex politically or economically defined series of time periods, a crude attempt is made to take each of the five postwar decades.

Prior to the 1940s the government's relationship with the motor industry was almost entirely arm's-length and regulative, in complete conformity to the tradition of the 'night watchman state'. The two main regulatory provisions were the McKenna duties and the horsepower tax. The McKenna duties were introduced in 1915 to protect the British industry from American imports. They were set at 33⅓ per cent on cars and, except for a break in 1924–25, remained in effect until 1967 providing a protected home market. The horsepower tax introduced in 1909 was revised in 1921 to a rate of £1 per annum per horsepower; the calculation of horsepower depended on a 1906 RAC formula which emphasized the base (width) of the cylinders. The tax therefore encouraged the production of low powered, long stroke engines which were unpopular abroad (the small cylinder diameter necessitated a long piston stroke which produced an engine which was inefficient and highly stressed at high speeds over long distances). The horsepower tax was abolished in 1947 in favour of a flat rate tax which ironically discouraged the smaller cars which at that time were exactly what was needed to meet demand from poor, war-torn Europe. The effect of the two measures was to produce a protected, inward looking motor industry with few prewar exports and no commitment to exporting.

This *laissez-faire* relationship was superseded by the war. The first detailed intervention came in 1936 when the industry was invited to participate in the shadow factory scheme and throughout the war motor factories were essential to the war effort. The companies were integrated into the planning network of the Ministry of Supply and the labour mobilization schemes of the Ministry of Labour.

In the immediate postwar period the industry was incorporated into the overwhelming priority of the export drive. In this it was outstandingly successful. By 1950 66 per cent of British car production was exported. In order to secure exports the government set export quotas and then allocated raw material supplies, especially sheet steel, to those who met their quotas. There were two drawbacks to this policy. First, exports were made in a spirit of short-term opportunism. It was a global seller's market; every car made could be sold with little regard to quality and after sales support. There is widespread agreement among students of the industry that very little attempt was made to serve the customer, to establish customer loyalty or to build up a decent distribution network. The wrong cars were exported to the wrong countries in the wrong spirit. This encouraged a continuing disdain for questions of quality and delivery and there also resulted a legacy of distrust and dislike of British products which has handicapped the export effort ever since.

The second drawback of the export policy was that industrial structure was frozen. Instead of a rationalization of the industry the quota system 'supported the weak and outdated manufacturers at the expense of the more efficient' (Dunnett 1980, p 35). As can be seen from Table 9.3, in 1950 8 per cent of total production

Table 9.3   Share of car production by company 1945–86 (percentage)

	Austin	Nuffield	Standard	Ford	Vauxhall	Rootes	Others	Total ('000)
1946	23	20	11	14	9	11	12	219
1947	17	27	9	18	10	10	9	287
1950	17	22	11	19	9	14	8	523
	BMC							
1955	39		10	27	9	11	4	898
1960	38		9	28	11	11	3	1 353
1964	37		7	28	13	12	3	1 868
		BLMC				Chrysler UK		
1970		48		27	11	13.5	0.5	1 641
1974		48		25	9.5	17.4	0.1	1 534
1975		48		26	8	17.9	0.1	1 268
						Peugeot		
1980		48		37	13.5	7	0.5	924
1985		45		30.5	14.5	6	4.0	1 048
		Rover Group						
1986		39.7		34.0	15.9	5.7	4.7	1 019

Notes: 'Others' covers the output of some twenty firms. In 1986 the largest were Jaguar, Rolls-Royce, Lotus (GM), Reliant and Nissan. The remaining firms were makers of either luxury cars such as Aston Martin and Bristol, or workshop built high performance cars such as Caterham and TVR. From 1985 'others' included Jaguar and from 1986 it included Nissan and Honda. From 1979 Peugeot made its UK-built cars under the Talbot name. In 1986 the Peugeot name itself was used.
Source: From data obtained from the Society of Motor Manufacturers and Traders (SMMT). Rhys, 1988, p 165

was still accounted for by small firms such as Singer, eventually purchased by Rootes in 1955.

These episodes provide the first examples of abiding features of the government-industry relationship. One such is the lack of technical expertise in government. As Dunnett (1980, p 36) commented, 'the government seemed unaware of the stranglehold their export policy had placed on industry structure'. He also notes the destructiveness of some aspects of that policy. For instance, since parts were not counted in the export quota, manufacturers were given an actual incentive to skimp on spares and service. A second feature is the obsessive desire of the civil service to treat all clients 'fairly'. This instinctive refusal to discriminate is a typical cultural trait of the British civil service. When applying natural justice in regulatory or social areas of administration it is laudable. In the economic sphere, however, fairness can be counter-productive. The opportunity to restructure the industry was not seized. Indeed, Rhys (1972, p 380) notes that 'reduction in steel quotas was never in practice used to force firms to export . . . firms failing to meet quotas were not penalised as governments were more afraid of being labelled unfair or as being cast as the prime cause of a firm's labour force being thrown out of work'. Thus we have early examples of the arm's-length relationship between government and industry preoccupied with notions of equity and respect for the autonomy of the firm.

Under Conservative governments after 1951 the remnants of wartime controls fell into disuse. The emphasis in economic policy moved away from microeconomic measures towards Keynesian demand management while the liberal economic policy establishment re-emphasized the importance of sterling and free capital movement. Although it was not immediately apparent, the government-industry relationship deteriorated badly as far as the motor industry was concerned. This was the beginning of the 'Stop-Go' era.

Much ink has been spilled over the analysis of Stop-Go economic policy. Most studies focus on the central policy actors in the Treasury and the Bank. Otherwise excellent studies, such as those by Samuel Brittan (1964, 1971), say very little about the practical impact of Stop-Go on individual industries; they deal in aggregates. They reflect, perhaps, the myopia of the times. As Pollard (1984) vigorously argues, Stop-Go had a devastating effect on investment, confidence and productivity. That effect was probably worst in the motor industry but the harm done was not officially acknowledged until 20 years later (in 1975, in evidence by the Treasury to the Trade and Industry Subcommittee, see TISC 1975, p 134).

In fact, put at its worst, demand management can be presented as deliberately destructive of the motor industry. The case as presented by the SMMT and quite widely accepted was that the Treasury was not unaware of the sensitivity of the motor industry to demand management. On the contrary, it exploited that sensitivity in the interests of preserving the exchange rate, and simply didn't care about the effect on the industry itself. Elite insularity taken to an extreme. In support of such a case it must be appreciated that motor cars are a consumer product which is susceptible to economic cycles and credit regimes. The cyclical expansion and contraction of the economy naturally affected the industry but the

Treasury went further and actually used the size and integration of the industry as a 'regulator' of economic activity. It achieved this mainly through hire purchase controls. Throughout the 1950s and 60s the Treasury manipulated demand for cars through the minimum deposit on hire purchase and the repayment period. Since most cars then and now are bought on credit these regulations had an immediate and significant impact. Extremes went from 50 per cent deposit with 24 months to repay in 1956 to 20 per cent and 36 months in 1961. The 'stop' phases saw actual contraction in motor vehicle production and it became apparent that 'demand for cars in Britain [was] cyclical with the rhythm conducted by the government' (*Economist*, 26 August 1961, cited in Dunnett 1980, p 91; for a fuller analysis see TISC 1975, particularly the SMMT evidence).

The 1950s also saw the creation of the BMC in 1952. Talks between Morris and Austin had begun in 1948 prompted by Ministry of Supply encouragement to standardize specifications and purchases. The government were not, however, involved in the eventual merger which, in fact, was an Austin takeover of Morris. Towards the end of the decade government influence on BMC and all manufacturers became more pointed as the industry expanded capacity and was obliged, under regional policy, to place its new factories in depressed areas. In 1960 manufacturers announced new capacity plans of 750 000 vehicles, creating 38 000 jobs in South Wales, Merseyside and Scotland.

The decade of the 1960s saw a move away from purely macroeconomic considerations towards a closer involvement of government with the structure and performance of the industry. The Stop-Go pattern of the 1950s continued but came into conflict with the indicative planning initiatives. The conflict was institutionalized between the planners in the NEDO and later in the DEA, and the Keynesians in the Treasury. Early in 1963 the NEDC approved the 4 per cent growth target and the motor industry section of the document saw 'no difficulty in providing the small additional physical capacity to meet the 4 per cent case' (NEDO 1963). The planning exercise encouraged further expansion of capacity but did not, of course, guarantee the demand. Through the Council and the Motor Manufacturing EDC the industry was able to express its needs and press demands upon the government, such as removal of trade barriers and provisions to enforce labour agreements. But while their demands may have convinced the planners they failed to make much impact on the Treasury nexus. This, of course, is a sub-plot of the great economic setbacks of the Wilson government associated with deflation and devaluation.

It did appear momentarily, however, that the case for a more stable, expanding home market was being taken seriously by the Treasury. After conversations between the Chancellor, James Callaghan, and the Chairman of Ford, Sir Patrick Hennessy, the government agreed to consider what could be done to ameliorate deflationary measures. A confidential Motor Industry-Treasury Joint Working Party was established. The group comprised eight civil servants (three Treasury) and eight company representatives. It met between September 1966 and November 1967. In effect the report accepted the harmful effects of discriminatory demand management but avoided any firm commitment to change policy. This perpetuated the frustrating stance of the Treasury which was one of resigned apology. Yes, they said, we know these measures are harmful but we really have no alternative. In a ludicrously apt piece of symbolism, the day after the Working Party Report was issued sterling was devalued and hire purchase controls were tightened on cars. The urgent totems of macroeconomic management had once again triumphed over the basic essentials of industrial investment and productivity. The home market stagnated and in 1969 was at its lowest level for seven years.

A more detailed involvement with individual companies took the form initially of acceptance of foreign takeovers. In 1960 the Conservatives agreed to Ford buying out its British subsidiary and in 1964 and again in 1966–67 Labour acceded to a two-stage takeover of Rootes by Chrysler. Both takeovers provoked considerable heart-searching and created a pressure to evaluate the future of the British-owned section of the industry.

In 1967 government's relationship with the motor industry moved on to a new footing. Both Tony Benn at the Ministry of Technology and Harold Wilson encouraged the merger of BMC and Leyland to produce a giant British motor manufacturer. The story has been well told by Graham Turner, who describes a dinner at Chequers in October 1966 to which Wilson and Benn invited Donald (now Lord) Stokes of Leyland, and Sir George Harriman of BMC. Discussions went on until well after midnight. 'The Chequers meeting created a profound impression on both men. . . . Now the Prime Minister had asked and they had both publicly committed themselves to the view that a merger would be good for the country. . . . "When the Prime Minister asks," said Harriman, "it's not a good thing to say no. After Chequers I did feel an extra compulsion to go ahead" ' (Turner 1971, p 122). The merger came to fruition in 1967 and was blessed with a dowry in the form of a £25 million loan from the IRC.

Three changes followed from the government intervention in the merger which created British Leyland. Firstly, Britain now had a national champion backed by the government. Secondly, that backing was to take an increasingly visible form in a series of loans, grants and equity contributions that developed a momentum of their own. Thirdly, for the next 20 years relations with the industry were to be politicized. Senior ministers concerned themselves with the motor industry, that was natural. What became more remarkable was the close personal interest of successive Prime Ministers in the series of interventions and crises.

It would be futile to attempt to summarize relations between government and the industry in the 1970s and 80s. Too much has happened and the reader can look elsewhere (see Dunnett 1980; Williams et al 1987; Quinn 1988; Wilks 1988). One or two comments are, however, necessary.

Initially, it can be observed that macroeconomic policy was periodically just as destructive as it had been in the two previous decades. The Barber 'dash for growth' increased the home market by 60 per cent in 1972–82. The industry could not gear up in time and imports made irreversible gains from 14 per cent in 1970 to 27 per cent by 1973. At the other end of the cycle the overvaluation of the pound in 1980–82 crippled the BL recovery, decimated exports and encouraged the build-up of 'captive imports' by Ford and Vauxhall. By 1983, 23 per cent of the car market was being supplied by captive imports (for a damning critique see Jones 1985).

Perhaps more noteworthy has been the way in which detailed intervention by government obliged it to adapt institutions and methods, and reproduced tensions within the government machine itself. Under Labour the Ryder plan rescue of BL and its subsequent trials and tribulations became almost the daily business of government. Ministers became intimately involved in decision making and would visit individual factories to make appeals to the workforce. It has been argued elsewhere that the Ryder plan, the TISC Report and the CPRS Report, all published in 1975, constituted the basis for a government strategy for the industry. The Chrysler UK rescue and subsequent reactive policy-making dissipated that opportunity but did not prevent important developments within Whitehall. Those developments included the build-up of expertise within the NEB and the DoI, allowing a more considered implementation of policy. One could distinguish three strategies of implementation. 'Government has been prone to support products, plans or people – the "three ps" ' (Wilks 1988, pp 190–1). Thus government supported the product (the Metro), a plan (the various corporate plans) or people (Sir Michael Edwardes). Emphasis has moved from the first to the last and has remained with 'people' under Mrs Thatcher in the form of the 'corporate heroes' whom John Lloyd sees as bastions of 'the Disestablishment' (*Financial Times*, 19 July 1988).

The build-up of expertise within Whitehall was not, however, translated into reform of the administrative machine. The coalition of interests in the NEB, the DoI and the Regional Departments in favour of strategic intervention (perhaps something approaching a 'modernizing' coalition in current usage) was transient. The important dynamic at work has been the relationship between the party, ministers and civil servants. Ministers have become very involved with the industry and have carried their officials partly with them. But such has been the rapidity of change of government, at least until 1979, that the basic administrative machine was not reformed. It retained the same liberal, generalist, arm's-length and 'fair' characteristics remarked upon earlier. This is a syndrome which suggests analysis of government-industry relations on two levels. The first level is the rhetorical level of principles, ideological policy pronouncements made by party activists and by ministers. The stuff of manifesto politics. The second level is an underlying reality of pragmatic adaptation of arm's-length policy by civil servants raised in a liberal tradition. The disjuncture between the two levels I have discussed elsewhere in terms of 'doctrinal policy' (Wilks 1988, pp 36–41).

Doctrinal policy-making continued into the first Thatcher Government. Despite the free-market rhetoric, interventionism continued virtually unabated (see Wilks 1985). In the second and third governments the adversarial pattern was broken and administrative practice began to converge with ministerial rhetoric. Here a 'fourth p' was added to the implementation portfolio – privatization.

Privatization has, of course, been successfully undertaken in respect of BL. Jaguar in 1984, Unipart and Trucks in 1987 and the Rover car group in 1988. The irony has been that privatization has been used as a justification for making substantial grants to BL which would otherwise never have been tolerated. The government subscribed £680 million in new equity when Leyland Trucks was taken over by DAF, and £800 million, reduced to £469 million by the Competition Directorate of the EC, when Rover was sold to British Aerospace.

In one sense privatization represents the apotheosis of the insularity remarked on above. Ministers have shown disdain for BL and barely hidden their single-minded concern to transfer it to the private sector. The casual way in which BL was offered to Ford, its major competitor, in February 1986 was a startling revelation of the way in which the government had washed its hands of the British-owned portion of the industry. On the other hand we are at least seeing a conscious and deliberate, if minimalist, policy at work. The market-dominated pattern of government-industry relations rejects subsidy and intervention, and seeks to minimize regulation. Yet it does retain an interest in competitive performance. It might be expected that ministers and civil servants will become more accessible, if less influential, than ever before. Similarly, the constant challenge to managers to become more professional and to establish their prestige is undoubtedly addressing one of the central problems of the industry. Finally, the government has produced a more competitive and challenging market not only for Britain, but for Europe as a whole, by encouraging Honda and Nissan. The welcome and the grants given to the Nissan factory in Sunderland are the single most important factor in provoking the productivity revolution now sweeping the British motor industry.

Inadequacies in the government-industry relationship

As a means of summing up, we can enumerate some of the problems which appear to have characterized government's dealings with the motor industry and, vice versa, industry's dealings with government. The following ten points (five on each side) are selected eclectically for their long-term importance.

Government Firstly, we can note the consistent priority given in government to the 'high politics' of macroeconomic policy over the 'low politics' of company investment. This is a theme which stresses Treasury dominance of economic policy-making and a Treasury insulated from the more concrete world of manufacturing industry. The theme has, of course, been examined in Pollard's (1984) excellent polemic and is amply confirmed in the motor industry case. Whether it was Keynesian defence of the pound (1967) or pursuit of growth (1972), or monetarist reduction of the money supply (1981), macroeconomic policy has repeatedly, blatantly and seemingly unapologetically done damage to the motor industry.

A second familiar theme concerns the inability of the state to define or pursue a credible 'modernization strategy'. This is a phrase which has been increasingly employed by writers of the left working with the concept of the 'unfinished (industrial) revolution' (see Gamble 1981). They argue that pre-industrial, liberal or class values continue to dominate the political parties and the administrative organs of the state, and that they have aborted effective industrial modernization. Hence the state has failed to articulate values of industrial investment and efficiency, it has failed to give priority to industrial activities and its policies have disregarded questions of industrial structure, trade, organization and productivity. This is, of course, one strand in the British decline literature and it is certainly not contradicted by the experience of the motor industry. This perspective may be insufficiently subtle to explain why attempts were made to modernize, and how intervention became relatively routinized but the broad conclusions about 'anti-industrial' priorities and policies can be confirmed.

A third problem lies in the closed, secretive and regulative nature of the civil service. Higher civil servants have little training in, familiarity with, or, one suspects, sympathy for manufacturing industry. They are well aware of their lack of business credentials and in dealing with industry frequently appear neutral and aloof. Groups of officials in the NEDO, the CPRS and the NEB have been more technocratic and assertive but they have been outside the mainstream of Whitehall. Study of the motor industry would indicate that civil servants, even in the pre-1988 sponsoring divisions, communicate badly with individual companies and lack confidence and expertise in making such contacts. There is nothing surprising in this. Officials are recruited as generalists and are brought up in the regulative and defensive traditions of the service. The old Board of Trade which dominated dealings with industry until 1964 had the reputation of being 'the last true bastion in Whitehall of Manchester free trade liberalism' (Bruce-Gardyne 1986, p 58). Its more interventionist successors have been attacked by industry, disarmed by Conservative governments, reorganized by every government and favoured with some of the most ideologically controversial ministers of modern times (e.g. Tony Benn, John Davies, Sir Keith Joseph, Norman Tebbitt and Lord Young).

The machinery of government presents a fourth problem. Whitehall is organized functionally and is badly placed to coordinate the range of policies which impact on the motor industry. The SMMT has called for a more adequate coordination of policies between Trade and Industry, Environment, Transport, the Treasury and Regional Departments. A whole range of seemingly tangential policies impact on the industry. A singular example is the Home Office's preference for an annual registration suffix which helps the police identify vehicles. Unfortunately it also distorts the whole pattern of vehicle demand, boosting August sales, when factories tend to have reduced holiday production, and allowing continental factories to shift their stocks to Britain.

The fifth problem concerns the question of information flow and expertise. One of the great handicaps of government in dealing with the periodic crisis interventions has been a simple lack of information about the company and about the industry. This has been compounded by a lack of in-house expertise, the DoI has 'bought in' accountants, merchant bankers and industry specialists. Expertise can be built up. The annual monitoring of the BL/Rover corporate plan became quite sophisticated but on the whole government has neither the capacity nor the inclination to acquire an in-depth understanding. This puts officials and ministers in the hands of corporate management. Presentation of information can determine outcomes. Thus, according to Stokes and Barber, the Ryder plan for BL was directly based on an internal company document that was questioned neither by Ryder nor by the DoI (see Wilks 1988, p 99). The ability of corporations to manipulate government through control of technical expertise is a theme of recent French literature (Joannides and Wilks 1988). That is bad enough when dealing with indigenous companies but when dealing with multinationals it seriously prejudices the government's bargaining position. Bargaining on the basis of a company's corporate strategy can be an effective way of securing national interests (Wilks 1989b) but it demands a competence in the analysis of corporate behaviour.

Industry   The motor industry also exhibits a series of features which hinder its relationships with government. First of all, it has a long tradition of suspicion, if not hostility, towards government. The motor magnates of the prewar years were Conservative and fiercely independent. Postwar suspicion was fuelled by what the industry saw as clear discrimination over demand management measures and by the abortive planning experiences of the early 1960s. Motor companies had responded positively to the exhortations to expand, only to be confronted with high cost excess capacity when the economy was deflated in the second half of the decade. Pollard is especially emphatic on this point. He argues that 'business had learned to adjust to a low-growth, low investment economy . . . businessmen's reactions were the cumulative result of thirty years battering. . . . In holding back investment, innovation and enterprise they not only did what the government expected them to do; they did what the government expressly wanted them to do' (Pollard 1984, p 106). But understandably this did not endear government to them.

A second problem has been the absence of a solid management cadre within the British-owned firms. A prerequisite of information flow and discussion is not only civil servants willing to listen but middle and upper management prepared to talk. The management ability was simply not there. BMC had no product planning in the mid-60s and, amazing though it seems, BL had no budgeting system as late as 1968 (Wood 1988, p 194). Orr-Ewing, who worked for Ford and Leyland, is quoted by Wood (1988, p 245) as saying that 'The world of Ford and that type of British company (Leyland) is so utterly and completely different, we are not talking about Ford versus BMC or Ford versus Standard-Triumph, we are really dealing with the difference between Earth and the planet Mars'. Even in the late 1970s Edwardes was intensely critical of BL management. If that management had no plans, did not know what condition their company was in, or what options would be best for them, how could they communicate those views to government? Ford was very different. It had graduates, training, budgets and plans. Its alumni went to senior positions throughout the industry and it negotiated directly with government. It has a forceful government affairs department and has been the most successful and profitable company in the British industry.

A third problem is posed by the unions. The position of the union leadership has been ambiguous, especially under Labour governments. In this industry, unlike others such as pharmaceuticals, union cooperation is a necessity. Yet unions have been treated most erratically by government and have similarly varied in their willingness to become constructively involved in tripartite discussion. Briefly in 1964–67, and again in 1974–78, attempts were made to produce a tripartite consensus over policy for the industry and for labour relations. Such transient episodes constituted perhaps the closest the industry came to some form of corporatism.

Fourthly, the weakness of industrial representation deserves emphasis. It has recently been argued 'that business remains politically weak, making it difficult for government to enter into a partnership relationship with business even if it wanted to' (Grant with Sargent 1987, p 8). The motor industry provides both exceptions to and confirmation of this general rule. The SMMT is a capable pressure group but is handicapped by divisions within the industry. When there is common cause, as over expanding the home market or restricting Japanese imports, it can be very effective. The JAMA-SMMT 'voluntary' import limitation of 10/11 per cent has been in place since 1975 and is an essential prop for the industry. But over many issues there is no uniformity and SMMT can only transmit a consensus, it appears unable to create one. The activities of individual companies vary. Ford has defended its interests very successfully and has secured spectacular financial assistance for its UK investments. Similarly, BL has occasionally managed to secure all the trump cards and virtually hold the government to ransom. But at the level of routine day-to-day representation and influence there is less mutual understanding than one might expect. For the mass of the industry, including the big component companies, their interests are represented to government poorly and their views appear scarcely to be heeded.

The fifth problem is that of internationalization. With the exception of Rover all the British truck and car assemblers are now foreign owned. Their corporate strategies are international, their links are within the group rather than within the country, the major decision loci are abroad, they can survive without Britain. This means that the motor companies are responding to a logic beyond the comprehension of the British government, as defined by a corporate executive beyond the reach of British officials. Such companies have extraordinary competitive advantages. Vauxhall's sheer existence is due to prolonged and extensive subsidization by General Motors; Ford can 'captive import' half of its sales to enable it to capture market leadership and at the same time make windfall exchange rate profits; Nissan and Honda can draw on their parent facilities to introduce technically advanced vehicles at minimal research costs to their British subsidiaries. Conducting a relationship with such companies, if desired, is skilful and demanding. The final irony may be that the Japanese companies expect to talk to government, just as they do at home. It is possible that they will import their government-industry relations and begin to bring British officials into the final quarter of the twentieth century.

Conclusion

This chapter has used the concept of insularity to convey the way in which government-industry relations are underdeveloped in the British motor industry. We can detect both substantive and procedural insularity. The former refers to the way in which economic or political events in any one institutional arena fail to impact on other institutional arenas. Thus the profitability of City institutions is barely affected by the decline of the industry and the career prospects of civil servants are unrelated to their effectiveness in dealing with the companies. Procedural insularity refers to the actual mechanisms of contact, joint discussion and attempts to build up sympathetic networks of those interested in the industry. Such channels exist but are transient and marginalized.

The perspective of insularity and its manifestations discussed above will appear relatively familiar to the reader. Many general discussions of Britain's relative industrial decline have emphasized traits such as a liberal, regulative civil service; an arm's-length relationship between government and industry; the individualism and voluntarism of company involvement in government initiatives and the discontinuities of industrial policy-making in a two-party system. It is probable that a similarity between general diagnoses of the British political economy, and the experience of the motor industry, originate from the importance and visibility of the industry as stressed above. It cannot be emphasized too strongly that characteristics undoubtedly vary in other industrial sectors. Examination of pharmaceuticals, oil, or even food processing would almost certainly yield significant variations. Even within this industry we can also see variations over time.

In the period 1945–55, and again in 1975–85 government and the motor industry became far more closely involved with one another. The concept of elite insularity was inappropriate. During both periods the economic performance of the industry became so important as to break through the boundaries of insularity and create a political reaction. An alternative conceptualization is needed and for that latter period the idea of 'doctrinal policy' is useful. This emphasizes that the politicization of relationships which took place was misleading. Ministers made political capital out of the motor industry and there were some dramatic Cabinet disputes (e.g. over the 'rescue' of Chrysler UK in 1975 and the 'second rescue' of BL in 1981). In reality, however, the administrative machine dealt with BL and Chrysler to the best of its capacity without materially changing that capacity. Officials did not become 'involved', the firms retained their autonomy, and the keynote was the 'monitoring' of the government's financial involvement. In the early 1980s civil servants were pointing out that 'BL is still a plc' and therefore that, legally, government was just another shareholder. Thus relationships operated on two levels, the ideological and the routine, the ministerial and the bureaucratic, the ministerial level having limited impact on bureaucratic procedures. Successful privatization of BL has brought this period to an end. It is fascinating to see how the Conservative Governments have returned government-industry relations to the historical certainties of a liberal, arm's-length posture and have re-created conditions of elite insularity. To what extent insularity continues to be reproduced depends on how successful Lord Young becomes in making the DTI more managerial and accessible to industry. Scepticism is in order.

Describing relationships is one thing, explaining them is more demanding. Why are relationships underdeveloped and institutions insular? We can conclude by briefly reintroducing the four points which were mentioned in the introduction and have recurred repeatedly in the body of the discussion. Each of these explanatory points are interrelated, all deal with historically derived attitudes which have been perpetuated in contemporary institutions, expectations and laws.

The autonomy of the firm is a first explanation for the insularity of relationships. The legal and behavioural individualism of large British companies is striking. In general they can be bought and sold as commodities. They have ownership independence from banks and the City; they have decision-making independence from their workers, the government and fellow companies. Government respects this autonomy and builds it into its dealings with companies. A 'weak state' tradition of public authority provides a second explanation. By this we mean a tradition of equality before the law and voluntarism in public affairs. The civil service, or government, does not embody a sense of national destiny as in the 'state-centred' traditions of West Germany, France or Japan. Hence businessmen have no natural inclination to defer to government or to automatically accept the guidance of officials. The 'fairness' referred to above reflects this traditional norm.

The third explanation arises from the long-standing internationalization of British financial and industrial capital. It is clear that British finance capital is global but industrial capital is also proportionately the most internationalized in the world. To this extent British big capital has been 'de-nationalized'. Industrial success rests as much on market success outside as within Britain. Relations with the British government become more problematic and less important. The discussion above emphasizes the progressive internationalization of the British motor industry.

The fourth explanation lies in the British two-party system and in the nature of the parties themselves. There has been in Britain a reluctance to face up to the need to modernize the economy and the institutions of the state. This has rested upon a failure of political leadership which in turn emphasizes the role of the parties. The way in which the Conservative and Labour parties have maintained ideologically polarized perspectives on industry (market versus planning) has helped to politicize dealings with the motor industry. It is at the root of the doctrinal policy syndrome discussed above. But this factor is part of a far wider weakness of institutional capacity affecting the British political economy. As such it provides gloomy portents. If one were to look for a model on which British industry could base its recovery one would look neither to the motor industry nor to the government–industry relationships to which it has been subject.

Acknowledgement

The author wishes to acknowledge the financial assistance of the ESRC.

References

Altshuler, A. et al. *The Future of the Automobile*, Allen and Unwin, London 1984
Beynon, H. *Working for Ford*, Penguin, Harmondsworth 1973

Bhaskar, K. with Rhys, G. *The Future of the British Automobile Industry*, Kogan Page, London 1979

Brittan, S. *The Treasury Under the Tories*, Penguin, Harmondsworth 1964

Brittan, S. *Steering the Economy*, Penguin, Harmondsworth 1971

Bruce-Gardyne, J. *Ministers and Mandarins*, Sidgwick and Jackson, London 1986

CPRS. *The Future of the British Car Industry*, Central Policy Review Staff, HMSO, London 1975

Dunnett, P. *The Decline of the British Motor Industry: The Effects of Government Policy 1945–1979*, Croom Helm, London 1980

Edwardes, M. *Back from the Brink*, Collins, London 1983

Friedman, A. *Agnelli: and the Network of Italian Power*, Harrap, London 1988

Gamble, A. *Britain in Decline: Economic Policy, Political Strategy and the British State*, Macmillan, London 1981

Grant, W. with Sargent, J. *Business and Politics in Britain*, Macmillan, London 1987

Hirsch, F. *The Social Limits to Growth*, Routledge, London 1977

House of Lords. *Report from the Select Committee on Overseas Trade*, Session 1984–85, HCP 238, HMSO, London 1985

Ingham, G. *Capitalism Divided? The City and Industry in British Social Development*, Macmillan, London 1984

Joannides, C., Wilks, S. 'Bringing the firm in to the comparative study of government-industry relations', paper to a Conference on *Politiques Publiques Comparées*, University of Grenoble, 1988

Jones, D. *The Import Threat to the UK Car Industry*, SPRU, Brighton 1985

Lewchuck, W. *American Technology and the British Vehicle Industry*, Cambridge University Press, Cambridge 1987

Leys, C. 'Thatcherism and British manufacturing: a question of hegemony', *New Left Review*, 1985, vol. 15, May/June

Lodge, D. *Changing Places*, Penguin, Harmondsworth 1975

Markovits, A. *The Politics of the West German Trade Unions*, Cambridge University Press, Cambridge 1976

NEDO. *Growth of the UK Economy 1961–66*, NEDO, London 1963

Pollard, S. *The Wasting of the British Economy: British Economic Policy 1945 to the Present*, 2nd edn, Croom Helm, London 1984

Quinn, D. *Restructuring the Automobile Industry: A Study of Firms and States in Modern Capitalism*, Columbia UP, New York 1988

Rhys, G. *The Motor Industry: An Economic Survey*, Butterworths, London 1972

Rhys, G. 'Motor vehicles' in P. Johnson, ed., *The Structure of British Industry*, 2nd edn, Unwin Hyman, London 1988

Streeck, W. *Industrial Relations in West Germany*, Heinemann, London

TISC. *The Motor Vehicle Industry*, Trade and Industry Subcommittee, Fourteenth Report from the Expenditure Committee, 1974–75, HC 617, HMSO, London 1975

Turner, G. *The Leyland Papers*, Eyre and Spottiswoode, London 1971

Wickens, P. *The Road to Nissan: Flexibility, Quality, Teamwork*, Macmillan, London 1987

Wilks, S. 'Conservative industrial policy 1979–82' in P. Jackson, ed., *Implementing Government Policy Initiatives: The Thatcher Administration 1979–83*, RIPA, London 1985

Wilks, S. 'Has the state abandoned British industry?', *Parliamentary Affairs*, January, 1986

Wilks, S. *Industrial Policy and the Motor Industry*, 2nd edn, Manchester UP, Manchester 1988

Wilks, S. 'Government-industry relations: progress and findings of the ESRC Research Initiative', *Public Administration*, 1989a, vol. 67, Spring

Wilks, S. 'Corporate strategy and state support in the European motor industry' in L. Hancher, M. Moran, eds, *Capitalism, Culture and Regulation*, Clarendon, Oxford 1989b

Wilks, S., Wright, M., eds., *Comparative Government-Industry Relations: Western Europe, the United States and Japan*, Clarendon, Oxford 1987

Williams, K. et al. *The Breakdown of Austin Rover*, Berg, Leamington Spa 1987

Wood, J. *Wheels of Misfortune: The Rise and Fall of the British Motor Industry*, Sidgwick and Jackson, London 1988

10 Scotch whisky: 1933–1988

Michael S. Moss

The record of the Scotch whisky industry in the last 50 years sets it apart from that of much of British manufacturing. Where other sectors can sometimes be characterized by declining markets, poor productivity, inadequate cost control, ineffective marketing and a lack of collective identity, the whisky industry experienced almost sustained export-led growth from the end of the war to the late 1970s. This achievement was not the outcome of past success, but of a long period of retreat and retrenchment. Although the distilling of malt liquor in Scotland dates back to at least the fifteenth century, the modern industry owes its origins to reforms in its legislative framework in 1822–23 and the invention of the patent still a few years later which allowed grain whisky (made originally from malt and unmalted barley) to be made continuously.[1] Soon spirit merchants began mixing the bland patent still grain whisky with the much more distinctively flavoured malt whiskies to produce prototype blends. The art of blending developed in the 1860s and 1870s with the establishment of many specialist concerns in Scotland's towns and cities.[2] The Distillers Company Limited (DCL) was formed in 1877 as a defensive amalgamation between the principal grain distillers to prevent over-production.[3] During the last 25 years of the nineteenth century, there was a great shortage of brandy and wines, due to the devastation of European vineyards by the phylloxera beetle. Spirit dealers looked to whisky to fill the gap left by the absence of brandy in the market.[4] Some began branding their product, building up a large worldwide bottled trade through aggressive marketing.[5]

The boom in whisky sales came to an abrupt halt at the end of the century, due to the changes in taste and overstocking.[6] The collapse in demand heralded a depression in the industry which was to last until the end of the Second World War. The background to this prolonged downturn was the Liberal government's budget of 1909–10 which imposed large increases in duty on whisky to help pay for its programme of social reform. Lloyd George, the Chancellor of the Exchequer, was a staunch teetotaller and believed passionately that whisky was the most dangerous of all alcohol drink.[7] When Britain did not achieve an immediate victory in the First World War, and the conflict became bogged down in a war of attrition, the government was quick to blame drink for having sapped the morale of troops. With the twin objectives of reducing consumption and raising revenue to help meet the escalating cost of the fighting, duty was greatly increased and, in the misguided belief that newly made whisky was injurious to health, regulations introduced prohibiting the sale of whiskies less than three years old and of more than 40 per cent alcohol by volume. Under these pressures, and with barley and other grains in short supply, production collapsed. During 1917, as a consequence of the German unrestricted 'U'-Boat campaign, pot distilling was prohibited altogether. Grain whisky was exempt from this ban because an important by-product was baker's yeast. The industry responded to these unprecedented attacks on its livelihood by forming the Whisky Association to defend it against further Government interference.[8]

Although output recovered in the aftermath of peace to replace stocks used up during the war, sales were sluggish, due to the continuing high rates of duty both at home and overseas, and the imposition of prohibition in the United States. By the mid-1920s the whisky industry was in crisis. After lengthy negotiations, DCL amalgamated in January 1925 with the three largest blending companies, John Walker & Sons, James Buchanan & Co, and John Dewar & Sons. Since 1917 DCL, under the able direction of William Ross, had made determined efforts to rationalize the industry by acquisition and merger.[9] By the time prohibition in America was repealed in 1933, DCL dominated the industry, running the majority of the most prestigious blending houses, all except two grain distilleries and about half the malt pot distilleries.[10] Output and sales increased sharply between 1936 and the outbreak of war as the world economy struggled out of recession. The best prospect for sustained growth in demand, was the American market, which had been successfully supplied during prohibition through off-shore agents in the Caribbean. This resurgence was short-lived; on the declaration of war, duty was increased and in February 1940 output was cut back by one-third on the preceding year's production by the newly established Government Committee on Brewing and Distilling. This decision came as a serious blow to most distillers who had already produced their quota by this time. Their remaining stocks of barley and other grains were requisitioned by the Ministry of Food and the men, thrown out of work, drifted into the forces.[11]

The Whisky Association immediately took precautions to conserve stocks by limiting its members' releases of whisky from bond for sale on the home market to 80 per cent of purchases in 1939. Further duty increases followed in April 1940 and, at the same time, the government encouraged blenders and distillers to export as much to the American market to help pay for badly needed war materials. The industry responded to this challenge by shipping nearly 7 million proof gallons to the United States in 1940, 2.2 million proof gallons more than the year before. With grains in very short supply, the patent distilleries all ceased production in 1941 and many pot distillers either went on to very short time working or closed. By 1942 there were only 44 pot distilleries working, less than half the number in 1939. Output collapsed to under 2 million gallons, a little more than a fifth of the total quantity of malt whisky distilled in the last year of peace. The industry, nevertheless, continued to be pressed to export as much as possible, shipping 7 million proof gallons in 1941, of which 5 million was destined for the United States.

Deeply troubled by the twin effects of the fall in production and the high volume of exports, the Whisky Association, early in 1942, restricted releases to 50 per cent of sales in 1939. By this time, with the advent of the lend-lease scheme, there was no longer the same pressure to export to earn dollars and shipments fell back.[12]

Any respite there may have been was short-lived. In the spring of 1942 the Ministry of Food expressed concern at the lack of supplies on the Home Market and threatened to force the industry to increase releases. The Whisky Association explained that supplies could only be raised if production was increased to replace stocks. The government responded by dampening demand by raising duty in the 1942 budget, pushing the cost of a bottle of whisky up by a colossal 60 per cent.[13] Later in the year, with the country's food supplies in jeopardy, supplies of grain for making whisky were cut off, and by the end of October 1942, all the distilleries were closed. In the face of this crisis the Whisky Association changed its name to the Scotch Whisky Association to identify explicitly with the Scottish distilling industry. Although the Association tried hard to fix retail prices in the home market, a black market developed in whiskies distributed by bottlers and wine and spirit merchants who were not members. There was another larger increase in duty in the 1943 budget in an effort to depress demand even further. By midsummer, with the war beginning to turn in the Allies' favour, the Ministry of Food asked the Scotch Whisky Association and the Pot Still Malt Distillers Association to review postwar prospects.[14]

Both organizations were firmly of the opinion that the industry would not be able to earn badly needed foreign exchange unless urgent action was taken to replace stocks. This plea fell on deaf ears and no whisky at all was made during 1943–44 as the government concentrated all its efforts on establishing the Second Front. It was not until August 1944, with the prospect of victory, that the Ministry of Food made a limited supply of grain available for distilling in the coming season. For its part, the Scotch Whisky Association and the Pot Still Malt Distillers Association undertook to secure the agreement of their members not to take advantage of the high unregulated black market prices for mature whisky.[15] Since June the Scotch Whisky Association had banned members from supplying stock to wholesalers and retailers who exceeded its permitted prices. The Association took even stronger action in October to curb the unregulated market by intervening in whisky auctions to buy all spirit offered for sale, irrespective of price. Not convinced that the trade would observe voluntary restraint when it came to placing orders for new make, the Ministry of Food fixed the price itself at the end of the year.[16] Further supplies of grains were released for distilling in January 1945 on the understanding that the industry would reserve a proportion of mature stocks for export. Thirteen grain distilleries were recommissioned during the season, producing 6 million proof gallons of whisky and 34 malt distilleries turning out 3.2 million proof gallons.[17] Knowing that lend-lease would cease when Germany was finally defeated, exports once more assumed a greater significance in government thinking. During April, only days before the peace, Winston Churchill, the Prime Minister, had lent his personal support to the industry:

On no account reduce the barley for whisky. This takes years to mature and is an invaluable export and dollar producer. Having regard to all our difficulties about export it would be most improvident not to preserve this characteristic British element of ascendancy.[18]

On this basis the Ministry of Food promised distillers in June an allocation of 300 000 tons of cereals, double the Pot Still Malt Distillers Association's estimate of postwar requirements made in 1943. Licences were issued immediately for the purchase of 130 000 tons of cereals. The likelihood of continuing favourable treatment was reduced by the election in July of the Labour Government, committed to improving living standards and tinged with anti-drink sentiment.[19]

By November 1945 it had become evident that the Ministry of Food had made wildly optimistic forecasts of the availability of cereals and the Ministry told the industry that, in view of the deterioration in the cereals position, it would not be possible to deliver even the 130 000 tons authorized earlier in the year.[20] The industry remained optimistic that this setback was temporary and made application to the Ministries of Works and Supply to release materials for the refurbishment of plant. Early in the New Year of 1946 the Minister of Food, Sir Ben Smith, brought unseasonal greetings when he announced a policy of 'Food Before Whisky'. Production was limited to three-sevenths of the make in 1939, forcing most distilleries to close for the remainder of the season. With demand rising and stocks falling, most blending companies and distillers were reluctant to raise releases to exporters for fear that, within three years, they would be unable to satisfy the custom they had generated. At home with releases still controlled, the unregulated market flourished and in June the Ministry of Food banned the auction of parcels of whisky. There was confusion about government intentions; many believed that the domestic market was to be curbed in order to raise exports to hard currency areas. The Scotch Whisky Association refuted such reports, maintaining that every bottle shipped abroad would be matched by a bottle sold at home. During October the Scotch Whisky Association met the Minister, who was unable to offer any cereals for the coming season because supplies barely matched the demand for feeding people and livestock. There was no alternative but for the Scotch Whisky Association, despite the promises to the customers, to cut back releases to the home market from January 1947 to 45 per cent of sales in 1939.[21] At the same time, the new Minister of Food, John Stratchey, announced a scheme for allocating grain for distilling in the future.[22]

In the face of the massive sterling crisis in 1946–47 the government once again looked to whisky as a major earner of foreign currency. Grain was only to be made available on the understanding that the industry would release stocks for export, principally to the United States. After negotiations with the Scotch Whisky Association, the home market was rationed to 25 per cent of sales in 1939 from May 1947. In a further move to reduce home demand, duty was raised by 21 per cent in November. Denied access to its domestic customers, the industry turned its attention to exports. During 1947 shipments totalled 6.7 million gallons with 3.9 million gallons going to the United States. This was less than John Stratchey had expected and he told the SWA that, unless there was a marked improvement, cereals would be diverted to cattlefeed to save imports. The SWA pledged the industry to releasing 10.5 million gallons of mature whisky in the coming year and immediately set about making it even more difficult for whisky to fall into the hands of those firms who refused to observe the regulations. After at times acrimonious discussion with the Pot Still Malt Distillers Association, it was agreed that the distillers would not sell any whisky until the customer had signed a pledge to observe the government quotas, not to sell stock before maturity and to maintain the prices fixed by the SWA. For its part, the government raised duty by a further 10 per cent in April and the following month cut releases on the home market to 20 per cent of 1939 sales.[23]

During 1948 exports fell just short of the target, but thereafter matched expectations. The government responded by making more cereals available which, in 1949, equalled the 1939 total. The export drive towards hard currency areas deprived other parts of the world, forcing many companies to withdraw from established markets. As elsewhere in the world, sales in the United States were handled entirely by agents who controlled the whole promotional activity, and often made badly needed funds available in the UK for laying down stock. By the 1949–50 season, there was sufficient barley available to meet the whole needs of the industry and in July 1950, the government abruptly abandoned control of purchases of home grown barley. The problem for blenders and distillers was to assemble sufficient funds to finance the refurbishment of plant and, more importantly, the laying down of stocks. Liquidity was further strained by a poor harvest in 1951, which drove up barley prices where they remained for over a year due to the refusal of the Ministry of Food to sanction imports which would have exacerbated Britain's deteriorating balance of payments. Output declined in 1952–53 before recovering sharply the following season.[24] This gain in production was achieved by the reconstruction and extension of existing distilleries. Despite the industry's crucial role as a foreign currency earner, such plans were hampered by the unwillingness of even the new Conservative Government to make copper available, as it had to be imported.[25]

The Conservative Government was, however, committed to dismantling control of distilling and sales of whisky. In August 1953, all regulations concerning home grown cereals were abolished.[26] Three months later, the system of agreeing export quotas to different overseas markets, particularly to the United States, were scrapped in return for an agreement that the SWA would administer a voluntary rationing scheme, giving greater flexibility, until stocks could be expected to be replenished in 1959. Distillers were free to import foreign cereals without restriction from 1955.[27] With the dismantling of direct government supervision, output advanced rapidly, leading to the construction of additional warehouses at nearly every distillery. A new grain plant was opened at the Ben Nevis distillery, Fort William, in 1954, and three years later Distillers Corporation-Seagrams Ltd of Montreal constructed the first malt distillery, Glen Keith, to be built in Scotland since the end of the nineteenth century. Seagrams had diversified into the Scotch whisky industry in 1947 through the acquisition of Chivas Bros, a small blending firm in Aberdeen. In the mid-1950s, Hiram Walker-Gooderham & Worts of Canada, who had constructed the Dumbarton grain distillery in 1938, purchased three malt distilleries. At the same time, National Distillers of America sold its whisky interests in Scotland to DCL.[28]

The passing of the Restrictive Practices Act in 1956 heralded the end of the fixing of prices for both new make and old grain and malt whiskies by the SWA and the Pot Still Malt Distillers Association, but not export prices of blend. The inability of the Association to maintain price discipline at home resulted in a rapid increase in the price of mature grain whisky during 1958 with the larger blenders including the DCL houses chasing all available parcels on the market. Three-year-old grain climbed to 41 shillings a gallon and five-year-old to 65 shillings, compared to a new filling price of 6 shillings and threepence.[29] Early in 1959 voluntary rationing came to an end and blenders and distillers were free in theory to sell their whiskies wherever they chose. In practice the industry was locked into the markets that had been nurtured since the war.[30] Despite declarations that the high level of duty in the domestic market imposed during the war was designed to dampen demand, the government refused to concede to the SWA's demands for a reduction to allow sales to recover now that stocks were plentiful. On the contrary, duty was increased in 1958, again in 1961, then every year from 1964 to 1966, and twice in 1968. Within a decade of relatively little inflation, duty doubled from 22 shillings and threepence to 44 shillings. Three of these increases were triggered by the so-called regulators introduced in 1960 to protect Britain's chronic balance of payments position and the value of sterling. These fiscal penalties, effectively, perpetuated the policy towards the industry established at the outset of the war.[31]

Exports continued to be orientated towards the United States where demand remained strong. Although there were hundreds of different blends on offer, marketing in America focused on 15 leading brands of which four had about 50 per cent of all sales in the 1960s. These prominent brands were 'J & B Rare' owned by International Distillers and Vintners; 'Cutty Sark' owned by Berry Bros & Rudd, the London wine and spirit merchants and blended by Robertson & Baxter of Glasgow; 'Dewars' and 'Johnnie Walker' owned by Distillers Company Limited. By the late 1960s the two DCL blends were overshadowed by 'J & B Rare' and 'Cutty Sark' which held some 15 per cent of the market each. DCL's weakness in the United States, which accounted for about 50 per cent of all whisky consumption, was due largely to the range of blends it was attempting to sell across the price range. The lower priced brands, often shipped in bulk to cut costs, earned insufficient margins to support effective promotion except through discounting and dented the company's marketing strategy for its premium products. By contrast, IDV and Berry Bros & Rudd concentrated all their attention on their two brands, both presented as light whiskies tailored to the modern palate and sold aggressively by their agents with targeted advertising and selective discounting. Other international markets were small in comparison and, with the exception of DCL's Johnnie Walker, no brand could claim worldwide appeal. Returns from exports to other countries were reduced by the increasing tendency to ship in bulk to gain penetration.[32] Total exports climbed from just under 10 million proof gallons in

1950 to a total value of £2627 million without any setback to almost 60 million proof gallons in 1968 to a total value of £176.55 million.

The second largest market outside the United States remained the United Kingdom which had traditionally been dominated by DCL brands, particularly Haig, Johnnie Walker, Black & White and White Horse. In the early 1960s, DCL ran into increasingly strong competition from the Glasgow-based William Teacher & Sons with Teachers, Seagrams with Chivas Regal, and Arthur Bell & Sons with Bells. The abolition of resale price maintenance in 1964 gave DCL the opportunity to strike back by cutting prices and offering across the board discounts. Since United Kingdom whisky drinkers were far more price sensitive than their foreign counterparts, a price war soon developed. The DCL's strategy was to use its size and the power of vertical integration to destroy the competition. In imitation of larger wine and spirit merchants, efforts were made from 1967 to streamline DCL's production and distribution with the aim of reducing the amount of stock wholesalers and retailers needed to carry. Shortly before the general election in May 1970, the majority of blenders increased their wholesale prices by £1.50 per case. DCL refused to follow suit and as a result captured much of the trade of their competitors. DCL relented during the summer but announced increases pitched below those of the rest of the trade. Not to be outmanoeuvred, their competitors restored the original price structure. By the end of the year it was widely reported that it was impossible to trade profitably at home. None of these tactics did anything to increase total sales of whisky which remained static due to the impact of regular increases in duty.[33]

The unprecedented growth in overall demand for whisky at around 10 per cent compound per annum in the 1960s, led the industry to forecast continual gains for at least a further decade. Production, particularly of grain whisky, was planned to generate stocks to sustain such expansion. Between 1959 and 1966 the output of grain whisky advanced from just over 41 million gallons to nearly 90 million gallons, largely achieved by the construction of three new distilleries – Invergordon on the Cromarty Firth, Girvan distillery in Ayrshire, and Inver House distillery at Airdrie. When complete these three distilleries had a combined capacity of about 20 million gallons a year.[34] Investment in new grain plant was encouraged by the shortages of mature grain that had forced up prices after the abolition of restrictive practices, leading to speculative buying from outwith the trade. When the new plants finally all came on stream in 1965, the price collapsed, falling from nearly £1.75p a gallon in 1964 to just 30p a gallon in 1968.[35] There was an even greater proportional expansion in malt production, but without such catastrophic consequences. Distilleries that had been closed since the interwar years were re-opened, like Glenturret, near Crieff, rebuilt in 1959–60, and Benriach distillery, near Elgin, Isle of Jura and Caperdonich distillery at Rothes, all reconstructed between 1963 and 1965. Four new malt distilleries were constructed – Tomintoul, financed by two Glasgow whisky broking firms; Tamnavulin, built by Invergordon Distillers; Loch Lomond distillery at Alexandria; and Glenallachie at Aberlour in Banffshire. Several established distilleries were enlarged.[36] Malt output rose from nearly 16 million gallons in 1955–56 to 51 million gallons in 1966. The price of 3-year-old malt steadied at £1.80p a gallon in 1969 and remained at that level until 1967. It slumped to £1 in 1968 and remained at that level.[37]

The more unstable economic environment of the early 1970s combined with changing consumer taste to prevent exports of Scotch whisky matching expectations. The United States market was seriously affected with a downturn in total sales from 1971 to 1974 and then a brief recovery followed by a further trough. During these years the top six brands enlarged their market, whereas the smaller brands that were bottled in Scotland were squeezed by a steady increase in shipments of bulk blend. The biggest threat to Scotch was not domestically produced spirits, but growing consumer preference for wines now being manufactured to a high standard in California.[38] The stagnation of the market that had been chiefly responsible for the rapid expansion of the industry since the war, forced whisky blenders to re-assess the potential of other areas of the world. In many countries customers and agents had been neglected in the headlong concentration on meeting the apparently insatiable demand from the United States. The DCL, which had maintained a semblance of representation worldwide, was able to switch quickly to other market areas, particularly central and southern America, Australia, Japan, Hong Kong, and the EEC countries.[39] Although sales of blend bottled in Scotland grew markedly in Japan, they were eclipsed by a massive increase in sales of bulk blend and malt which more than quadrupled from 2 million gallons in 1971 to almost 9 million gallons in 1976. Much of this bulk export was used as admixtures for locally produced whiskies. Expansion outside the United States ensured that exports maintained their upwards trend, albeit at a slower rate, to the end of the decade, moving up from 182 million litres of proof alcohol in 1971 to 277 million litres in 1978. Even the home market began to advance in line with other spirits, encouraged by a small reduction in the rate of duty between 1973 and 1975. Following further sharp increases imposed by the Labour Government between 1975 and 1977, progress was curtailed.[40]

In addressing the obvious latent demand in EEC countries after the United Kingdom gained membership in 1973, the whisky industry was hampered by the Commission's attitude to the long established system of sole distributors/agents appointed for different specified geographical areas. In return, the agent shouldered the burden of brand promotion and protection, and of financing stocks. The agent was left to determine the price structure to cover the cost of these services. When questions were raised about the legality of these arrangements, less scrupulous wholesalers in the United Kingdom, where price competition was severe due to the activities of the DCL, began parallel exporting, particularly to Europe and, to a lesser extent, to Japan. This action threatened to undermine the position of the leading brands throughout the world, as it allowed them to appear on the shelves at a discount to those sold by the recognized agents with their substantial overheads. The industry went to the European Court seeking ratification of the long established agency system under article 85(3) of the Treaty of Rome. Since the whole concept of parallel trading is fundamental to the EEC, proceedings were inevitably slow.[41] The DCL, which was most vulnerable, was unable to wait for the outcome and withdrew its leading export brand, 'Johnnie

Walker Red Label' from the UK market in 1977 and priced up its other labels. The effect was dramatic, with a sharp fall in market share, allowing independent blenders, like Whyte & MacKay and Highland Distilleries with its 'Famous Grouse' blend, to build their brands at home before setting their sights on export markets. It was not until 1983 that the Commission announced that a favourable decision would be made, but, even then, the industry had to wait a further 2 years for formal confirmation.[42]

The changing pattern of overseas and domestic sales in the 1970s was accompanied by structural changes in the industry. The Glenlivet and Glen Grant Distilleries Ltd, Longmore-Glenlivet Distilleries Ltd and blenders, Hill Thomson & Co. Ltd, amalgamated in 1970 to form Glenlivet Distillers Ltd. Seven years later Seagrams acquired the company. Sir Hugh Fraser's Scottish & Universal Investment Trust bought Dalmore-Whyte & MacKay in 1972 and added Tomintoul Glenlivet Distillery Co. in 1973. DCL took over Mackinlays & Birnie, owners of Glen Albyn and Glen Mhor distilleries at Inverness in 1972 and in the same year Invergordon Distillers Ltd acquired two malt distilleries. Increasingly, whisky companies found themselves part of large integrated drinks groups. Watney Mann, the brewers, purchased International Distillers & Vintners in 1972, before being absorbed by Grand Metropolitan later in the year. In 1975 Allied Breweries bought William Teachers & Son and Whitbread took over Long John International from the American concern, Schenley Industries Ltd.[42]

Falling prices and increased fuel costs after 1974 forced distillers to improve efficiency through mechanizing malting, better mashing, technique and insulation of stills. At the grain distilleries, malt drying was eliminated by using green malt direct and, instead of grinding maize, it was cooked whole. The green malt and cooked maize was then mixed and fermented and the resulting alcoholic porridge put straight through the still. Some distilleries adopted continuous mashing and began using high gravity mashes to reduce the amount of heat required in distillation. The process of malt whisky distilling changed less radically, but at many distilleries traditional open mash tuns were replaced by German Lauter tuns, which were thermally more efficient and gave higher rates of extraction of maltose than the traditional open tuns. Wooden wash backs were replaced by stainless steel to reduce risk of bacterial infection and new strains of yeasts developed to make fermentation more predictable. The whole production process was automated and controlled from central consoles, raising labour productivity.[43]

Weakness in current demand, coupled with soaring interest rates, depressed production of both malt and grain whisky. Malt whisky output reached a peak in 1974 of 204 million litres of proof alcohol, falling to 169 million litres by 1977. Grain whisky output peaked a year earlier at 272 million litres of proof alcohol, dropping to 195 million litres in 1976. This decline worried many observers, who believed that, by the early 1980s, when an upturn was confidently predicted, there would be a serious shortage of stock.[44] As a result, despite the financing problems, production was stepped up from 1977 for grain and from 1978 for malt. Total output for malt in 1978 exceeded the peak of 1974, and by 1979 grain production had come back almost to the level of the early 1970s. This recovery was short-lived as the recession at the end of the decade began to bite and companies could not mobilize funds to lay down additional stocks even if they believed demand could be sustained into the late 1980s. Output of both malt and grain whisky retreated sharply, collapsing by 1983 to their lowest levels since the end of rationing in 1959. Many distillers were placed on part-time working and the number of people employed by the industry in Scotland fell from 25 000 in 1978 to just under 18 000 by 1984. Some distilleries closed permanently.[45]

The recession in the world economy disguised underlying changes in consumer preference for alcoholic drinks, which was moving away worldwide from whisky towards blander style spirits and to wine. Overall, there was a decline in demand for all alcoholic beverages, partly through pressure on discretionary spending, but more significantly in the long term, in response to a revival in calls for temperance based on medical evidence of the consequence of immoderate drinking.[46] The industry took some time to recognize these factors, believing that the setback was due to economic rather than structural factors. This argument was given some credence by an upturn in sales in 1982 which encouraged the industry to predict growth of 3 per cent per annum for the rest of the decade.[47] It was almost certainly on this assumption that the Conservative Government did nothing to help the industry in the domestic market, continuing to raise duty in line with inflation and doing little to alleviate the burden of paying duty before income from sales was received. The government seemed content to continue the policy of holding up domestic prices to encourage exports, even though this was no longer either appropriate or necessary. Sales worldwide resumed their downward path in 1983 and the decline continued for the next 2 years. The industry lost confidence in predicting future demand and all the Distilling Sector Working Group of the National Economic Development Council was prepared to commit itself to in the autumn of 1984 was that sales were 'believed to be capable of recovering from their depressed level in due course, and the end of the present decade may see sales levels rise towards the peak level of the late 1970s'.[48]

With clear signals that there was a secular decline in demand worldwide, the industry re-assessed its sales strategy. The success of Highland Distilleries' premium priced 'Famous Grouse' in the UK market had demonstrated that well thought-out and targeted promotion could win market share as effectively as price competition. Others, including DCL, quickly followed suit, becoming more selective in discounting, concentrating their efforts on positioning their brands as far up the price range as prudent. This strategy inevitably led to the withdrawal of support for brands at the lower end of the market where returns were negligible.[49] Although some commentators believed that the sole agency/distributor system was the only way of achieving effective worldwide sales coverage, there were growing doubts within the industry about the continuing viability of the system, particularly since many agents/distributors were being assumed into large international drinks conglomerates.[50] The DCL was most exposed to such changes in ownership. During 1983, following the appointment of a new chairman, albeit from the ranks of the executive directors, there was a massive reorganization of DCL management. The outmoded committee structure was abolished to give greater individual responsibility and the marketing strategy overhauled with the recruitment of experienced staff to revitalize promotional campaigns. Early in 1984 Somerset Importers, the distributors in the United States of 'Johnnie Walker Red Label', was acquired, heralding a policy of direct representation in larger export markets. The underlying strategy was to raise the value of sales rather than as it had been in the 1960s and early 1970s, to shift bulk. By the end of 1985 there was plenty of evidence that DCL was not only earning higher returns, but also clawing back market share at a time when overall sales of Scotch whisky were falling.[51] Throughout the second half of the year there had been regular press reports that the Argyll Group, whose principal business was food retailing in the UK, intended to bid for the company. Egged on by the press, the Argyll Group made a formal offer on 2 December for the company that still dominated the industry with 40 per cent of sales worldwide.[52]

DCL rejected the bid outright on the grounds that the two companies were totally incompatible. The management was disappointed that shareholders and the institutions equivocated in offering support. The Conservative Government, wedded to its free market philosophy, refused to refer the bid to the Monopolies Commission, even though in its first year of office in 1980 a much smaller bid by Hiram Walker for Highland Distilleries had been disallowed after referral. Uncertain of their chances in a straight contest, the DCL board chose early in 1986 to recommend a rival offer from Guinness plc, which had acquired Arthur Bell & Sons after a tough fight the previous year. The attraction for DCL in Guinness was its expanding team of marketing and sales executives deployed in 26 of the largest export markets.[53] There followed one of the most bitterly contested and acrimonious takeover battles in recent times which seemed likely to set a new pattern in corporate behaviour. Guinness emerged victorious in April, but by the end of the year, serious questions had been raised about the legality of the bid. The Guinness board was reconstructed under a new chairman responsible for welding the two companies into an integrated international drinks group. Despite the extensive press coverage, or perhaps because of it, whisky sales were not damaged by the Guinness affair. In fact, worldwide they increased during 1986 and remained buoyant into 1987. This upturn was characterized by sustained growth in premium priced blend and single malts, and a decline in export sales of bulk blend and malt, either for overseas bottling or as admixtures to locally produced whisky. The outlook, however, remained confused. During 1987 Invergordon Distillers, with healthy profits and the potential of the Mackinlay brand acquired in 1985, was bought out by the management from Hawker Siddely, while Whyte & Mackay was sold by Lonrho, reportedly because it was not making an adequate return, to Brent Walker. Some analysts discounted the effect of medical evidence about the dangers of alcohol and suggested a squeeze on discretionary spending in the anticipated downturn would not affect sales. Others were less optimistic.

The performance of the Scotch whisky industry as a whole since 1945 stands in marked contrast to its experience before the war. Although much of its achievement in export markets resulted from government policy in the immediate postwar years, successive governments have done little directly to encourage sales or protect markets until late in the day. Policy, if it exists at all in a formal sense, is governed by engrained temperance attitudes that on the flimsiest of evidence, condemned whisky as far more injurious than other types of alcoholic drinks. This, combined with the use of the price mechanism to hold down domestic demand during the time of scarcity up to 1959, has left whisky bearing far higher rates of duty per unit of alcohol in the United Kingdom than imported alcoholic drinks, particularly table wine. Despite the undoubted success of the whisky industry, it has shared many of the failures of other sectors, particularly after the abolition of resale price maintenance in 1964, a preoccupation with buying domestic market shares at whatever price and the reliance on export marketing strategies using sole agents/distributors evolved in the age of slow communication but less appropriate in major overseas markets with the coming of transcontinental air services. Unlike many other UK industries it could afford these mistakes and a lack of developed government thinking because the labour force was small and dispersed and imported raw material costs relatively low.

Notes

1. Moss, M.S., Hume, J.R. *The Making of Scotch Whisky – A History of the Scotch Whisky Distilling Industry*, James & James, Edinburgh 1981, pp 69–74
2. Ibid., p 98
3. Weir, R.B. *The Distilling Industry in the Nineteenth and Early Twentieth Centuries*, unpublished PhD thesis, University of Edinburgh, 1974, pp 325–8
4. See, for example, Moss, M.S., *History of Robertson & Baxter, Wine and Spirit Merchants, Glasgow* (to be published 1990), chapter 2 'The biggest brokers: 1879–1894'
5. See, for example, Weir, R.B., op. cit., pp 498–560, for description of John Walker & Sons, John Dewar & Sons, and James Buchanan & Co.; Brian Spiller, *The Cameleon's Eye*, James Buchanan & Co. Ltd, London and Glasgow 1984, and MS statistical notebook of Sir Peter Jeffrey Mackie in the possession of United Distillers Group, Glasgow, showing sales of the White Horse brand, 1895–1923
6. Moss and Hume, op. cit., pp 133–6
7. Ibid., pp 138–9, and Wilson, R., *Scotch The Formative Years*, Constable, London 1970, pp 62–116
8. Wilson, R., op. cit., pp 168–242, and Ross, W.H., unpublished history of DCL, 1923, chapter XIV 'The Great War and its consequences to the company'
9. Wilson, R., op. cit., pp 430–42, and Ross, W.H., op. cit., chapter XXI 'The big amalgamation'
10. Moss and Hume, op. cit., pp 155–7
11. Wilson, R. *Scotch Its History and Romance*, David & Charles, Newton Abbot 1974, pp 75–7, and Weir, R.B., *The History of the Malt Distillers' Association of Scotland*, pub. priv., 1974, pp 110–11
12. Moss and Hume, op. cit., pp 162–3

13. Weir, R.B. *History of the Malt Distillers*, op. cit., pp 113–14
14. Ibid., pp 115–16, and Wilson, R., *Scotch Its History*, op. cit., pp 81–5
15. Ibid., pp 119–20
16. Ibid., p 121, and Wilson, R., *Scotch Its History*, op. cit., p 86
17. Idem, and Moss and Hume, op. cit., p 166
18. It has not been possible to locate this reference amongst the Government files at the Public Record Office, but it is quoted in Ross Wilson, *Scotch Its History*, op. cit., p 92
19. An account of cereals supply to the industry and by extension government policy towards Scotch from 1940 to 1950 is to be found in PRO MAF/75/14, Home Grown Cereals – Alcohol, 'Permanent Record of Operation', 1940–50
20. Weir, R.B. *History of the Malt Distillers*, op. cit., p 122
21. Ibid., pp 123–4, and Wilson, R., *Scotch Its History*, op. cit., pp 93–4
22. Described in detail in PRO MAF/75/14, op. cit.
23. Weir, R.B. *History of the Malt Distillers*, op. cit., pp 124–31
24. These events are described in PRO MAF/75/15, Home Grown Cereals – Alcohol, 'Permanent Record of Operation', 1951–54
25. See, for example, Moss, M.S., *100 Years of Quality – A Hundred Years of the Highland Distilleries Company plc 1887–1987*, to be published 1990, chapter 5, 1938–1959, description of difficulty of securing copper to repair the stills at Tamdhu at this time
26. See PRO MAF/75/15, op. cit.
27. Wilson, R. *Scotch Its History*, op. cit., pp 108–11
28. Moss and Hume, op. cit., pp 167–8
29. Roger Mortimer Research Ltd, *The Scotch Whisky Industry*, 1970, pp 6–7, 17–18
30. Ibid., pp 10–15, and Wood Mackenzie & Co., *The Distillers Co*, January 1971, pp 13–15
31. *Distilling – Scotch Whisky*, prepared by the Distilling Sector Working Group, National Economic Development Office, London 1978, sections 41–7, and Roger Mortimer, op. cit., 1970, p 13
32. Wood Mackenzie & Co., op. cit., 1971, pp 8–17
33. Roger Mortimer, op. cit., 1970, pp 13–14
34. Moss and Hume, op. cit., pp 168, 171
35. Roger Mortimer, op. cit., 1970, pp 7–8, 18
36. Moss and Hume, op. cit., pp 171–2
37. Roger Mortimer, op. cit., 1970, p 18
38. Wood Mackenzie & Co., *Scotch Whisky and The DCL. Growth Prospects Re-assessed*, July 1976, pp 13–19
39. Ibid., 23–4, and Wood Mackenzie, *The Distillers Company – Brand and Price Leadership*, 1979, pp 3–22
40. *Scotch Whisky in the '80s*, prepared by the Distilling Sector Working Group, National Economic Development Office, London 1984, pp 9–25
41. Ibid., pp 39–41, and Wood Mackenzie, *Scotch Whisky/The Distillers' Company – Facing up to the Challenge*, 1983, pp 52–3

42. Moss and Hume, op. cit., pp 175–6
43. These developments and others are discussed in detail in Moss and Hume, op. cit., p 179
44. See, for example, Wood Mackenzie, op. cit., 1976, pp 30–1
45. *Scotch Whisky in the '80s*, op. cit., pp 28–9, 43
46. Ibid., pp 24–5
47. Wood Mackeznie, op. cit., 1983, p 6
48. *Scotch Whisky in the '80s*, op. cit., p 147
49. Wood Mackenzie, op. cit., 1983, pp 60–2
50. Ibid., pp 68–9
51. *This is about the future of one of Britain's largest exporters*, circular by DCL, 30 December 1985
52. *The Argyll Offer*, Argyll Group plc, 17 December 1985
53. *Guinness is Good for Distillers*, Guinness plc, April 1986

11 The British government and foreign multinationals before 1970

Geoffrey Jones

I Introduction

This paper examines the policies of British governments towards inward foreign direct investment in the United Kingdom before 1970.[1] The subject is an important one because, arguably, the activities of foreign companies in Britain have been one of the few sustained success stories in that country's twentieth-century business history. If government policies can be shown to have substantially facilitated this multinational investment, it would represent a considerable achievement for industrial policy.

The growth of multinational investment in twentieth-century Britain has been striking. By 1900 a number of American and Continental companies had already established manufacturing operations in the United Kingdom. The 1900s and 1920s, in particular, saw a considerable expansion in such investments. By the Second World War some 240 American companies alone had established factories in Britain, and United States direct investment in British manufacturing had reached nearly £70 million.[2] Inward direct investment further accelerated after 1945, most of it before the 1960s originating from the United States. By 1963 foreign-controlled companies accounted for just under 10 per cent of net output of all manufacturing, 13 per cent of total UK capital expenditure, and 7 per cent of total manufacturing employment.[3] By 1987 foreign-controlled companies in Britain accounted for 20 per cent of net output, 21 per cent of capital expenditure, and 15 per cent of manufacturing employment.[4]

Although the measurement of the impact of foreign multinationals on the British economy raises complex problems, the few available studies of the subject suggest those firms had a net positive effect, at least up to the late 1960s.[5] This view has rested on a number of (partly interrelated) characteristics of the population of foreign companies in Britain. First, they had a long-run tendency to be concentrated in the newer and more dynamic business sectors. Before 1945, foreign-owned manufacturing companies were clustered in the fast-growing and/or high technology industries such as electrical engineering, telephone equipment, motor cars and domestic electrical equipment. A similar pattern prevailed after the War. In 1965, 67 per cent of the net assets of foreign firms in British manufacturing were in the technology-intensive sectors of chemicals, engineering, electronics, and vehicles.[6] Secondly, subsidiaries of foreign firms exhibited signs of greater efficiency than their indigenous counterparts. One analysis showed that foreign-controlled companies had higher rates of return on capital invested than domestically quoted companies in manufacturing in every year between 1960 and 1968: more significantly, rates of return within the same industry (especially chemicals and mechanical engineering) were significantly higher for foreign firms. The larger size of foreign subsidiaries was one significant influence in this differential.[7] Thirdly, after the Second World War foreign companies exhibited a higher export propensity than their British equivalents. In 1966 foreign-owned affiliates accounted for 12 per cent of the net assets of all manufacturing companies in the UK, yet they were responsible for 19 per cent of visible exports.[8]

Between the 1900s and the 1960s, Britain was an increasingly popular outlet for foreign direct investment. She received a significant share of world direct investment[9] and was a favoured destination for American companies. Table 11.1 shows

Table 11.1   Proportion of total US foreign direct investments (fdi) by area 1950–70 (weighted averages)

	1950–59	1960–69	% change
UK share of US total fdi	7.5%	10.3%	+37.3
UK share of US total fdi in Europe	47.4%	36.9%	−22.2
UK share of US manufacturing fdi	15.0%	17.0%	+13.3
UK share of US manufacturing fdi in Europe	56.5%	43.3%	−23.4

Source: Calculated from M.D. Steuer, *The Impact of Foreign Direct Investment on the United Kingdom* (Department of Trade and Industry, 1973), pp 204–5

that Britain in the 1950s attracted nearly half of United States direct investment in Europe, and over half of such investment in manufacturing. In the following decade these proportions declined, but the British levels nonetheless remained high. In 1950 American direct investment in Britain was £303 million (of which £194 million was in manufacturing and £44 million in petroleum). By 1969 American direct investment was £2983 million (of which £1898 was in manufacturing and £651 million in petroleum).

If one adds to this picture the substantial role that foreign-born individuals have played in certain British industries,[10] it can be seen that there had been a significant and growing foreign participation in British business over the twentieth century. This phenomenon offers one possible solution to the little-discussed problem of how the United Kingdom remained a major industrial economy in the twentieth century despite the chorus of complaints from some contemporaries and many later business historians that indigenous British entrepreneurs and managers were ill-educated, conservative and incompetent.

The remainder of this chapter discusses British government policies towards foreign multinationals. The next section examines very briefly the initial response to multinationals before 1945, a period when the broad outlines of future policy were formulated. The third section surveys policies between 1945 and 1970. The concluding section assesses the achievements and limitations of these policies and, in particular, asks how far the British government was responsible for both attracting inward investment and for its apparently positive impact on the British economy.

II British government policies towards foreign multinationals

There was no explicit British government policy towards foreign multinationals before 1945. Statistics on either inward or outward direct investment were not collected: the estimates for the size of American investment in Britain are all based on data assembled by the US government. Officials were aware that foreigners were establishing factories in the United Kingdom but this was not usually regarded as a matter on which the government needed a policy. Given that academic economists made no clear distribution between direct and portfolio investment before the 1960s – and that the actual word 'multinational' was not coined until 1960 – the lack of focus on the issue by policy-makers was hardly surprising.[11] There was certainly no general wish to discourage inward direct investment. Indeed, it is widely acknowledged that it was the introduction of protectionism in the interwar years which provided a major stimulus to the flow of multinational investment into Britain.[12] There is no suggestion, however, that this was anything but an unexpected consequence of the imposition of tariffs.

There were regular flickers of interest in the subject among the public and, sometimes, policy-makers. The American assault on the British tobacco industry at the beginning of the twentieth century provoked much public debate about an alleged American invasion of British industry. At the end of the 1920s there was another flurry of public anxiety about American takeovers of British firms. Various British companies, notably GEC, attempted to introduce provisions into their articles of association designed to restrict the voting rights of foreigners at shareholders meetings.[13] The Governor of the Bank of England, Montagu Norman, became concerned about this issue, partly as a result of complaints from the Federal Reserve Bank of New York about British discrimination against American shareholders.[14] On his initiative, a meeting was held at the Bank of England on 15 May 1929 between senior Bank and Treasury officials, which was probably the first and last time in the interwar years that the question of inward direct investment was systematically discussed within government (or quasi-government) circles.[15]

The May 1929 meeting is of particular interest because it articulated most of the main trends of British official thinking on foreign multinationals, which were to remain remarkably consistent over the next 40 years. Three points were made during the meeting. First, it was established that foreign direct investment in Britain was growing, and that it was 'undesirable' to interfere with it. The gains to the economy were held to outweigh any costs, although no empirical evidence was produced to support this view. Fears were expressed, however, that American-dominated industries might locate all their research and development activities in the United States. Secondly, it was held that any serious restriction on inward investment was highly risky because of the 'possibility of retribution by foreign countries and of its serious effect for the United Kingdom as a larger investor in foreign undertakings'. As recent research has made clear, Britain itself was the world's largest multinational investor before 1939 – and remained the second largest afterwards.[16] Concern not to provoke retribution against Britain's vast overseas business interests has remained a major reason for maintaining a liberal policy towards inward direct investment.

It was only within this framework that the May 1929 meeting sounded a third, more restrictive, note. Arguments were put forward that there were 'key or strategic industries' which 'should not be allowed to pass under foreign control'. Thus was opened a Pandora's Box of uncertainty, for the definition of what exactly these industries were has continually shifted, and British governments have displayed an aversion to listing them in any published official document. Nevertheless, it is clear that the primary concern, in 1929 and thereafter, was with companies working in the financial and defence-related industries, very broadly interpreted.

The May 1929 meeting identified five 'key or strategic' areas: South American railways 'or other like companies, providing large orders for British industry', shipping companies, armament firms, British-owned banks operating overseas, and the 'Bank of England and other large British Banks'. Over the following decade Montagu Norman offered various additions to this list. In the early 1930s, for example, he became concerned about a possible loss of British control over the Central Mining and Investment Corporation, a British company which controlled around 40 per cent of South African gold output, but which had a large French shareholding. In 1934 the Bank of England took up 300 000 Preference Shares in a new issue in order to counterbalance the French shareholders and maintain British voting control.[17] In the mid-1930s Norman and Sir Horace Wilson, chief industrial adviser to the Board of Trade, facilitated and encouraged the American-owned General Electric Company to turn its majority shareholding in Associated Electric Industries (AEI), one of the three large British electrical companies, into a minority stake.[18]

Foreign-owned companies established in Britain were treated identically to indigenous companies in law and for tax purposes. Usually the question of ownership only arose in instances when 'national security' was involved. In the early 1920s Western Electric may have been denied a leading share in the supply of automatic telephone exchange equipment for the Post Office because of its American ownership.[19] The British Security Service (MI5) maintained a wary eye on Italian-owned electricity undertakings in Britain in the late 1930s. 'No public utility concern of vital national importance', one of its officials noted in July 1939, 'should be allowed to remain in the hands of foreigners even during peacetime.'[20] The British Admiralty denied AEI 'very secret work' because of fears that 'information regarding it might be transferred to the USA'.[21]

Another feature of Britain's post-1945 policies towards foreign multinationals had made an appearance before the War. In certain 'key or strategic' industries governments sought not to prohibit a foreign presence, but to promote an indigenous national champion which could prevent the industry from falling under foreign domination. The classic example was the British government's support for the Anglo-Persian Oil Company (later British Petroleum) and the acquisition of a majority equity stake in the company in 1914, which was retained until the Thatcher privatization programme of the 1980s. The desire to secure cheap fuel oil for the Admiralty was the major stimulus behind this investment, but a pervading theme in official discussions of the time was suspicion of the Standard Oil Company of the United States and the Shell Group, in which British interests were in the minority compared to Dutch ones. Recent research has demonstrated the inconsistencies, ignorance, anti-semitism and interdepartmental rivalries behind the making of British oil policy. Various schemes between 1916 and 1924 to promote an even greater national oil champion by merging Anglo-Persian with one or more independent British oil companies and the Shell Group were ill-conceived and unproductive.[22] Nevertheless, the government did succeed in encouraging and sustaining a wholly-British owned oil company which, by the late 1920s, had become one of the 'seven sisters' which dominated the oligopolistic petroleum industry. This set a pattern for state promotion of national oil champions which was subsequently widely followed by many European governments, if not those of Japan or the United States.[23] There are parallels with government policies in other industries. The official encouragement of the creation of ICI in 1926 was motivated by the desire for a major indigenious chemicals company able to compete with the Americans and Germans.[24]

As in many areas, the Second World War provoked officials into re-assessing their views on inward direct investment, and towards the end of the War there was a serious discussion on the issue. In May 1945 there was a suggestion from Treasury officials that there might be a case for legislation requiring a majority British shareholding in any manufacturing company in Britain. Foreign subsidiaries were seen as useful providers of employment, but their value to the balance of payments – emerging already as a key concern – was held to be 'less clear'.[25]

This protectionist sentiment found little support. The gains from inward investment were still generally held to outweigh the problems and, in particular, it was widely believed that foreign-owned companies had exercised a beneficial impact on their sluggish British competitors, though actual evidence on this matter did not rise above the anecdotal. This point was made when the question of disposing of sequestrated German companies was discussed at the end of the War. Several of those companies, a meeting of officials in June 1945 was told, had exploited 'ingenious and sometimes revolutionary German plant or processes. They are not infrequently much disliked by their English competitors who rely on more orthodox though possibly more costly machinery and ideas.'[26] The most important consideration which militated against any restrictive policy against foreign companies continued to be Britain's own position as a major multinational investor. Britain, it was argued, dare not impose restrictions in case foreign countries imposed similar controls on Britain's multinationals.[27] By September the tentative Treasury proposal had been dropped.

III   Policies between 1945 and 1970

Between 1945 and 1970 the principles of British policy towards foreign multinationals remained broadly on the lines developed in earlier decades. Interesting comparisons can be made with Japanese policies on the same issue. In both countries there were strong continuities between the pre- and postwar periods. First, both the British and the Japanese governments believed that foreign companies offered benefits to their respective economies. Already before 1945 the possibility of technology transfer had been identified as a major gain. This seems to have been the major preoccupation of Japanese governments. British officials had also identified other potential gains, such as employment, serving as a competitive stimulus to local firms, and especially from the late 1940s, a means to improve the balance of payments. Secondly, the Japanese made a sharp distinction between indigenous and foreign-owned companies. They had, therefore, a strong preference for attracting foreign technology by arms-length licensing agreements, and for forcing foreign firms to take local partners in joint ventures. British governments were much less concerned with nationality of ownership, and were generally happy to see foreign firms owning and controlling businesses in Britain, except in a few 'key' areas. Some of the gains from foreign companies British governments identified as important, such as employment, could indeed only be transferred in the short term by direct investment. Thirdly, British governments, again both before and after the Second World War, felt obliged to adopt liberal policies towards inward investors because of Britain's large foreign investments. Japan felt no such constraint given that its emergence as a substantial capital exporter and multinational investor did not begin until the 1970s.[28]

In Britain, the major difference between the pre- and postwar periods was that the introduction of extensive exchange controls gave the government an opportunity for 'screening' of foreign investment proposals. Criteria were developed as to what constituted a desirable investment, as well as where it should be located. Those policies continued to be based on fragile empirical foundations. Until the 1960s the government declined to collect data on the size of inward investment in Britain, despite questions in the House of Commons and articles on the subject in journals such as *The Economist*.[29] The Board of Trade sponsored J.H. Dunning's study of *American Investment in British Manufacturing Industry*, published in 1958, but the first systematic (and also officially sponsored) study of the impact of inward investment only came in 1973 with the report by M.D. Steuer and colleagues on *The Impact of Foreign Direct Investment on the United Kingdom*.

Government policies towards multinationals after the War focused on control over entry into the United Kingdom. The key legislation was the Exchange Control Act of 1947. This Act, which remained in operation until October 1979, required Treasury permission for any imports of capital, whether for the purchase of management *control* over existing firms or greenfield direct investment.[30] This permission was given if the proposed investment met certain criteria, the emphasis in which changed and generally became less restrictive over time. The Treasury emerged as the major influence on government policies towards multinationals. The Bank of England was also involved in policy, especially through its 'informal' contacts with British banks and companies.

The main initial concerns of the Treasury was that any proposed inward investment had a net effect on the balance of payments and/or had a positive impact on industrial efficiency in the United Kingdom. The balance of payments concern led to the favouring of schemes which involved the import of capital rather than local borrowing; where there was the prospect of substantial exports to hard currency (in effect, dollar) areas; and which did not entail the import of foreign equipment or technicians.[31] Some imports of equipment or components were permitted on occasion but, as a Board of Trade memorandum noted in 1954, 'we normally require steady progress to 100 per cent British manufacture and we have in no case agreed to guarantee imports over an indefinite period in the future'.[32] Investments were permitted in any industry so long as they met these requirements. The industrial efficiency criteria were vaguer and carried much less importance in decisions, and the exact interpretation of their meaning and scope varied between individual officials and departments. A 1949 Treasury memorandum thought that the 'right type of investment' might make a valuable contribution 'either by the provision of foreign know-how and technique not otherwise available, or by injecting a desirable element of competition into a monopolistic or sleepy industry'. Conversely, schemes were discouraged if they involved 'cartel arrangements of a restrictive character' or if they brought strategically important industries under 'foreign control'.[33] Essentially, however, while Japanese governments looked to foreign companies to provide technology (preferably at arms length), postwar British governments were primarily concerned with their balance of payments impact.

The problem with official screening of investment proposals was that it had the potential to be restrictive and become a deterrant to prospective investors, especially as in the first couple of years after the 1947 Act a variety of government departments and agencies became involved in inward investment policy. By December 1949 an intending investor had to secure up to six official consents and approvals. These included permission from under the foreign exchange regulations which were operated by the Bank of England; permission from the Treasury's Capital Issues Committee if the Company was raising more than £50 000 locally under certain conditions; approval of the relevant government Production Branch, without which access to rationed raw materials would be unforthcoming; location approval from the Board of Trade; and local planning approvals and a building licence if a new factory was planned.[34] These bureaucratic controls, which were exacerbated by uncertainties about the criteria on which each department based its decisions, led to a steady flow of complaints from American government and business circles that the British government was discouraging foreign investment.[35]

Given the government's underlying belief in the benefits of foreign investment, from an early date considerable attention was devoted to simplifying these administrative procedures. In November and December 1949 a Board of Trade Working Group examined the reasons for delays in decision making. The report made clear that the overriding aim was to attract, rather than to hinder, American investment. Departments, it advised, 'should be asked to make every effort to give a degree of priority to the consideration and handling of U.S. investment cases'.[36] As a result of this report, the Board of Trade took responsibility for coordinating official negotiations with foreign companies, and ensuring that they did not have 'separate interviews with different Departments covering similar ground'.[37] In a further measure to attract investors, from 1 January 1950 direct investors were allowed to repatriate the funds from their original investments and any proceeds from the sale of such investments.[38]

In 1954, after an outburst from Lord Bilsland, Chairman of the Scottish Council, about the government's alleged unhelpful attitude towards foreign investors, further liberalization steps were taken. It was decided that instead of having the onus on the inward investor to demonstrate that his investment would be advantageous to Britain, projects would henceforward be approved unless the government could show that they would be 'positively disadvantageous'. Officials continued to find it 'difficult to lay down . . . precisely what constituted a positive disadvantage', but various criteria were suggested, including if the planned production was only for the Sterling Area or if 'no worthwhile new techniques would be introduced'.[39] Vagueness, therefore, remained the order of the day, but there can be no doubt that in the mid-1950s there was a further softening of official attitudes to inward investors.

The screening powers under the Exchange Act and other regulations were not used merely to make straightforward admission or exclusion decisions. Instead a bargaining process developed, with government departments encouraging companies to adapt their original proposals in ways considered desirable from the point of view of the British economy. The process was described by one Treasury official in 1950:

> when a project first comes up in a form which is, on balance, unattractive, there is nothing to be gained, and may be much to be lost, both for us and for the American investor, if we return a flat No. Instead we tell the prospective investor what is wrong with it, and suggest he could make it more palatable to us. . . . I think it is true to say that in almost every case of American investment in the UK in the last two years we have in this way succeeded in improving on the original proposals from the point of view of benefit to the United Kingdom.[40]

The details of the individual negotiations have rarely survived, but it seems likely that this process was the most significant element of the whole screening process in these years. However, the changes in conditions were usually marginal rather than fundamental, for wherever there was any danger of a valued project being lost the government retreated. In 1947, for example, there was some pressure on Anglo-American Oil Company to locate a new refinery on the Clyde or at Stranraer rather than to erect one adjacent to its existing Fawley one, but this pressure was soon relaxed on the realization that 'if the Fawley site is not agreed it must be accepted that the American Company will not proceed with their proposals'. Almost any proposal which involved the possibility of balance of payments advantages attracted strong government support. Ford of England, for example, received the foreign exchange it required in the late 1940s because of its role in enhancing British exports.[41]

Consistent data on the number of inward investment proposals which were declined in late 1940s and early 1950s is unavailable. It is clear that there were a significant number of rejections in the early years, and the claim by one author that there were 'less than half a dozen refusals' between 1945 and 1974 is a serious underestimate.[42] In 1949 the Board of Trade approved 31 applications and rejected 14 whose total investment was £180 000.[43] Between January and September 1954 9 out of 74 cases were rejected, involving a total investment of £100 000, all from the United States. In 4 of the rejected cases insufficient assurances were given on exports. In 2 cases the value of the technological transfer was doubted: one of these was a proposal by an American company 'to open up in Oxford Street a kind of beauty parlour to "slenderise" the gentler sex' using special slimming mints. One proposal to build flats in Bournemouth was held to have involved excessive local funding; an investment in Scottish whisky failed because there were 'numerous UK blenders and exporters'; and 'no advantage was seen' in a project to manufacture salted popcorn.[44]

From the beginning of the postwar period some encouragement was given to intending foreign investors to locate factories in the regions as part of the general policy to promote industry in certain 'Development Areas' of high unemployment, mostly located in Wales, Scotland, Northern Ireland and the North. A leading instrument of regional policy between 1947 and 1981 was Industrial Development Certificates (IDCs), which had to be obtained from the Board of Trade for new industrial buildings and extensions, and which were often refused for congested areas such as London while granted for areas where investment was considered desirable. However, in the first decade after the War informal encouragement, rather than manipulation of IDCs, was the main strategy used to lure foreign investors to the regions. Companies were advised of the potentialities of the Development Areas when they approached the government for permission to invest in Britain, but there was no attempt to either force or induce firms to invest there.[45] Some officials suggested that the government had no impact at all on location decisions, putting forward the implausible argument that the substantial postwar North American investment in Scotland was for 'sentimental rather than economic' reasons.[46] In fact there were always some material incentives: the large majority of American industrial investments in Scotland between 1945 and 1955, for example, were in government-financed trading estate factories built under the Distribution of Industry Act.[47] From the mid-1950s IDC controls were also used more strongly, while legislation in the early 1960s provided the government with a wide variety of financial incentives (such as free depreciation of capital expenditure) to offer to firms investing in Development Areas.[48]

Government policies exercised an influence on the spatial distribution of inward investment into Britain. As the data collected by C.M. Law and shown in Table 11.2 illustrates, in contrast to the interwar period, after 1945 new inward direct investment showed a marked preference for the outlying regions, at least until the late 1960s.

Table 11.2   Location of initial foreign manufacturing investment in Britain, 1918–71

	1918–44	1945–51	1952–59	1960–65	1966–71
No. of factories	162	55	77	126	174
Percentage of total					
South East	70.3	16.4	20.1	18.3	36.2
North West	11.7	14.5	13.0	11.1	7.5
North	0.6	5.4	7.8	7.9	9.2
Wales	0.6	20.0	9.1	4.8	7.5
Scotland	3.7	36.4	24.7	29.4	20.1
N. Ireland	–	1.8	7.8	11.9	6.8
Other	13.1	5.5	17.5	16.6	12.7

Source: Calculated from C.M. Law, *British Regional Development Since World War I* (Newton Abbot 1980), Table 33, p 175

Both the data in Table 11.2, and its interpretation, need to be treated with caution. The statistics do not cover expansion or transfers by foreign-owned firms already with Britain: the epic moves of Ford and Vauxhall to Merseyside in the early 1960s, for example, find no reflection in the Table. The regional impact of the investment in terms of jobs and local linkages is problematic, although a recent study concludes that foreign direct investment 'made a substantial contribution towards a reduction in regional employment inequalities' in the 1960s.[49] An even greater difficulty is to determine the exact contribution of government policies in influencing the geographical location of foreign investment. Greenfield investors had a lack of commitment to any British region, which probably meant that they gave a heavier weighting to factors such as cheaper land than their domestic counterparts.[50] Moreover, it is hard to correlate shifts in official policy with location trends. One study of job creation showed that between 1945 and 1951 44 700 jobs were created by new foreign investors. Two-thirds of these went to Scotland, but subsequently Scotland's relative share declined.[51] Yet this was just as more assertive regional policies were being introduced from the mid-1950s.

The provisions of the Exchange Control Act of 1947, and the resulting screening and bargaining processes, were the main instruments of government controls over multinational entry into Britain between 1945 and the 1960s. The other potential instrument was the Monopolies Commission, established in 1948, which had powers over anti-competitive behaviour generally in the economy. In the late 1970s and 1980s the Monopolies and Mergers Commission has been used to some extent to screen unwelcome foreign takeovers of British firms, such as the Hongkong Bank's bid for the Royal Bank of Scotland in 1982.[52] There is very little evidence of any such use of the Commission before the late 1960s. Only six of the Commission's reports concerned foreign companies between 1960 and 1970, and in all cases they were treated entirely as local firms, with no mention or investigation of their foreign parents. In 1965 the British government took power to vet and control proposed mergers, establishing the Mergers Panel to investigate if a particular case deserved reference to the Commission. This provided a potential device to screen foreign takeovers of British firms, but in practice between 1965 and 1969 only one such case was referred to the Commission, and this was allowed.[53]

In a small number of cases, the British authorities took the view that certain companies were so 'key or strategic' that foreign takeovers were effectively prohibited, although this prohibition continued to be in practice rather than in law or any published document. In 1959, for example, the Governor of the Bank of England made clear his opposition to any sizeable block of shares of Burmah Oil being transferred into American interests. Burmah Oil held a large shareholding in British Petroleum, which British governments between 1914 and 1987 held to be so important that it had to be kept in British hands.[54] The financial sector was also protected from foreign takeovers. Foreign banks were always permitted to open representatives or branches, and a range of American and Continental institutions were represented in London from the late nineteenth century, well before the surge in foreign bank activity in Britain from the late 1960s.[55] However, all the forms of indigenous banking institutions were rigorously, if informally, protected from foreign control or – as Montagu Norman put it in 1926 – the American 'scorpions'.[56] No foreign bidder was permitted for a British clearing bank until the National Australia Bank was allowed to acquire Midland Bank's Scottish and Ulster subsidiaries in 1986. The Bank of England also exercised pressure to prohibit foreign encroachments on the merchant banks. During the early 1960s, for example, Brandts got into serious financial difficulties, and approached the Bank of England about the possibility of 'linking up with a firm on the Continent'. The firm was 'warned against foreign control – at least if they wanted to preserve the position of their House as one of our merchant bankers whose bills were taken at the Bank of England'.[57] This was a powerful threat at the time for it meant expulsion from the Accepting Houses Committee. In 1973 the acquisition of a large shareholding in another merchant bank, Antony Gibbs, by the Hongkong Bank, was followed by Gibbs' expulsion from the Committee.

During the 1950s and 1960s the Bank of England also worked assiduously to keep the weakest segment of the banking community, the British overseas banks, out of American control. To some extent this can be viewed as part of a more general set of policies that hesitated in opening the door to American capital in areas considered to be part of British 'spheres of influence'. The small, under-capitalized overseas banks, usually operating in developing economies, became increasingly vulnerable to the international expansion strategies of the large American banks such as Citibank and Chase Manhattan.[58] Several of the British banks also wanted access to dollar funds and were prepared to seek alliances with North American institutions. In the late 1950s, the Bank of England acted discretely to keep the Mercantile Bank of India under British control for, as an official noted in October 1956, 'we don't want the Mercantile to fall into non-British hands'.[59] In 1959 there was outright hostility at the Bank when Standard Bank of South Africa floated the idea of taking an American partner.[60]

In the 1960s the Bank of England softened its views in response to the increasingly desperate pleas from the overseas banks themselves for additional capital and, especially, for dollar funds. By 1965 the Bank of England's policy had become 'that an overseas bank wishing to take a participation in a U.K. bank should not hold more than 15 per cent of the issued capital'.[61] As a result, in that year, Chase Manhattan were allowed to buy a 15 per cent stake in Standard Bank of South Africa, and Mellon Bank an equivalent amount in the Bank of London and South America.[62] By 1968 policy had been further liberalized and Citibank was allowed to acquire 40 per cent of National and Grindlays, but only on the conditions that British control was retained, and that the Americans did not purchase further shares without the agreement of the Governor of the Bank of England.[63]

Once established in Britain, foreign-owned companies continued to be treated by the government almost exactly as if they were indigenous firms. The major exception in the first decade after the War was in the area of local borrowing. Section 30(3) of the 1947 Exchange Control Act prohibited British concerns controlled by non-residents from borrowing in the Sterling Area without official permission. The aim was to prevent foreign firms building up 'assets in the United Kingdom involving a future foreign exchange liability for profits, on the basis of loan capital raised here'.[64] In practice, the Bank of England allowed British banks to lend quite freely to provide finance for trade movements, but exercised tight control over requests for loans to provide fixed or working capital.[65] However, in 1954 the Treasury – eager as ever in this period to see an increase in British exports – permitted Vauxhall (owned by General Motors) to borrow up to £15 million for 15 years to expand production capacity. The usual requirement that the parent should pay for the fixed assets was waived, GM merely agreeing to provide £2.75 million from the United States, repayable out of profits in 5 years' time. The Bank of England, anxious to abandon the irksome task of reviewing a large number of applications for small loans, used the opportunity of the Vauxhall case to force a reluctant Treasury to abandon this form of control over foreign-owned companies. It was initially agreed that loans not in excess of £50 000 were to be permitted without official approval and, from early in 1955, foreign subsidiaries were permitted to borrow freely from banks.[66] In practice, however, for some years there remained a – in the words of a Bank of England official in 1957 – 'somewhat inconsistent' monitoring of local borrowing exercised by the Capital Issues Committee, which continued to encourage foreign parents to supply at least a part of any subsidiary's capital requirements.[67]

The primary concerns of British governments were the foreign exchange and foreign trade implications of multinationals, but these issues were treated in rather a broad brush fashion. For example, there was no attempt at more sophisticated regulations to control or investigate transfer pricing between foreign parents and British subsidiaries, even though inter-firm transfer prices were an obvious way of violating foreign exchange controls. Perhaps British governments lacked the administrative machinery to explore such matters. Only in the case of the pharmaceuticals industry, where the government – through the National Health Service – was in a special quasi-monopsonist position, was a serious investigation mounted. In 1973 a Monopolies Commission investigation established that the Swiss firm Hoffman La Roche had charged its British subsidiaries over forty times the production cost for the supply of ingredients for tranquilizers. The Swiss company was ordered to repay excess profits from sales to the government and reduce its profits.[68] This remained an isolated case, however, and no thought was given to any general survey as to the extent and implications of transfer pricing policies among multinationals as a whole.

British governments made few efforts to positively attract foreign multinationals. There were several calls for the government to play a more dynamic role. *The Economist* in 1954 argued that 'the advantage of manufacturing in Britain is something that Britain now has to sell',[69] but it was not a message that persuaded Whitehall, which was prepared to relax constraints on foreign investments but to do little more. The one exception was the oil industry, where postwar British governments did strongly encourage American companies to establish refineries in Britain, both for defence reasons and for their dollar-saving/dollar-earning pro-spects. In response to a suggestion that a publicity campaign was needed to attract inward investment, one Treasury official in 1954 observed that Britain was 'traditionally a capital-exporting country and he doubted the need for American capital. He saw no necessity for a special campaign.'[70] Eight years later a small British Industrial Development Office was established in New York to attract American investment to Development Areas, but this did not indicate any radical departure from the previous passive strategy. The ill-fated National Plan in 1965 forecast that 'a special effort will be made to attract those companies whose exports to Britain have already secured them a firm base in the British market to start local production', but nothing was done on these lines.[71] A positive British policy to attract inward investment cannot really be dated before 1977, when the Invest in Britain Bureau was started.

During the 1960s British policy showed some shift in emphasis. While, on the one hand, many of the foreign exchange restrictions of the first postwar decade had been relaxed, on the other hand there was stronger emphasis on negotiation with inward investors, and a renewed concern to promote national champions. There were several factors behind this policy change. The volume of inward direct investment was continuing to rise, and foreign-owned companies were growing in prominence in the economy. The fact that economists had by then identified 'multinationals' as a distinct phenomenon may have led to a change of atmosphere in which a more 'positive' policy response seemed appropriate. Finally, the existence of a Labour government between 1964 and 1970 probably encouraged greater state activity in this area.

The era of the British government seeking 'assurances' from multinationals is often dated to 1960, when in return for allowing Ford to buy out the minority British shareholders in its British subsidiary, the government extracted a series of commitments on imports, employment, management, dividends, capital invest- ment and exports.[72] In fact, the 'assurances' policy can be dated back to at least Texas Oil's acquisition of the British-owned Trinidad Oil in 1956, when a number of very general 'conditions' concerning both Britain and the colony of Trinidad had been specified.[73] During the 1960s more 'assurances' were sought in the cases of important foreign takeovers. Chrysler's acquisition of a minority shareholding in Rootes Motors in 1964, followed by full control in 1967, was accompanied by a range of 'assurances' to the British government. The 1967 terms, negotiated by the Labour Minister Wedgewood Benn, committed the company to a number of policies, including maintaining a majority of British directors on the Board of Rootes and expanding exports to the extent that 'the export percentage' of the firm 'should be at least as high as the average for the British Motor Vehicle Industry as a whole'.[74]

The 'assurances' policy was completely ineffective. As the Steuer Report noted in 1973, the government relied on 'the good faith and social responsibility of the companies concerned'.[75] No attempt was made to monitor whether firms lived up to their specific assurances.[76] The disinclination of successive governments to take real coercive measures against foreign companies – probably because of worry about reciprocal action being taken against British firms – left them helpless when those companies chose not to act in 'good faith'. Chrysler, for example, secured large government grants by making withdrawal threats in 1975. In 1978 it sold its British subsidiary to Peugeot-Citroen – and the British government was left to read about the sale in the newspapers.[77]

A renewed attempt to promote national champions had more positive results, at least in the short term, although it was prone to unfortunate long-term consequences. Among the manifestations of this policy was the encouragement given to the formation of British Leyland Motor Corporation and International Computers Ltd (ICL) in 1968.[78] However, one of the most interesting demonstra- tions of this policy was in the ball bearings industry, when the Industrial Reorganisation Corporation (a government agency in operation between 1966 and 1971) intervened to block Swedish-owned SKF's purchase of a leading British company, and eventually underwrote a merger of a number of independent British firms to form RHP. A fairly efficient independent indigenous enterprise in ball bearings was created in this fashion.[79] Concern at engineering capacity constraints within the economy probably lay behind this policy, but the intellectual case underpinning it was far from convincing. According to IRC's 'semi-official' history, a Board meeting was held when news of SKF's intending purchase broke, and 'it was decided that the importance of the industry, and the danger that there could soon be no major U.K. bearings company, clearly warranted IRC involvement'.[80] Why the industry should remain in indigenous hands does not appear to have been discussed.

Underlying all the government policies in the 1950s and 1960s was the continuing assumption that inward investment was (except in a few cases) a positive net benefit to Britain. This remained much more an article of faith than a proven fact, but the faith was widely shared. As one study of the attitudes of senior civil servants and politicians towards multinationals in the 1964–70 Labour government showed, there was a widespread consensus about the benefits of inward investment. This was reinforced by the fact that most of this investment was still American and thus perceived as less 'foreign' than if it had been Continental or Asian.[81]

IV Conclusions

The attitudes underlying British government policies towards inward investment between the 1900s and 1970 show strong continuities. It was widely assumed that such investment brought net benefits. There was no discernible difference between mainstream politicians of all political parties on this issue. The policy response was passive – confined to regulating proposed investments rather than attracting investors – and characterized by an unwillingness to define hard and fast rules as to what categories of investment were desirable or otherwise. Before 1945 'policy' was confined to scattered attempts to protect various 'key or strategic' industries. After the War more coherent policies emerged because governments had to screen intending investors under the 1947 Exchange Act. Entry to Britain became a matter of negotiation, and policies towards multinationals became entwined with several industrial policy goals, such as promotion of Development Areas. The primary policy concern was the balance of payments implications of foreign multinationals. The possible contributions of foreign companies in improving industrial efficiency or enhancing competition were mentioned, but not awarded great priority. British governments showed a notable lack of concern about foreign ownership of businesses in Britain, except in the 'key' financial, defence and oil sectors. This was a very marked contrast with Japan, and also various other European countries such as France.

Given the passive nature of government policies, there can be no suggestion that they played an active part in making Britain such a favoured location for inward direct investment, apart from protectionism which was an obvious stimulus. The size and growth of the British market, the use of English, and patent laws were among the factors attracting foreign multinationals to Britain. However, the overall policy orientation of British governments – the long-term liberal attitude towards inward investment, the ownership-neutral characteristic of industrial policies, the (on the whole) harmonious diplomatic relations with the United States, and overall political stability and bureaucratic competence – was a significant 'permissive' factor in attracting direct investment to Britain. Studies of the factors encouraging foreign pharmaceutical companies to locate in Britain have suggested that overall political stability and the quality of the drug regulatory regime were highly important.[82]

British governments influenced the structure and performance of inward investment between 1945 and the late 1960s, but only at the margin. The government did not affect the industry distribution of inward investment by favouring applicants in 'technology-intensive' sectors and rejecting those in basic industries. The industry distribution merely reflected the overall pattern of multinational activity in this period. On the other hand, the screening of investments may have encouraged a bias in inward investors towards exporting activities, and thus help to explain their higher export propensity compared to their British equivalents. Government policies may also have been one factor in encouraging foreign multinationals after 1945 to locate in the regions. Whether these balance of payments and regional employment goals were in fact desirable is another matter. They might also have been better achieved by a Japanese-style emphasis on licensing and joint ventures rather than allowing comparatively unrestricted direct investment. It has been and can be argued that the presence of foreign multinationals merely disguised underlying economic weaknesses, and delayed efforts to make indigenous business more competitive.[83]

British policies were rarely satisfactory when they attempted to take specific positive steps rather than to provide an overall attractive environment and some regulation. The attempts to set performance requirements through securing promises at the time of 'screening' and, from the mid-1950s, the 'assurances' policy were ineffective. The national champion strategies usually rested on a weak intellectual basis and, as a result, were rarely effective in the long term. The cartelized and uncompetitive (if stable) British banking system before the 1970s was not a good illustration of the benefits of protecting 'key or strategic' companies from foreign takeovers.

The intellectual basis for British policies was not impressive. Occasional consideration was given to important issues surrounding multinational investment – such as technological dependence – but there was no sustained interest in such matters. It is debatable whether the vagueness of inward investment criteria which so irritated American business in the late 1940s and early 1950s rested on a wish to be flexible or on sheer inability to decide what a 'key or strategic' industry was. The reluctance to adopt positive measures to stimulate inward investment seems to have originated more from lethargy or perhaps ignorance than anything else, as does the unwillingness to compile basic statistical data on the subject. Underlying the whole liberal thrust of inward investment policies was the belief that it was vital not to provoke any attack on Britain's overseas business activities. Yet the benefits of British outward investment remained unexplored at least until the Reddaway Report in 1967, and the gains to the British economy of acting as a home economy to so many multinationals still remain unclear and debatable.[84]

The British government's contribution to the success story of inward investment, therefore, was limited. The kind of failings visible in other areas of industrial policy were visible here also. Perhaps the most that can be said is that the government managed not to obstruct the flow of investment, and may have marginally improved the terms on which it entered Britain. Much empirical research and theoretical modelling remains to be undertaken, however, before it can be conclusively shown that the British 'open economy' strategy of permitting extensive inward and outward direct investment was the most effective response to the economy's long-term decline in competitiveness.

Acknowledgement

I would like to thank the editor of this volume, Tony Corley, Helen Mercer and Mira Wilkins for their helpful comments on an earlier draft of this chapter.

Notes

1. A foreign direct investment involves ownership (in part or whole) and management of a foreign operation. It is conventionally contrasted with portfolio investment, which involves the acquisition of foreign securities or institutions without any control over or participation in the management of the companies concerned. Multinational companies engage in production across national boundaries through the mechanism of foreign direct investment

2. On foreign multinational activity in Britain before 1945 see, especially, J.H. Dunning, *American Investment in British Manufacturing Industry*, London 1958, and G. Jones, 'Foreign multinationals and British industry before 1945', *Economic History Review*, XL, 1988

3. Steuer, M.D. et al. *The Impact of Foreign Direct Investment on the United Kingdom*, Department of Trade and Industry, 1973, pp 189–90; Young, S., Hood, N., Hamill, J. *Foreign Multinationals and the British Economy*, London 1988, p 91

4. *OECD Economic Surveys: UK*, 1988

5. Jones 'Foreign multinationals', p 45; Steuer *Impact*, p 12; Young *Foreign Multinationals*, p 99, which, however, suggests that the net benefits may have declined in the more recent period

6. Dunning, J.H. *Multinational Enterprise, Economic Structure and International Competitiveness*, Chichester 1985, pp 17–18. For the foreign share of employment in particular British industries in 1963, see Steuer, *Impact*, p 196

7. Steuer,*Impact*, pp 198–9. For similar evidence for the early 1980s on net output per head, see Young, *Foreign Multinationals*, p 49

8. Steuer *Impact*, p 186

9. Dunning, J.H. 'Changes in the level and structure of international production in the last one hundred years' in M. Casson, ed., *The Growth of International Business*, London 1983, p 88

10. There is no systematic survey of the role of foreign-born but British resident individuals in British business. However, anecdotal evidence suggests a considerable stream of such activity extending from the founding fathers of most of Britain's merchant banks in the nineteenth century through to such prominent contemporary (or near contemporary) figures as David Alliance, Graham Day, Michael Edwardes, Robert Maxwell, Sir Eric Pasold, Tiny Rowland

11. Dunning, J.H., Cantwell, J.A., Corley, T.A.B. 'The theory of international production: some historical antecedents' in P. Hertner and G. Jones, eds, *Multinationals: Theory and History*, Aldershot 1986; Corley, T.A.B. 'Multinational studies, at Reading and elsewhere, 1960–80', *University of Reading Discussion Papers in International Investment and Business Studies*, No 100, 1986

12. Dunning *American Investment*, p 37; Jones 'Foreign multinationals', pp 438–9

13. Dunning *American Investment*, pp 40–1. For British concern about American investment in the early 1900s, see M. Wilkins, *The Emergence of Multinational Enterprise*, Cambridge, Mass 1970, pp 70–1. For the late 1920s, see F.A. Southard, *American Industry in Europe*, Boston 1931, pp 180–3

14. Telegram from Harrison to Norman, 12 March 1929, Bank of England Archives (hereafter B of E), G1/326

15. Note of meeting held at Bank of 15 May 1929, G1/326, B of E

16. Jones, G., ed., *British Multinationals: Origins, Management and Performance*, Aldershot 1986, p 3; M. Wilkins 'European and North American multinationals, 1870–1914: comparisons and contrasts', *Business History*, 1988

17. Secret Memorandum on Central Mining and Investment Corporation, 18 June 1931; Minutes of Committee of Treasury, 9 May 1934; Memorandum, 23 September 1942, G1/193, B of E

18. Memorandum on AEI, 14 March 1933; handwritten note, 16 March 1934; Felix Pole to Montagu Norman, 4 January 1935; Felix Pole to Montagu Norman, 8 November 1935. For essential background on AEI (but no mention of the moves to reduce American shareholding in the mid-1930s) see R. Jones and O. Marriott, *Anatomy of a Merger*, London 1970, chapter 8

19. Young, P. *Power of Speech: A History of Standard Telephones and Cables, 1883–1983*, London 1983, pp 37–40

20. Colonel Sir Vernon Kell to Ministry of Transport, 7 July 1939, Ministry of Power records (hereafter POWE) 13/101, Public Record Office (PRO). See also L. Hannah, *Electricity before Nationalisation*, London 1979, p 290

21. MI5 to Ministry of Transport, 23 October 1936, POWE 33/101, PRO

22. The history of the oil industry and its relations with the British government in this period are now very well documented. There are two high quality company histories, R.W. Ferrier, *The History of the British Petroleum Company*, vol. I, Cambridge 1982, and T.A.B. Corley, *A History of the Burmah Oil Company Vol. I: 1886–1924*, London 1983 and *Vol. II: 1926–66*,

London 1988. See also G. Jones, *The State and the Emergence of the British Oil Industry*, London 1981, and *idem,* 'The "old aunts": governments, politicians and the oil business' in J. Turner, ed., *Businessmen and Politics*, London 1984

23. Samuels, R.J. *The Business of the Japanese State*, Ithaca 1987, pp 45–64
24. Reader, W.J. *Imperial Chemical Industries: A History*, vol. 1, London 1970, chapter 19; *idem* 'Imperial Chemical Industries and the state, 1926–1945' in B. Supple, ed., *Essays in British Business History*, Oxford 1977
25. Extract from R (I.E.) 45, 3rd meeting, 14 May 1945, BT 11/2589, PRO
26. Meeting of 17 June 1945, BT 60/80/12, PRO
27. Memorandum by R.J. Shackle, 17 July 1945, BT 11/2589, PRO
28. For Japanese government policies see R. Davenport-Hines and G. Jones, 'British business in Japan since 1868' in Davenport-Hines and Jones, eds, *British Business in Asia since 1860*, Cambridge 1989, pp 219, 237–8; A.E. Safarian, *Governments and Multinationals: Policies in the Developed Countries*, Washington, DC 1983, pp 24–9
29. Question by J. Grimmond to Chancellor of Exchequer, 3 March 1953, *House of Commons Debates*, vol. 512, No. 65; *Economist*, 5 June 1954
30. Exchange Control Act, 1947; Steuer *Impact*, chapter 9
31. See, for example, Dollar Exports Council, 'Some notes for intending United States investors in the United Kingdom', BT 258/567, PRO
32. Memorandum on Imports of Equipment and Components, October 1954, BT 258/568, PRO
33. Treasury memorandum on US Investment in the Sterling Area, 1949, Treasury files (hereafter T) 231/474, PRO
34. Report of the Board of Trade Working Group on UK Administrative Procedures, 31 December 1949, T 231/471, PRO
35. Report by the Exchange Control Division, 3 November 1949, T231/471; A.J.W.S. Leonard to R.L. Sharp, 7 July 1954, BT 258/567, PRO
36. Report of the Board of Trade Working Group, 31 December 1949, T231/471, PRO
37. Board of Trade memorandum, 23 June 1950, BT 258/567, PRO
38. Board of Trade memorandum, 10 January 1950, T231/471, PRO
39. Board of Trade meeting, 8 October 1954, BT 258/568, PRO
40. Memorandum by A.E. Drake, 15 February 1950, T231/474, PRO
41. Home Refining in the U.K. Brief for Minister, July 1947, POWE 33/2211, PRO; M. Wilkins and F.E. Hill *American Business Abroad*, Detroit 1964, pp 381–2
42. Hodges, M. *Multinational Corporations and National Government*, Farnborough 1974, p 79. This figure is repeated in M. Brech and M. Sharp, *Inward Investment: Policy Options for the United Kingdom*, London 1984, p 9
43. G. Parker to J.G. Owen, 29 December 1949, T 231/471, PRO
44. North American Investment in the UK. Summary of cases not supported (Jan–Sept 1954), BT 258/568, PRO
45. Memorandum of 8 May 1954, BT 258/567, PRO

46. Memorandum by R.W. Daniel, 13 November 1952, BT 258/567, PRO
47. Memorandum by A.L. Burgess, 28 January 1955, BT 258/568, PRO
48. Young, Hood, Hamill *Foreign Multinationals*, p 112; Hodges *Multinational Corporation*, pp 88–90
49. Young, Hood, Hamill *Foreign Multinationals*, p 113. See also C.M. Law, *British Regional Development Since World War I*, Newton Abbot 1980, pp 177–8
50. Steuer *Impact*, p 104
51. Dicken, P., Lloyd, P.E. 'Geographical perspectives on United States investment in the United Kingdom', *Environment and Planning*, 1976, pp 696–7
52. Young, Hood, Hamill *Foreign Multinationals*, pp 210–17
53. Hodges *Multinational Corporation*, pp 97–108
54. Corley, T.A.B. *History*, vol. II, pp 222–3
55. Channon, D.F. *British Banking Strategy and the International Challenge*, London 1977, chapter 8; W.F. Spalding 'The foreign bank branches in England, and their influence on the London Money Market', *Economic Journal*, XXII, 1917
56. M. Norman to General Sir Herbert Lawrence, 17 August 1926, C40/120, B of E
57. Memorandum, 20 October 1964, C48/21, B of E
58. Jones, G. *Banking and Oil. The History of the British Bank of the Middle East*, vol. 2, Cambridge 1987, pp 73–6
59. Memorandum, 11 October 1956, C48/395, B of E. Mercantile was acquired by the Hongkong Bank in 1959, with the Bank of England's blessing. Jones *Banking and Oil*, pp 78–81
60. Memorandum, 13 February 1959, C48/157, B of E
61. Memorandum by Mr Hilton Clarke to Deputy Governor, 5 August 1965, C48/156, B of E
62. On Chase's investment in Standard Bank, see J.D. Wilson, *The Chase*, Boston, Mass 1986, p 170
63. M.H. Parsons to Lord Aldington, 18 December 1968, C48/153, B of E
64. Report by Exchange Control Division, 3 November 1949, T231/471, PRO
65. Bank of England Memorandum, 25 August 1954, T231/729, PRO
66. Memorandum of 21 January 1955, T231/729, PRO
67. Bank of England to J.G. Owen, 7 February 1957; Memorandum, 15 February 1957, T231/729, PRO
68. *A Report on the Supply of Chlordiazepoxide and Diazepam*, Monopolies and Mergers Commission, 1973; Hodges *Multinational Corporations*, p 75
69. *The Economist*, 5 June 1954
70. Note of a meeting held in the Treasury on 1 March 1954, BT 258/567, PRO
71. Robert W. Gillespie 'The policies of England, France, and Germany as recipients of foreign direct investment' in F. Machlup, W.S. Salant and L. Tarshis, eds, *International Mobility and Movement of Capital*, New York 1972, p 423

72. Hodges *Multinational Corporations*, pp 186–91; Safarian *Governments and Multinationals*, Washington, DC 1983, p 30

73. Speech by H. Macmillan, House of Commons Debates, 14 June 1956

74. Hodges *Multinational Corporations*, pp 191–4, 202–9

75. Steuer *Impact*, p 180

76. Hodges *Multinational Corporations*, p 82

77. Young, S., Hood, N. *Chrysler U.K.: A Corporation in Transition*, New York 1977; J.M. Stopford and L. Turner *Britain and the Multinationals*, Chichester 1985, p 230

78. For a useful evaluation of these mergers (from a 1980 perspective) see K. Cowling et al., *Mergers and Economic Performance*, Cambridge 1980, pp 170–90, 272–89. On ICL see also Hodges, *Multinational Corporations*, chapter 6

79. Cowling *Mergers*, pp 95–104

80. Hague, D., Wilkinson, G. *The IRC – An Experiment in Industrial Intervention*, London 1983, p 38, and chapter 6

81. Hodges *Multinational Corporations*, chapter 4

82. Brech and Sharp *Inward Investment*, pp 47–8

83. Young, Hood, Hamill *Foreign Multinationals*, p 251

84. Hood, N., Young, S. *The Economics of Multinational Enterprise*, London 1979, pp 311–21

12 The warm welcome for foreign-owned transnationals from recent British governments

Roger Sugden

I Introduction

Down the years a vast literature has evolved on the influence of transnational corporations. A clear lesson is that they tend to be very important in modern Britain. Hence there is good reason for analysing the policy of British governments towards transnationals over the last 25 years or so. This paper pursues such an analysis.

More specifically, it focuses on the attitude of governments towards foreign-owned firms producing in Britain. Section II describes the attitude throughout the period. It makes no attempt to chronicle every event and scrutinize each policy item, details which can be sought in the likes of Hodges' (1974) account of the 1964–70 Labour administration or in OECD's (1987) survey of member countries' policies as of August 1986. Rather, the Section draws on these and other studies to characterize Britain's attitude. In particular it is argued that foreign-owned firms have essentially received a warm welcome from successive governments, be they Labour or Conservative. This Section also uses comparisons with other so-called developed countries to reveal this attitude all the more clearly.

Similarly existing studies and comparisons with elsewhere are used in discussing government's reasons for acting as they have, the concern of Section III. Here it is suggested that governments have been seriously misguided. For example, it is argued that governments have never supported their belief in the beneficial consequences of foreign-owned firms with adequate information. Moreover, whilst a paper which focuses on the relationship between government and foreign-owned firms is an inappropriate place for a detailed assessment of the pros and cons of inward investment – something which warrants separate attention and which can be pursued in the likes of Cowling and Sugden's (1987) analysis of a world dominated by transnational corporations – the sources of foreign-owned trans-nationals alleged advantages to Britain are severely undermined in the Section. In short the outcome of Section III is a series of simple arguments which leave the justifications for recent policy in tatters.

II The attitude of governments

For practical purposes official policy has been typified by the following statement from Patrick Jenkin, then Secretary of State for Industry, speaking in 1982: 'This government, like its predecessors, welcomes inward direct investment into the UK. Since the lifting of exchange controls in 1979, non-residents have needed no official permission to invest in this country other than those, such as planning consent, which are required of all investors. Foreign investors are assured of receiving equal treatment with their UK counterparts and are eligible for the full range of incentives and benefits provided to investors generally.'[1] When it comes to detail it might be argued that Conservative governments have offered an even warmer welcome to foreign-owned firms than Labour administrations – for instance Hodges (1974) suggests the welcome was 'perhaps even less qualified' in Heath's government than in its Labour predecessor. However, the existence of a Labour or Conservative government has made no real difference. This can be seen, for example, in Graham's (1982) discussion of the '70s. He argues that in opposition the Labour Party criticized the Heath government's encouragement to foreign investors, seeing its attitude as too relaxed, yet the formation of a new Labour government in 1974 caused no genuine policy change; whilst initially the new government at least seemed to be seeking a firmer line this never really materialized and it ended up actively encouraging new investment by foreign-owned transnationals.

This is not to deny that Britain – like just about every other country in the world – has had some restrictions and vetoes over incoming investment. These have focused upon non-manufacturing activity, see OECD (1987), the detailed review in Safarian (1983) and the shorter discussion of Stopford and Turner (1985). For instance, the restriction of air transport licences to nationals unless the Secretary of State determines otherwise, the reserving of broadcasting for UK and EEC residents, special requirements for insurance companies with their headquarters outside the EEC, and limits on foreign share ownership in recently privatized concerns such as British Telecom. But even manufacturing has not been ignored. For example, when the 1947 Exchange Control Act was in force it was used to secure undertakings from some incoming investors, for instance in the infamous Chrysler case (which we will explore in a moment). Also, the 1975 Industry Act provided for the relevant Ministry to stop a takeover of an important manufacturing firm by a non-resident if this would serve the 'national interest'. And foreign takeovers of British companies have been referred to the Monopolies and Mergers Commission and rejected because of the desire to preserve domestic ownership. This happened in the case of Highland Distilleries in 1980, for example.

However, the instances of restrictions and vetoes are isolated and indeed pale into insignificance alongside the overall policy perspective typified by Patrick Jenkin's statement (although not everybody agrees with this characterization[2]). This perspective can be illustrated in a number of ways.

More revealing than the fact that foreign takeovers of British companies could be referred to the Monopolies and Mergers Commission is that in almost every instance they have not been. For example, Stopford and Turner (1985) report that between 1978 and 1981 a mere 2.2. per cent of acquisitions were referred. This is similar to the proportion of referrals involving acquisitions by domestically-owned companies, 1.6 per cent. On the admittedly superficial basis of these statistics it would seem that foreign-owned firms have had no more to fear than their British-owned rivals and that no firm has been under anything like a considerable threat. Likewise, the potential of the 1975 Industry Act has hardly been exploited; in his 1983 publication Safarian reports that its provisions had not yet been used.

It is perhaps even more telling to consider the operation of the 1947 Exchange Control Act, see again Hodges (1974) and Safarian (1983), also Steuer et al.'s (1973) chapter on regulating inward investment. The Act meant that Treasury permission was needed for the import of capital to set up a new firm or to take over an existing one. In principle, there were two criteria that determined whether or not permission was given: firstly, concern over the effect on foreign exchange reserves and hence the balance of payments; secondly, the wider implications of inward investment. Potentially the legislation was quite radical; it conferred considerable power to monitor incoming investment and even laid a basis for its control. Indeed it seems that at times control was sought. For example, when the American car giant Chrysler wanted to take over Rootes, the government secured various undertakings as a condition of permission. For instance, Chrysler was to keep a majority of British directors on the Rootes board; confirm expansion plans at various factories, especially Linwood; and achieve an export percentage at least as high as the average for the British motor industry. However, even in cases like Chrysler the government had no effective control; the undertakings attached to permission had no bite because the Act provided no systematic review to ensure they were satisfied and no sanction for breach.

One view is that the government was trying to control foreign-owned firms but that the legislation had a gross omission. But it is such an obvious fault that even this view decries any suggestion that use of the legislation represents a genuinely firm line with foreign investors. It certainly contrasts with what has happened in France, where conditions attached to inward investments have been followed ûp to see that they are met. In fact, another view is that the omission was deliberate; this underlines Britain's true policy even more clearly. Hodges (1974) claims that officials from the Treasury and (the now defunct) Ministry of Technology have suggested that one reason for Chrysler's undertakings was that 'they acted as a political escape-valve to reduce the possibility of criticism of permitting UK companies to come under foreign control'. This is plausible and would explain the lack of follow-up: why check what Chrysler has done if it is all a mere public relations exercise and actually giving the undertakings is sufficient to serve this purpose? As for France, it has happily discriminated against foreign investors to promote domestic firms and, according to Dicken (1986), has screened inward investment more than anywhere else in Europe. In short, the French have not given transnationals a particularly warm welcome, which is why they have seen that undertakings are satisfied.

Moreover, the Chrysler case can easily be taken out of context. It is exceptional.

Even ignoring the fact that it was not a genuine attempt to control a foreign-owned firm, it was so unusual that it should not alter the opinion that British governments have given inward investors a warm welcome; at best, Chrysler would be an exception that proves the rule. This is certainly in line with Hodges' (1974) opinion, for instance. Following a very detailed analysis of the 1964–70 period he concludes that the Exchange Control Act's balance of payments criteria for determining permission presented little or no barrier to most potential investors and that the more general second criteria was apparently never used to stop any inward investment.

Another very revealing illustration of Britain's policy perspective is the strenuous efforts it has made to sell itself to foreign investors. For example, in 1977 the Invest in Britain Bureau was set up in the Department of Trade and Industry to promote Britain as a whole; see the discussion in Dicken's (1986) survey. It has advised and assisted particular investors and produced a glossy booklet – *Britain the Preferred Location* – focusing attention on Britain's alleged advantages, for instance government policy 'aimed at providing maximum encouragement for private business'. The Bureau has also attempted to coordinate the activities of regional organizations, the likes of development agencies in Scotland and Wales. As Dicken (1986) again points out these regional organizations have been very active. For example, the Scottish Development Agency has established overseas offices in New York, San Francisco, Zurich, Brussels and Tokyo. It has also engaged in keen competition with other countries, especially Ireland. Moreover, it has even competed with the Welsh Development Agency!

Not that Britain has been alone in seeking inward investors; this has been a priority for many countries. However, there again there are interesting comparisons. For example, whilst Britain has preferred the carrot rather than the stick France has shown more aggression. This is illustrated by the 1982 Poitiers affair, when imports of Japanese videorecorders were controlled by an order that they must pass through a remote customs post. Such aggression has been argued by some French government officials to be responsible for their recently claimed success in attracting Japanese investment; see the newspaper articles by de Jonquieres (1986 and 1987). Moreover, a stark contrast is provided by Japan itself. Far from seeking investors, before the 1970s Japan used the 1949 Foreign Exchange and Foreign Trade Control Law and the 1950 Foreign Investment Law to virtually deny foreign firms setting up production facilities, although via carefully screened licensing and domestically controlled joint ventures there was substantial imported technology focused on selected sectors, see Safarian (1983) and Dicken (1986). More recently this attitude was relaxed – moving from what Safarian has called 'prohibition in principle' to 'freedom in principle' – but even then retained sufficient flexibility to leave Japan and not foreign investors undoubtedly in charge. At most the Japanese have given inward investment a welcome that is polite yet careful and firm.

Other comparisons and illustrations could also be given to depict Britain's perspective. For example, no mention has been made of its pro-transnationals stance in the EEC, something noted in Hellmann (1977) and Robinson (1983), or indeed of its behaviour in international organizations more generally. But there is nothing to gain in pursuing these as it would simply be labouring the point: throughout the last 25 years or so Britain has given foreign-owned transnationals a warm welcome.

III   Reasons for the attitude

The broad explanation for this attitude is a simple view that has characterized all governments throughout the period: the presence of foreign-owned firms is beneficial to Britain, therefore they warrant a warm welcome. This view is badly misguided.

Consider first the notion that inward investment is beneficial. For a start, governments' belief in this has been on insecure ground because the quality of their information has been very poor. Hodges (1974) argues that to the extent inward investment had its drawbacks 'they were not readily apparent' to the 1964–70 Labour Government, 'particularly since there existed no machinery for giving special scrutiny to the activities of multinational companies, and in most areas there was inadequate information on which to base a coordinated policy towards them'. He explains this as a result of divided responsibility for industrial policy across various government departments, none having a significant interest in transnationals. But even accepting Graham's (1982) report that the 1974–79 Labour Government concentrated policy towards transnationals in the Department of Trade and Industry, inadequate information has always remained a problem. There has never been a systematic monitoring of inward investments. This is in vivid contrast to other countries. For instance, in 1973 Canada established the Foreign Investment Review Agency; see McCulloch and Owen's (1983) illustration of the Agency's activities, Safarian (1983) and Dicken (1986). The Agency's brief was to review the implications of foreign investment for such things as employment, productivity, exports, technological development and competition. It covered a wide area, for instance the esttablishment of all new activities and all but the smallest acquisitions of Canadian-owned companies (albeit growth in firms already established in Canada only if they were diversifying).

Nothwithstanding the lack of information – or perhaps because of it – there is clear evidence of Britain's belief that inward investment is beneficial. For example, to again cite Hodges (1974), he conducted in-depth interviews with 28 senior civil servants in 1970–71 and concluded that they all saw inward investment as conferring net benefits, in line with the conclusion that he reached from examining the speeches of Ministers in the 1964–70 Government. Likewise, Fayerweather (1982) surveyed legislators and permanent government officials in 1970. He found that they saw inward investors as having a fairly large effect which erred on the good side. Graham's (1982) survey of British Members of Parliament and senior civil servants in 1975 was similar to Fayerweather's and reached virtually the same conclusion; the vast majority of respondents saw the presence of foreign investors as at least to some extent good. Admittedly these results are not confined to the views of the government of the day but they provide a clear indication of beliefs.

More specifically, various sources of alleged benefit can be identified. Among these prominence has been given to the claims that foreign investment directly implies improved balance of payments, greater employment and a superior technology base; see the detailed discussion of the Treasury in Bridges (1964), also Hodges (1974), Graham (1982) and de Jonquieres (1986). It has also been thought indirectly beneficial because a country which wants to gain from itself investing overseas can hardly be seen to reject investment from other countries. This was recently illustrated very clearly when the Swiss giant Nestlé made a bid to take over the confectionery manufacturer Rowntrees. The government refused to refer the bid to the Monopolies and Mergers Commission. Lord Young, the Trade and Industry Secretary, told the House of Lords that British-owned firms were creating an 'empire' by investing abroad, that Britain was 'buying up the world' and accordingly that foreign bids for British companies should not be blocked, see the press reports by Waller (1988) and Riddell (1988). If they were, Britain's imperialist ambitions would not materialize because others would reciprocate by denying British investments.

However, an assessment of these alleged benefits reveals very insecure foundations for Britain's attitude. For instance, Lord Young's empire-building is surely immoral; it is no better than a gangland leader arguing that gang wars are beneficial simply because he has the most powerful gang. In contrast, the argument about superior technology has some appeal but even there it should be remembered that this is not necessarily a benefit of inward investment. This is revealed by Nestlé's takeover of Rowntrees: it does not seem that this will result in the British confectionery industry gaining better technology. Moreover, left unfettered, inward investment's contribution to employment and the balance of payments is beneficial in at most a superficial sense.

When an inward investor sets up a new plant, it tends to be assumed that the resultant jobs can only reduce dole queues. But it is important to realize, for example, that such investment tends to be footloose, see Hymer's (1972) path-breaking vision of the international division of labour and Cowling's (1986) analysis of deindustrialization. A foreign-owned firm that is enticed into Britain brings no long-run commitment; given a free rein it will be more than willing in the future to run down British production in favour of development elsewhere. Even such an apparently well-established company as Ford has continually threatened that unless workers do as they are told it will cut back English car manufacture in favour of other European countries and indeed in the early 1980s did so with a vengeance, see the evidence in SMMT (1984), Jones (1985) and Cowling and Sugden (1987). Accordingly, inward investment tends not to provide long-run, stable employment, something which needs the development of firms with a commitment to a particular country. Furthermore, this also has implications for the balance of payments. In the short run problems might be mitigated by financing industrial development using foreign currency and so on. But firms prone to leaving a country at the drop of a hat tend not to provide lasting, secure export potential.

220

Indeed, it is not simply that left unfettered inward investment provides no long-run solution; it at least sows the seeds of severe employment and trade difficulties, see Cowling and Sugden (1987). For instance a firm can use its time producing in Britain to secure monopoly power in the British market and then exploit this power using imports and hence overseas employment. This is illustrated by Ford having used its association with Britain to exploit 'Buy British' sentiments when selling cars it has produced elsewhere, e.g. the case of German-made Ford Granadas being bought as British in GLC (1985).

Thus governments' belief that inward investment is beneficial is badly founded both in terms of the information they have had available and the validity of alleged benefits. Put another way, the insinuation of the analysis so far is that policy would have been well founded if only governments had acted on a systematic, detailed monitoring of inward investments and had recognized that whilst the presence of a foreign-owned firm is sometimes beneficial – for instance because of its consequences for the technology base – this is not always the case.

This undoubtedly implies that Britain's warm welcome has been ill-advised; a more cautious approach would have been appropriate.

Nor is this the end of the matter. Even if the view that the presence of foreign-owned firms is beneficial to Britain is accepted, it is unjustified to argue that therefore such firms warrant a warm welcome. What is meant by the view that foreign-owned firms are beneficial is that their advantages outweigh their disadvantages; see Hodges (1974), Fayerweather (1982) and Graham (1982). Believing this yet nevertheless extending inward investors a warm welcome is to do nothing about these disadvantages. This is again misguided.

Essentially there are two reasons for tolerating the disadvantages, and neither of the reasons is a good enough basis for such inaction.

The first is the view that disadvantages are so insignificant they are irrelevant. This is probably the view of the Thatcher Government, at least. The earlier comments in this Section doubting alleged benefits should be enough to dismiss this naive approach but anybody needing to be convinced any more should be satisfied by looking at the experience of other countries. Nowhere else seems to have been quite as relaxed about inward investment as Britain. For example, even the United States – in many respects the champion of transnational corporations – has taken the problems of foreign-owned firms seriously enough to have established the Committee on Foreign Investment, see Safarian (1983). Amongst other things this Committee was given the task of reviewing inward investments which might have serious implications for the national interest. It was also to analyse proposals for controlling such investments.

The other reason for tolerating disadvantages – and the one that has at any rate been more prominent amongst Labour rather than Conservative governments – is that the costs of their elimination outweigh the benefits. At least this approach takes the disadvantages seriously. Essentially it amounts to the fear that if inward investment is not accommodated warts and all, it will be non-existent; i.e. that the cost of a country making any attempt to control foreign-owned firms is that the firms will take their investment elsewhere (and as their advantages outweigh the disadvantages this would be undesirable). The fear can be seen in the comments of Sir Richard Clarke, then Permanent Secretary at the Ministry of Technology: 'The government of the recipient country *must* accept that the multinational company *must* lay out its resources as *it* thinks right; and that if the performance of the local subsidiary is bad, *nothing* can stop the multinational company from drawing its own conclusion. . . . If governments get sensitive about this, they might be put in a quandary if they put pressure on a multinational company and that company refuses to cooperate. . . . *The basic question is: do we want foreign investment? If we do we must accept the consequences.*'[3] But such fear is misplaced, a point made in Sugden's (1988) discussion of a negotiating strategy to ensure transnational corporations follow a government's wishes. Indeed the point has already been implied in this paper by the earlier comparison with policy in other countries, for instance the success claimed by France in attracting Japanese investment despite its relatively aggressive policy – in fact because of its aggression!

IV Conclusion

This paper has focused on the attitude of recent governments towards foreign-owned firms producing in Britain.

Having recognized that Britain is typical of just about every country in the world insofar as it has had at least some restrictions and vetoes over incoming investment, Section II characterized the attitude of governments by concentrating on various illustrations. Particularly detailed consideration was given to the operation of the 1947 Exchange Control Act and to Britain's strenuous efforts to sell itself to overseas investors. It was claimed that instances of restrictions and vetoes are isolated and indeed insignificant; insofar as they appear to suggest Britain has taken a firm hand this only goes to show how appearances can be very deceptive. Nothing illustrated this better than the Chrysler example. The truth of the matter is that Britain has extended inward investors a warm welcome.

Section III argued that a simple view provides the broad explanation for this attitude; the presence of foreign-owned firms is beneficial to Britain, therefore they warrant a warm welcome. It examined each part of this view in considerable detail.

Governments' belief that inward investment is beneficial was said to be badly founded because of inadequate information and misjudgements over alleged benefits. Moreover, even ignoring this, nothing has been done about inward investment's admitted disadvantages. In short it was argued that Britain's policy over recent years has been ill-advised.

Notes

1. Quoted in Stopford and Turner (1985)
2. For instance, Government of Canada (1976) seems to believe Britain has not been very open, unlike the United States, West Germany and others; rather

222

Britain seems to be seen as a country which has wished to attract foreign investment but which has bargained about terms and conditions of entry. In truth bargaining has occurred but to see Britain as having been anything other than very open is at best a very superficial view

3.   Reproduced from British North-American Committee (1970). Emphasis added

References

Bridges, Lord *The Treasury*, Allen and Unwin, London 1964

British North-American Committee   'Guidelines for multinational corporations: a government view', *British North-American Committee Paper* BN/M–12, London July 1970

Cowling, K. 'The internationalisation of production and deindustrialisation' in A. Amin and J. Goddard, eds, *Technological Change, Industrial Restructuring and Regional Development*, Allen and Unwin, London 1986

Cowling, K., Sugden, R. *Transnational Monopoly Capitalism*, Wheatsheaf, Brighton 1987

de Jonquieres, G. 'Europe's quest for foreign investment. A war of diminishing returns', *Financial Times*, 10 November 1986

de Jonquieres, G. 'Inward investment. US arrivals spur mobility', *Financial Times*, 25 March Survey, 1987

Dicken, P. *Global Shift*, Harper and Row, London 1986

Fayerweather, J. 'Elite attitudes toward multinational firms' in J. Fayerweather, ed., *Host National Attitudes Toward Multinational Corporations*, Praeger, New York 1982

GLC. *London Industrial Strategy*, Greater London Council, London 1985

Government of Canada. 'Policies of governments towards foreign direct investment' in K.P. Sauvant and F.G. Lavpour, eds, *Controlling Mulitnational Enterprises*, West View Press, Boulder, Colorado 1976

Graham, N.A. 'Developed countries and multinational corporations: threat perception and policy response in France and the United Kingdom' in J. Fayerweather, ed., *Host National Attitudes Toward Multinational Corporations*, Praeger, New York 1982

Hellmann, R. *Transnational Control of Multinational Corporations*, Praeger, New York 1977

Hodges, M. *Multinational Corporations and National Government*, Saxon House, Farnborough 1974

Hymer, S.H. 'The multinational corporation and the law of uneven development' in J.N. Bhagwati, ed., *Economics and World Order*, Macmillan, London 1972

Jones, D.T. *The Import Threat to the UK Car Industry*, University of Sussex, Science Policy Research Unit, 1985

McCulloch, R., Owen, R.F. 'Linking negotiations on trade and foreign direct investment' in C.P. Kindleberger and D.B. Audretsch, eds, *The Multinational Corporation in the 1980s*, MIT Press, Cambridge, Mass 1983

OECD. *Controls and Impediments affecting Direct Investment*, OECD, Paris 1987

Riddell, P. 'Ministers defend takeover policy', *Financial Times*, 26 May 1988

Robinson, J. *Multinationals and Political Control*, Gower, Aldershot 1983

Safarian, A.E. *Governments and Multinationals: Policies in the Developed Countries*, British North-American Committee, London 1983

SMMT. *The Motor Industry of Great Britain 1984*, Society of Motor Manufacturers and Traders, London 1984

Steuer, M.D., Abell, P., Gennard, J., Perlman, M., Rees, R., Scott, B., Wallis, K. *The Impact of Foreign Direct Investment on the United Kingdom*, HMSO, London 1973

Stopford, J., Turner, L. *Britain and the Multinationals*, Wiley and Sons, Chichester 1985

Sugden, R. 'Industrial strategy, transnational corporations and British volume car manufacture', Mimeo, May 1988

Walker, D. 'Young sets stage for counter to Nestlé bid in Rowntree fight', *Financial Times*, 26 May 1988

Index